AF531668

HUMAN RIGHTS ISSUES AND OTHER RADICAL ESSAYS

Mrs. Ellen Roy, M.N. Roy and the Author
(The author made M.N. Roy stand up after he recovered from the first attack of cerebral thombosis in winter 1952)

HUMAN RIGHTS ISSUES AND OTHER RADICAL ESSAYS

Rai Mohan Pal
(R.M. Pal)

Human Rights Issues and Other Radical Essays
Rai Mohan Pal

First Published, 2010

ISBN 978-93-5002-025-8 (Hb)

Published by
AAKAR BOOKS
28 E Pocket IV, Mayur Vihar Phase I, Delhi-110 091
Phone : 011-2279 5505 Telefax : 011-2279 5641
aakarbooks@gmail.com; www.aakarbooks.com

Printed at
Arpit Printographers, Delhi-110 032
arpitprinto@yahoo.com

Dedicated to
Madhuri Pal

Acknowledgement

I am grateful to my wife Madhuri Pal, who collected my old writings and sent them to the publisher. My good friend Mr. Paul Jacob of the Indian Social Institute, New Delhi, was kind enough to type out the entire material for which I thank him. The final selection has been done by my daughter, Sangeeta Mall (former Managing Editor, *Radical Humanist*) who has also been good enough to write a preface. I thank her. I am also grateful to my close friend Mr. G.S. Bhargava, who was kind enough to go through the entire manuscript and make necessary corrections wherever necessary.

My thanks to Chandrakant Dange, who has been helping me by way of rendering secretarial assistance for the last several years and in organizing material for the book. Last but not least thanks to Mr. K.K. Saxena of Aakar Books, who has taken keen interest in bringing out the book. But for his encouragement, this book would not have seen the light of day.

Contents

Preface

In 2002 a strange thing happened to my father. He was in hospital, comatose after a paralysis attack that almost killed him. A retinue of visitors visited him continuously. One of these was a well-known Dalit leader about whom I had read many things in newspapers. Because of his strident activism and the resultant threats from Hindutva radicals, the government had given him Z class security, and so he came with gun-toting commandos, looking very important. He strode straight into the ward without seeking any kind of entry pass or permission from the nursing staff. Visiting hours were in the evening, between five and seven, but to him that didn't matter. He was too important to come at the regular time. The commandos dwarfed him but added to his consequence, so that he didn't walk so much as strut with arrogance. But as soon as he saw the patient, all his arrogance dissolved in a pool of tears, and he started sobbing loudly. He cried as a child cries at the loss of a parent. It occurred to me much later that even I, his own daughter, hadn't seen a grown man cry in a long time, and it struck me as a comical sight. However, the incident made an impression on me and I looked for its source. I couldn't ask my father why this self-important man should cry, since he was too sick to talk, and later more pressing matters, like the state of his health, obscured this episode. The Dalit leader was controversial because of certain utterances he had made, and I tactfully kept quiet about my curiosity. Nonetheless his demeanour at my father's illness had left a deep impression upon me, and I couldn't let go of the matter.

After a few months, when things had become more settled, I chanced upon some old issues of *PUCL Bulletin*, and started reading the editorials penned by my father. The People's Union for Civil Liberties was formed in 1976 during the Emergency to fight human rights abuses. Its bulletin keeps members informed of the various campaigns being run across the country. Most of these campaigns are to do with issues of civil liberties. It is quite obvious from the various reports published in it that the people sending these reports are both passionate and dedicated about their work, and through these reports they hope to excite public indignation at the various atrocities. My father became the editor of the bulletin in 1990.

Since the focus of each issue is on activism, as against intellectual analysis, thus making the Bulletin a truly report-oriented journal, the editorials written by my father stood out. Their tone was distinctive and more analytical than anything else in the monthly. The attempt was to examine the malaise and not just the symptoms. So while various writers were reporting on the activities of the organisation in distant parts of India, the editorials took a look at the thread that connected these seemingly disparate atrocities. And even if one were to skip the reports, one could not but help read the leader to understand both, why some human beings were committing heinous crimes under the garb of culture, and what could be done to prevent these crimes.

Neither of these issues of analysis is an easy subject matter. The issue of cause is highly debatable, and reams of philosophy have been devoted to just this topic. And because debates are heated, and the subject of culture is an especially sensitive one, writers choose to steer away from cause to more innocuous theories of environmental influences. It is easy to blame the crime on the inhospitable terrain, or the extent of poverty, rather than examine the nature of society which allows the crime to take place, at times even encourages it. Such an approach will not find favour with some members of that society. In the absence of an honest attempt to find the cause, the discovery of a suitable remedy can hardly be expected. A family of an upper caste man is killed, a Dalit is identified as a probable susoect, he is arrested and promptly sentenced to death. Nothing in such a description of the sequence of events should be liable to questioning, except the fact that in the Indian judicial system, every individual has the right to a fair trial and should be defended by a capable lawyer. In the case of this hypothetical Dalit, both conditions are probably missing. And yet, it would need courage to point out that the Dalit must not be condemned out of hand, that due process must be followed before conviction and sentencing. Such courage is the hallmark of the activists who scour the countryside to find victims of human rights violations. But is it enough to merely point to the absence of due process? Shouldn't a question be asked about why due process wasn't followed?

I read about fifteen of the editorials, and discovered that they all asked this question. And because they asked this question, the writer also went on to look for an answer. The way forward couldn't be mapped without a look at the past.

There was a pattern to all the editorials. Then they began with the description of the situation. Then they were linked to the reports that came in. They went on to examine the root cause and then, with this in mind, suggested a remedy. In most cases, neither the root cause nor the remedy was politically correct.

The writings were thought-provoking and provocative in their approach. They were written as though they were being spoken, and the speaker wasn't standing on a pulpit but sitting across from one in a drawing room, a small one at that. They were intimate in their tone, and yet they left one with an uneasy feeling in the gut, as though there was a pile of something unmentionable in the middle of one's living room, which everyone could see but refused to talk about, except the writer. The something unmentionable was really the plethora of problems that India was faced with, particularly the whole gamut of societal violations of human rights, caste and communal divisions. For almost a quarter of a century, the writer had been speaking about these issues, openly questioning many shibboleths that we Indians held close to our hearts, thus making himself a thoroughly unpopular man.

The outspokenness was tinged with irony. Almost every article made reference to the hypocrisy that is the hallmark of the Indian middle class without naming names, unless they were public figures. But one could easily guess at the people's identity and laugh a little at their folly, which these articles exposed so cleverly. The absence of tact in my father's conversation and writings was not conducive to polite talk, but according to him, there was little sense in polite talk when there was so much work to be done. And to expose the double standards of the establishment was a necessary step in the move towards a philosophical renaissance that he believed India could not do without.

But above all, these articles reflected the genuine sense of anger that their writer felt at the systemic abuse of human rights in India. He openly questioned the premise that laws could correct society and through his writings, proved how society needed reform on a radical scale, a 'philosophical revolution' as he put it, in order to achieve even a semblance of equality for the downtrodden in India, particularly the Dalit. He minced no words in censoring the Hindu scriptures, the *Bhagvad Geeta*, the *Manusmriti*, and the *Rig Veda*, for propagating inequality. Such forthrightness did not make him popular with his Hindu friends– and most of his friends, let it be said, were Hindu at heart, in spite of wearing their atheism on the sleeve– but won him many admirers from amongst the Dalits. They recognised in him a kindred soul who genuinely rebelled against doctrinal inequality, while claiming to be part of no group except the Radical Humanists.

The writer's personal journey was perhaps what made him such a fierce defender of human rights. Propelled into adulthood by the fires of the Partition, Pal refused to allow politeness to hide the enormity of the crime that was the separation of two religions by the separation of their physical terrains. His rationality demanded a reason why the clash of a handful of egos ended in the loss of a million lives. On the emotional front, his writings, demonstrated the desolation he felt at the wilful destruction of the composite fabric of Indian society.

Rai Mohan Pal's wasn't an easy life, and it was made tougher by his unwillingness to soft soap anyone. He wasn't polite or well-mannered, and he ascribed his acerbity to his rustic roots.

No one, he claimed, was more honest than a villager. It was a view that was unpopular with his urban colleagues, made more so by his impatience with their circumlocution. He was neither adult nor child when he made the transition from his village to the city, and his life consisted of none of the romance that such a transition is supposed to entail. Instead, all he encountered was pedestrian struggle to get an education, one that would allow him to support himself and his impoverished family. He got more than he bargained for when M N Roy took him under his wing. It was a fair bargain. Roy, in his old age, found a young man to take care of him and his wife, Ellen. In return, my father discovered the delight of being in the company of one of the best brains of the country. He was poor still, but he got what all the money in the world couldn't have paid for, the knowledge and wisdom of a man who had lived one of the most exciting lives that anyone could ask for, travelling across the world, being a member of the Comintern, living in prison and analysing Indian society through his writings. The rustic villager found himself in the presence of one of the most modern individuals of the time, and the influence ran deep. M.N. Roy's company did for my father what no university could have achieved. It made him an intellectual. He could overcome his lack of a sophisticated education because of his association with Roy.

This relationship was peculiar, to say the least. The peculiarity itself contributed to many of Pal's beliefs. By the time my father came in contact with Roy in the late forties, the latter had undergone a radical change in his convictions. His lengthy association with Communism had ended, his political ambitions had come to nought, and India no longer needed his thoughts on the way forward. Independence had been declared, the Constitution was well on its way to being promulgated, and the parliamentary system of democracy was well-entrenched. Roy, on his part, recognised that India was on the cusp of a huge change but showed no signs of adopting its new personality of a modern nation-state. Apart from a few leaders, no one really understood that now the good old days were gone forever. The same practices continued, and in an agony of frustration, Roy disbanded his party of devoted followers and exhorted them to inculcate the spirit of change in the populace. It was a good concept except that no one was listening. And before Roy could effectively lead his troopers, he died.

There was a lot of heartburn and introspection on the way forward for the 'Royists', and for Radical Humanism as an idea relevant to India. Somewhere along the way, Royism got conflated with Radical Humanism, and there was a feeling that the spread of Radical Humanism would end with the physical attrition in the numbers of Royists. A lot of chest-beating took place on this theme periodically, and the resultant seminars and conferences organised by the Royists were primarily concerned with the growth of the movement in the absence of the core team. The underlying text was that the core team was absolutely necessary to the spread of Radical Humanism. Along the way, many new organisations were set up, some of them thriving in the freedom of the post-Emergency days. One of these was the People's Union for Civil Liberties, one of whose founders was V M Tarkunde, a leading Radical Humanist, and one of Roy's inner circle of advisors. Many Radical Humanists found common cause with PUCL, and embraced its goals. One of these was Raimohan Pal. Pal was not a devoted Royist, in that he didn't equate Radical Humanism with Royism, and after seeing some success in his efforts to get *Selected Works of M N Roy* edited by S N Ray, another senior Royist and renowned intellectual, published by Oxford University Press, started taking more interest in the whole question of human rights, particularly in the context of India's unique problems of caste and communalism. He openly acknowledged Roy's debt in pointing him in this direction through his writings on Indian sociology.

In his capacity as editor of the *PUCL Bulletin*, Pal, by the early nineties, had become a vocal human rights activist, and one of his key contributions was to make the National Human Rights Commission, then a fledgling organisation, sit up and take notice of societal violations in the sectors of health, education, caste conflicts and communal riots. Through seminars and brainstorming sessions, in which the NHRC was happy to participate, seeking as it did closer cooperation with NGO's, these issues came to the fore, and became a part of the Commissions's main activity.

Many of the articles in this book were written more than a decade ago. Yet their universality is proven by their appropriateness in today's India, and never more so than today. The pride that has overtaken everyone on India becoming a nuclear power completely overshadows the fact that India chose the path of violence by exploding a nuclear device, completely against the precept laid down by the Father of the Nation. Yet no one dare say so for fear of spoiling the party. How many people are there in this country who recognise the supefluity of acquiring sophisticated weapons of mass destruction while hosting almost fifty percent of the world's most poor people? In 1998, apropos of the nuclear explosion at Pokhran Pal wrote "Human rights violations – reminiscent of Hiroshima and Nagasaki perpetrated by the USA – and nuclear weapons (the bomb), which have the capacity to wipe out all life from earth, are intimately connected with one another. Opinion makers, political formations and their leaders, intellectuals, and the media, while almost wholeheartedly welcoming the explosions and tests at Pokhran in May 1998, have not referred or have chosen not to refer, to this aspect of the explosions." Ten years on there is no change in the attitude. If at all it has become even more virulently in favour of India's 'nuclear autonomy', with complete disregard for human safety and the phenomenal cost of going nuclear, as the ongoing discourse on the nuclear deal shows.

But even more than the hypocrisy engulfing the Indian middle class, what comes through in some of these essays, is the problem of majority communalism, and its consequences for the unity fof the country. There is passionate criticism of the role that Hindu fundamentalist political parties have played in fuelling the fires of communal hatred, especially since the demolition of the Babri Masjid in 1992, and time and again the essays reason why Hindu fundamentalism is a threat to the unity of the country, and why, if India is not to dissolve into a fractured polity, the state must step in to curb the rhetoric of violence. The state hasn't stepped in, whether in Gujarat or Mumbai or Jammu, and communalism has become more overt, with fundamentalists going about their business with almost total impunity.

All the essays in this compilation have been published elsewhere, over a period of a decade and a half. Why then have them in a book? Firstly because their message is worth repeating and any thinking person will find herself in agreement with what they have to say. But more importantly, it would be hard to find another book that so succinctly describes the pitfalls that lie ahead for India as a strong and unified nation. With topics ranging from 'The Mischief of Party Politics' to 'Reconversion 'Movement' With A Vengeance', the topics in this book will help the reader in developing a sense, both of chronology and history, of the issues surrounding human rights and civil liberties. In a country of the size of India, it isn't hard to find people who champion the cause of the depressed and the downtrodden. There are many human rights activists and experts. They have each found a niche in which to operate. This book on human rights in India moves away from any kind of specialisation to create a discourse that will revolve around the cause rather than merely the symptom. The quotidian and mundane events of daily life have been used, in these essays, to highlight the grimness of the future that we face, and thus become all the more poignant.

This book's release is a timely reminder that putting out small conflagrations will not control the blaze of dissension and disintegration unless we are able to question every assumption that we hold dear and examine it in the light of cold rationality.

October 2009 **Sangeeta Mall**

Introduction

This is a compilation of 33 of my writings published between 31 May 1994 and 16 June 2001, a period of nearly seven years. Although several of the articles had appeared in *Mainstream*, edited by my young friend, Sumit Chakravarthy, the range of their publication is fairly wide. Daily newspapers like the *Pioneer* and *The Statesman*, among others, had carried quite a few of them. Each article has been duly acknowledged to the newspaper/journal where it first appeared. Nevertheless, I deem it my duty to offer my thanks to all of them for their implicit permission to bring them out in this compilation.

Two aspects of this little volume stand out: the accent of the articles on human rights and human rights movements at home and abroad, and the subjective thread running through them. Even if I have often used the expression 'this writer'—which was the style in those days—I have never believed in hiding my light under a bushel.

Having been intellectually drawn to **M.N. Roy** from my formative years—as student and later as lecturer—I had the privilege of studying intensely his writings and reports of his speeches and seminars. I was further lucky to spend time with Roy during his last years at his household at Dehra Dun, where he lived with his second wife, Ellen, *nee* Gottschalk (Roy). In the process, I was fortunately thrown into contact with political leaders and celebrities. Roy's companions and friends of his Comintern days, like Ruth Fischer who had become a rabid anti-Communist, were among the visitors to the Roy home. The lovely garden that Mrs. Roy maintained at their Dehra Dun bungalow was a magnet to visitors, including Nehru, not to mention Indira Gandhi. Incidentally, Mrs. Roy and Indira had hit it off famously. Ellen Roy stayed with Indira at the Prime Minister's residence when she visited New Delhi.

Among other Indian visitors, I recall Dr. Shyama Prasad Mookerjee, who had just then founded the Bharatiya Jana Sangh, forerunner of the BJP. Dr. Mookerjee greeted Roy in the traditional Hindu way of touching the feet of the elder. Roy was in a happy mood and recalled Dr. Mookerjee's dig at Nehru in the Lok Sabha, that it was not the birthright of the Prime Minister to lose his temper! (Dr. Mookerjee had resigned from the Nehru cabinet to launch the Jana Sangh. A few months later, he died while in detention in Jammu and Kashmir.)

Another caller at the Roy household was Suresh Majumdar of *Anand Bazar Patrika*, which regularly published Roy's writings and paid him a handsome honorarium. A veteran Congress leader of Bengal, Surendra Mohan Ghose, who was a member of the Lok Sabha, had also come to meet Roy, who had started his political career as a nationalist.

My passion for promotion of civil liberties also finds unfailing expression in these writings. I was closely associated with the People's Union for Civil Liberties (PUCL) of which Nehru was president before Independence, when it was called the All-India Civil Liberties Union. Subsequently, Jayaprakash Narayan, as general secretary of the Socialist Party, revived it as an adjunct of the party, with K.K. (Krishna) Menon, joint secretary of the Socialist Party as the moving spirit. He was associated with the All-India Civil Liberties Union in the pre-Independence days also. Later, when Jayaprakash Narayan joined the Sarvodaya movement, he launched the PUCL as a champion of partyless democracy. Justice V.M. Tarkunde, who resigned from the Bombay Bench and became a close companion of M.N. Roy, was heading it at that time.

As a PUCL activist I had come into contact with our opposite numbers in Pakistan, especially Justice Dorab Patel, who initiated the non-governmental human rights movement in Pakistan.

In the process, we were able to forge non-official value-based links between the two countries. It is my fond wish that this collection of my articles becomes instrumental in promoting the values of non-sectarian democracy.

R.M. Pal

7 B, Regency Park
Eden Woods, Thane (W) 400 601
September 4, 2009

I. Issues of Human Rights

CHAPTER 1

Human Rights Panel Spreads its Wings

By becoming more open to suggestions from voluntary organizations, the National Human Rights Commission will gain credibility.

Scepticism greeted the establishment of the National Human Rights Commission (NHRC) in September 1993. It was pointed out at that time, and rightly so, that the Commission was being set up under pressure from foreign funding agencies.

The idea was that such an institution, whatever be its power, might deflect criticism off government for human rights abuses. We, in the human rights movement, had suggested that if the government were honest about preservation of human rights, it should talk to activists to start the exercise of establishing the Commission with a clean slate. That hope was belied.

The home minister had only a one-point programme: the Commission will be set up to "counter the false and politically motivated propaganda by foreigners and Indian civil rights agencies" against the state. It was not a very dignified way, to put it mildly, of establishing the Commission's bonafides in the matter.

What the government ought to have done, but did not do, the NHRC has now made a beginning to accomplish: a dialogue and discussion with human rights leaders and activists and NGOs. Let us hope that it becomes an ongoing process.

The first such meeting was held at the invitation of the Commission on May 23, 1994. The NHRC Chairman, Justice Ranganath Misra, his colleagues Veerendra Dayal and Justice

Kang, and the Secretary General, R.V. Pillai, had a frank and free discussion with human rights activists.

An omission on the part of the NHRC, which should have been avoided, was not inviting any social activist from among the Dalits (SCs and STs) and Muslims, both of whom have been at the receiving end of violence. Still, that such an encounter has taken place is itself a sign of hope.

Justice Misra was forthright in his opening remarks. He said he wanted support and assistance from activists in the discharge of the Commission's responsibilities. V.M. Tarkunde responded by saying that the human rights situation in the country can be improved if voluntary organizations cooperate with the Commission in spreading awareness among the masses so that the aggrieved will be increasingly encouraged to knock on the Commission's doors.

Also, activists and voluntary organizations can highlight government lapses and expose efforts, by the establishment to use NHRC as a cover for such lapses. Of course, problems and hindrances would exist. For example, the jurisdiction of the Commission. It is very unlikely that the Andhra Pradesh Police will allow the Commission to enter the state.

The Punjab scene was highlighted against the background of the Commission's recent visit to the state, and Justices Misra and Kang's impression that law-enforcing agencies in the state had begun to develop respect for the rule of law. The optimism, however, was not shared by the others present at the meeting.

Facts and figures were cited to substantiate the appraisal that the police continues to use unnumbered vehicles, advocates defending "terrorists" are still being warned and in some cases, they "disappear" mysteriously and custodial deaths have not ended. It was felt that the Commission did not seem to have gone the right way during its visit to Punjab, where the police chief functions as the de facto chief minister and where the police are a "law unto themselves", as observed by the Supreme Court.

Justice Misra set the tone for the Commission's attitude towards voluntary organizations: "We are prepared to do what you tell us." Given such an approach, it was felt the Commission might ultimately overcome the infirmities with which it was conceived.

It was in this spirit of cordiality that certain important topics were raised and the Commission displayed some seriousness about acting according to them. First and foremost is the question of transparency, i.e. how the Commission works.

There should be interactions with voluntary organizations. In this context, the government's allergy to voluntary organizations from abroad is a striking point. It was suggested that the Commission should take the initiative in inviting organizations like Amnesty International and Asia Watch to be part of the Commission's investigating teams in some specific cases about which they claim to have authentic facts, details, or which, according to them, needed to be investigated.

There should be no legal difficulty in this since the NHRC (Procedure) Regulations framed by the Commission state, "the Commission may in any given case appoint an appropriate number of outsiders to be associated with the investigation either as investigators or observers".

Veerendra Dayal made the startling revelation that no organization has yet forwarded any complaint of child labour or bonded labour. The Commission, however, has taken up the issue in right earnest on its own. It is indeed surprising that some high profile activists, well known in international circles, have not found the Commission a fit enough forum for lodging complaints in a formal way. It has not, however, deterred some of them from making serious representations to various fora abroad on child labour.

The Secretary General said that a beginning has been made with regard to human rights education. A conference was held recently at the Central Reserve Police Force (CRPF) Academy at Mount Abu, where he and some activists addressed a gathering of CRPF officers on the subject. The Commission has also written to Vice-Chancellors of universities, asking them to take steps to introduce human rights as a subject of study.

One of the first things the Commission did on assuming office was to write to chief secretaries of all state governments and union territories, asking them to direct district magistrates, and superintendents of police to communicate to the Secretary General of the Commission incidents of custodial deaths and custodial rapes within 24 hours of their occurrence.

This decision was taken "in view of the rising number of incidents and the reported attempts to suppress or present a different picture of these incidents with the lapse of time".

The Commission has also been pursuing with the Law Commission of India the question of bringing about changes in custodial laws. In this context, it was some consolation that the Commission is very unhappy with recent Supreme Court judgements upholding TADA (Terrorist and Disruptive Activities (Prevention) Act, 1990—provisions of TADA and human rights are contradictions in terms, it was said.

Human rights activists hoped that the Commission would never come under the pressure of the government. Justice Misra said the Commission would never yield to any pressure; national interest, yes but never to government interest. The chairman may be trapped, for there is a very thin line between them in practice in our country.

The first annual report of the Commission, which is expected to be submitted to the Home Ministry soon, will, it is hoped, reflect that the values relating to human rights are being appreciated. It should indicate the sensitivity and commitment of those at the helm of affairs, like the Commission members and officials.

"Unless you have sound attitude of mind, a right psychology, you cannot construct or reconstruct anything that will endure."

Whatever be the views of activists, the political rulers, as also of bureaucrats and law-enforcing agencies, the Commission is on test before the bar of public opinion.

[Courtesy: *The Pioneer*, New Delhi, 31 May 1994, p. 10]

****

CHAPTER 2

NHRC and People's Movements

The National Human Rights Commission (NHRC) has not put into practice one of the most important statutory obligations. Section 12(i) of the Protection of Human Rights Act 1993 states clearly: "The Commission shall... encourage the efforts of non-governmental organisations and institutions working in the field of human rights." Which means that the Commission must have regular interaction with activists and dissident intellectuals involved in people's movements—now known as non-governmental organisations (NGOs). It is here that the Commission has failed; and this failure has caused tremendous damage to the growth of the Commission as an institution independent of the government. Let us be clear. The Commission as an institution can survive only if it chooses to be part of a people's movement. If it does not identify itself with people's causes, it cannot grow as an institution.

It is in the above context that the present Chairperson, Justice Venkatachaliah, has taken a positive step, even though belated, which should be welcomed. One hopes at least one meeting takes place before Justice Venkatachaliah's term comes to an end in October 1999. About this a little later.

Almost immediately after the Commission came into existence, I made a suggestion to the Secretary-General to start the process of interaction with activists. I drew his attention to the then Union Home Minister's one-point programme: the Commission will be set up to "counter the false and politically motivated propaganda by foreigners and Indian civil rights agencies" against the state. It may be appreciated, I added, that the scepticism with which the establishment of the Commission was greeted— namely, that it was to shove the sins of the government under the carpet—was not without any foundation. The Secretary-General welcomed the suggestion and almost immediately the Commission invited a few well-known activists from across the country. That was in 1994.

The participants raised a number of questions like human rights violations by the Punjab police, the government's allergy to NGOs from abroad, TADA, the question of transparency in the working of the Commission, and so on. The discussion was frank and forthright. I got the impression that the Chairperson and members of the Commission listened to the NGO intellectuals and activists with considerable seriousness and attention. For example, with regard to Punjab, the Chairperson and another member expressed the view that the law-enforcing agencies in the State had begun to develop respect for the rule of law. This optimism was at once questioned. Facts and figures were cited to substantiate the appraisal. The Commission noted this and gave the impression that they were quite prepared to overcome the infirmities with which the Commission was conceived and brought forth.

There was one omission to which I had drawn the attention of the Commission: no activist/intellectual from among SC/STs and Muslims was invited to this meet.

The meeting ended with an assurance from the Chairperson that this kind of interaction with NGOs would be a regular feature. Regrettably, the 1994 meet was the first and the last!

In an informal meeting with the present Chairperson, Justice Venkatchaliah, about a year ago, I referred to Section 12(i) of the 1993 Act and the total indifference on the part of the Commission in this regard. The Chairperson spontaneously welcomed my suggestion about reviving the 1994 experiment and issued instructions to his staff that a meet with NGOs be organized. He even asked me to help the Commission in drawing up an agenda. I spent half a day! In spite of the Chairperson's desire and keenness, it has not materialized. Obviously some people in the Commission are having second thoughts with regard to such an experiment!

*

To get back to Justice Venkatachaliah's proposal in this regard. He has now set up an "NGO (Liaison and Service) programme" in the Commission with a view to giving effect to the provisions of Section 12(i). The Commission recognizes the fact that "the lack of good governance is a reflection of the lack of empowerment of the civil society" in our country, and that "the work of NGOs is considered a source of empowerment of the civil society". It is for this reason that, as an important component of the ideal of promotion of human rights, the Commission is called upon by the statute to

> encourage the efforts of NGOs and institutions working in the field of human rights. In this area a mere expression of good intention does not advance the cause. A proper system needs to be evolved and put into operation in the Commission towards this objective.

A programme like this can be successful only if the functionaries of the scheme welcome dissident intellectuals and activists. The problems that the Commission is likely to face in this regard are that all sorts of impediments put up by the bureaucratic culture and tradition; the entire machinery in the Commission is drawn from the bureaucracy; and the Commission has to rely heavily on this machinery for implementation of any scheme. The fact remains that the values cherished by human rights intellectual-activists and the mindset of a bureaucrat are likely to clash. And, as we have seen since 1947, in a clash between the civil society/the people, and the bureaucracy, the latter has always had the upper hand—all these years it has dictated the terms. The Chairman and members of the Commission must have experienced this clash/confrontation. In a situation like this, it is important and urgent that the civil society stands up and takes a strong position; and if the Commission has the courage to put its foot down, the civil society must stand by the Commission. If the Commission does not stand up, it will end up like other Commissions which are mostly sinecures.

For reasons of space we may give only a couple of examples of intolerance on the part of bureaucrats. Sometime back the Commission invited a few NGOs to meet a delegation of human rights officials and activists from an African country. They wanted to know the state of human rights in India. In the course of discussion, an Indian NGO, in the context of non-implementation of Article 45 of our Constitution and child labour, made critical comments about a Supreme Court judgement (the 1996 judgement). A very senior bureaucrat from the Commission got so upset and angry that the speaker was asked not to make such comments—in plain and simple language, "keep your lips sealed"! On another occasion, at an all-India seminar in 1998, another senior bureaucrat got terribly upset on hearing a Dalit intellectual, a well-known academic, criticizing the Brahminical religion, which has been responsible for human rights violation in our country. He took it that a criticism of the Brahminical religion meant criticism of individual Brahmins. He was told that no individual was under attack; it was a system which was being discussed. He would not be pacified. The institute (an NGO) which organized the seminar is now in his bad books! The Commission will appreciate that this is certainly not the way to participate in people's movements which should be helped in their pursuit of protection and promotion of human rights. Justice Venkatachaliah writes himself:

> The civil society in India is a heterogenous amalgam of different groups, stratified vertically and horizontally in social and economic terms and consisting pf groups which are not unoften in conflict with each other.

The bureaucrats do not understand—one hopes the Chairperson and members of the Commission do—that if SC/STs and minorities do not form part of the mainstream, our pride in being Indians, pride in nation-building, will be undercut. The Commission, it is regrettable to note, has not taken any initiative on its own to have interaction with SC/ST intellectuals and activists and minorities.

Let us give another example as to why it is necessary for the Commission to have regular interaction with dissident intellectual/activists. As history tells us, communalism of any kind, like the hierarchical system, gives rise to dissension, divisiveness and then disintegration, apart from the worst form of human rights violation. Majoritarian communalism is more heinous. It is unfortunate that the Commission has not placed this on its agenda.

It is hoped that the Commission's NGO liasion and service programme will organize periodic meetings with activists and have the patience to listen to them and look at the other side of the coin. If, however, the Commission and its officials want to listen, in the age-old Indian tradition, to only "pleasant" things and be in the company of only those who are pliable, they might as well not open another shop in the Commission.

[Courtesy: *Mainstream,* Vol. XXXVII, No. 45, 30 October 1999, pp. 29–30]

****

CHAPTER 3

NHRC's "Confidential" Document

The National Human Rights Commission (NHRC) set up a seven-member Advisory Committee under the chairpersonship of Justice A.M. Ahmadi, a former Chief Justice of the Supreme Court, to make necessary recommendations about amendments in the Protection of Human Rights Act 1993 (PHRA). The Committee consisted of former judges and lawyers (as if only judges and lawyers can take care of human rights!)

The Committee had fifteen meetings between the period 3 June 1998 and 16 October 1999. It submitted its report, and produced a new draft bill "proposing some salient amendments to the PHRA" months ago but the NHRC has not released the report on the ostensible plea that it is a "confidential" document! (One should have thought confidentiality and human rights culture which the NHRC seeks to promote are contradictions in terms!) Since the possibility of the report being made public in the foreseeable future is remote, I give below a summary of the major recommendations, made after a couple of meetings.

1. The Committee has suggested amendment to Section of 3 of PHRA—instead of three judges as at present, there should be two judges (chairperson; and one judge member), and three members having human rights background and experience. Out of these five, the Committee has recommended that one member should be a woman. Further, the Chairperson of the NHRC should also be a member of the Selection Committee for appointment of members whenever a vacancy is to be filled. It may be noted that though, even according to the NHRC, societal violation of human rights (of SC/STs) has been on the rise, the

Committee has not recommended the appointment of a member from these communities.

2. At present the Commission does not have the power to appoint its staff. The Committee has recommended that the NHRC should have the discretion to appoint its staff.

3. The Committee has suggested amendment to Section 12. The Commission, according to the proposed amendment, should have the power to visit jails, police lock-ups and other custodial institutions without giving any prior information to the government.

4. According to the proposed amendment, the NHRC can publish its annual report without waiting for months and years; if the annual report is not tabled in Parliament within three months of its receipt by the government, the NHRC can publish its report.

5. In respect of Section 19 of PHRA (procedures with respect to armed forces), one regrets to note that the Committee treats the armed forces as a holy cow in that it has not found it advisable to bring the armed forces under the jurisdiction of the NHRC. The Committee had studied Human Rights Acts of other countries—it could not have missed the fact that even in a country like the Philippines, the armed forces come under the jurisdiction of the Commission. It has excluded the para-military forces like the CRPF and BSF from the armed forces; the para-military forces will be under the jurisdiction of the NHRC, according to the proposed amendment.

6. The Committee has recommended amendment to Section 36 "to enable the NHRC or the State Commission to enquire into any matter after the expiry of one year from the date on which the act constituting violation of human rights is alleged to have been committed, if there had been sufficient reasons for not filing a complaint within the said period". It is regrettable that the Committee has not recommended unqualified deletion of the one-year clause. In a country like India, where most of the victims are illiterates, this alone should be sufficient reason for not being able to file reports in time.

It is also regrettable that the Committee does not propose any change in Section 6(3), which reads:

> On ceasing to hold office, a Chairperson or a member shall be ineligible for further employment under the Government of India or under the government of any State.

All the members of the Committee were aware of the fact that some members of the Commission had been appointed Governors of States. The argument the members who accepted the post of Governor advanced is that the office of a Governor is not a government job! Is this the spirit of this provision? But this Committee would not go into this aspect! No wonder, learned Indians are known as people who have specialized in the job of rationalizing the irrational!

Section 30 of the PHRA on the subject of Human Rights Court has disturbed human rights activists and even the NHRC since its inception. The existing provision reads:

> For the purpose of providing speedy trial of offences arising out of violations of human rights, the State Government may, with the concurrence of the Chief Justice of the High Court, by notification specify for each district a Court of Session to be a Human Rights Court to try the said offences.

The provision does not, as is clear, define offences, nor does it lay down any procedure, etc. The Committee does take note of this Section but only to say that

> The Committee recommended the constitution of Human Rights Court…..the Human Rights Court will have the same jurisdiction and power as that of a Court of Sessions….

Have we been made any more wiser by the Committee! Why should a committee—former judges and eminent legal experts—be silent on one of the most important aspects which relate to remedial measures?

[Courtesy: *Mainstream*, Vol. XXXVIII, No. 17, 15 April 2000, pp. 28–29]

****

CHAPTER 4

Right to Information and Empowerment of the People

The BJP-led Union Government has announced that it proposes to introduce a Bill, "The Freedom of Information Bill", in Parliament in the current session. The bill is

> to provide for freedom to every citizen to secure access to information under the control of public authorities, consistent with public matters, in order to promote openness, transparency, and accountability in administration and in relation to matters connected therewith or incidental thereto.

It is said the draft bill with the above objective is ready—in fact the draft is in circulation.

An important question that needs to be answered is: why do we need a separate law for freedom of information since it is already provided for in Article 19(1)(a) of our Constitution? This Article reads:

> All citizens shall have the right to freedom of speech and expression.

Freedom of information, it is obvious, is guaranteed by the above Constitutional provision.

One simple answer to this question is that in spite of Constitutional provisions, which guarantee Fundamental Rights, we have not been able to create a culture and climate where values of freedom, rights and a dramatic way of life are respected. What we have achieved is that we have erected a fairly impressive-looking structure on a very shaky foundation, a foundation made of, as Jayaprakash Narayan said, in a different context, democratic governance. One of the purposes of making laws like the right to information, which is primarily a human right, is to help create this culture.

Another immediate question that would arise from the above assumption is: can laws create a climate for a democratic way of life? Laws by themselves are not adequate; what is needed is that such progressive laws must be backed by people's movements. A law for right to information can be made effective only through people's movements. We may recall what Raja Rammohun Roy said in the context of abolition of the *sati* system:

> A mere enactment of a law, without creating people's movement, will not succeed in abolishing the cruel system.

Let us be clear in this regard. In spite of all the pious wishes and laws, we have not been able to make widow remarriage a reality, abolish untouchability, reduce atrocities committed on Dalits and Tribals, uplift women, introduce compulsory basic education, and so on, even though all these are the sources of the worst type of human rights violations. The fact remains that the mindset which stands in the way of progress has to be changed; social movements backed by an appropriate philosophy, a philosophy of freedom, can bring about a change in the mindset.

It is in the above context that we may examine the whole question of right to information which has a larger purpose than merely seeking information from the government. It is often said that a demand for right to information is made only by the middle class or that it will bring benefit only to the privileged section of our people. This is a totally erroneous view. The movement started, for example, by the Mazdoor Kisan Shakti Sangathan (MKSS), a grass roots organization founded by Aruna Roy, Shankar Singh, and Nikhil Dey in rural Rajasthan, should make it clear that it is the poor and marginalized sections of our people who need the right to information. (Soon after its registration in 1990, the MKSS' ranks grew—all its members are marginal peasants and landless labourers.) It is common knowledge, for example, that government grants meant for the relief of the poor do not reach them. In fact, this is even acknowledged by the government and its agencies.

The MKSS started organizing *jan sunwais* (public hearings)—a new methodology—for fighting corruption. A *sunwai* would start with the demand that people must have the fundamental right to information about all actions and decisions of the government and its agencies. They would demand copies of all documents which concerned the people for a people's audit. This demand leads to a larger aspect of the movement.

The next important aspect of the *jan sunwai* organized by MKSS is that the so-called illiterate people realized that they ought to depend on themselves and solve their own problems—in short, they realized that they can make their own destiny. This confidence—that man makes his own destiny—would lead to the establishment of a new system of genuine democratic governance on a solid foundation based on the concept of decentralization of power—power to the people.

The MKSS' experiment centres around total decentralization—power to the people, power to the village unit. The MKSS movement, in course of time, would lead to the establishment of a decentralized state of local republics which will be mini-states in their functions as they affect local life. In this sphere all the members of the society would be able to participate directly and effectively in the decision-making process. Most of our intellectuals and activists do talk about democratic alternatives, but vaguely; their alternatives are within the present system which has degenerated into an unprincipled and diabolical scramble for power, and has given rise to criminalization and corruption in electoral politics. What the MKSS is trying to do is to bring about a revolution from below. It is a genuine people's movement in that it does not aim at capturing power; it is making efforts to empower the people. Help the people to help themselves. Once empowered the people will be able to solve their own problems by themselves. Such a movement backed by a philosophy of freedom and self-reliance, will usher in a revolution from below with a view to establishing a government of the people, by the people, but not for or on behalf of the people. Such a structure will lead to decentralization of power. The MKSS movement ought to convince the status-quoists that the ideal of decentralization—power to the people—is not an unattainable goal, not an El Dorado which will remain in the realm of imagination only.

Given this form of government, people can fight corruption directly and effectively. The Right to Information movement should be viewed in the context of the common people in our country, even though illiterate, being capable of thinking for themselves and of making their own destiny. Our common people do not need a "leader", they want philosopher-guides.

In the light of people's power discussed above, we may examine the draft Bill, "The Freedom of Information Act 1999", specially with regard to certain categories of information that are exempt from disclosure (Exemption from Disclosure of Information). These include: (i) information that would "prejudicially affect the sovereignty and integrity of India"; (ii) information which would "affect the conduct of Centre-State relations"; (iii) information relating to Cabinet papers; (iv) internal working papers containing notes and correspondence; (v) information which would "prejudicially affect public safety and order"; (vi) information relating to trade or commercial secrets; (vii) information which would "prejudicially affect the management of personnel of public authorities and their operations"; (viii) information which would "result in the breach of privileges of Parliament or the legislation of a State, contravention of an order of court of competent jurisdiction".

As I have already mentioned, the right to information is guaranteed by Article 19(1)(a) of the Constitution. This Fundamental Right can be curbed only in accordance with the provisions of Article 19(2) which reads:

> Nothing in sub-clause (a) of clause (1) shall affect the operation of any existing law, or prevent the state from making any law, in so far as such law imposes reasonable restrictions on the exercise of the right conferred by the said sub-clause in the interest of the sovereignty and integrity of India, the security of the state, friendly

> relations with foreign states, public order, decency or morality or in relation to contempt of court, defamation or incitement to an offence.

It should be obvious that the exemptions included in the draft bill go far beyond what Article 19(2) prescribes. Furthermore, "subject to morality" is a dicey proposition. What is "immoral" today may not be so tomorrow. Then, why should information exchanged between the Centre and the States be not available? After all, matters relating to centre–state decisions affect the public; and yet such decisions will not be made public. There is a limit to the authoritarian mindset! We may also remember that the founding fathers of the Constitution did not include "the sovereignty and integrity of India". To think that political bosses and bureaucrats can think so thoughtlessly: that only they have the exclusive right to preserve the integrity of the country!

In fact, a close scrutiny of the exemptions would indicate that almost everything under the sun can be brought under these provisions by a clever lawyer/bureaucrat/politician whose basic philosophy is: it is dangerous to trust the people. One need hardly add that this philosophy and mindset has failed our Constitution and progressive laws. It is hoped, therefore, the government, specially the Minister of Information and Broadcasting, Arun Jaitley, will make amendments in the Bill keeping in mind that the right to information and a law to give this right to the people can be effective only if the government trusts the people. This writer had the privilege of working with Arun Jaitley during the latter part of the infamous Emergency of Indira Gandhi, and then after her defeat in the 1977 general elections during the Janata Party rule in 1977-80. Both of us were members of the People's Union for Civil Liberties. Arun hardly ever missed the regular meetings of the PUCL. He was one of the most radical amongst us, would never compromise with freedom and human rights; he was never apologetic in exposing human rights violations and infringement on civil liberties.

He was one of those who had refused to apologize to the dictatorial government of Indira and Sanjay Gandhi and preferred to spend nineteen months in jail (unlike quite a few stalwarts of the then Jana Sangh and RSS). One fondly hopes that a man of this background will definitely present a progressive Bill in Parliament, a law which will ensure a genuinely democratic form of government in which the people will exercise sovereignty. In those days people like Arun Jaitley trusted the people. It will be most unfortunate if they are today guided by misplaced patriotism and nationalism. Trust the people, and things will begin to change—to change for the better.

[Courtesy: *Mainstream*, Vol. XXXVIII, No. 20, 6 May 2000, pp. 21–23]

****

CHAPTER 5

"Missing" Prisoners in India and Pakistan

"*Mubarakbad!* Roop Lal is all set to return on Friday April 14 by PK 270. Do kindly request the media to cover this event and treat it in a humane manner by emphasizing compassion and humanity. His release should help us in building the bridge of understanding [between Pakistan and India]."

This fax message and contents of an earlier telephone call to this writer from Brigadier (Retd) Rao Abid Hamid of the Human Rights Commission of Pakistan (HRCP), a non-governmental organization based in Lahore, was the most cheering news in the context of human rights and in "building the bridge of understanding" between India and Pakistan.

A large number of Indians in Pakistani jails and Pakistanis in Indian jails have been languishing for years and years together. But, first a brief account of Roop Lal's escape from death in Pakistan.

Roop Lal was a soldier in the Indian Army. He resigned sometime in 1971. He entered into the territory of Pakistan in 1971. He was arrested on charges of espionage in 1974, and put on trial. He was sentenced to death. Roop Lal's son-in-law, Krishan Kumar, who came to know of the death sentence, succeeded in establishing contact with Roop Lal. Krishan Kumar approached this writer. Krishan Kumar had come to know of me through the *PUCL Bulletin*. I then wrote to Brigadier (Retd) Rao Abid of the HRCP. Roop Lal owes his life to Brigadier Rao Abid and the HRCP in that they succeeded in getting Roop Lal's death sentence commuted to life imprisonment.

A significant point that emerges from the Roop Lal case is the important role played by non-governmental voluntary organizations in rescuing victims of foreign origin. It is no secret that a large number of Pakistanis have been languishing in Indian jails on espionage charges. Sometimes, even after they have served their terms of imprisonment, they are not released. I may refer to one such case by way of example.

A couple of years ago, the HRCP wrote to the well-known human rights activist in India, Rajindar Sachar, a former Chief Justice of the Delhi High Court and former President of the People's Union for Civil Liberties (PUCL), drawing his attention to a number of Pakistanis who had served their sentence but were not, it was alleged, being released by the Indian authorities. Justice Sachar at once got in touch with our National Human Rights Commission and the Government of India. The Government of India then informed Justice Sachar that they wanted to release the Pakistanis but the Government of Pakistan did not come forward to accept them. On hearing from Justice Sachar, the HRCP put pressure on the Government of Pakistan, which then accepted the released Pakistani prisoners.

A few years ago, a Bangladeshi came to Ajmer pilgrimage. He was alleged to have been taken away to a police station. The Border Security Force was said to be involved. He was never traced. It is suspected that he was killed by the police or the BSF. A habeas corpus petition was filed in the Calcutta High Court; it was dismissed on grounds of jurisdiction. The Rajasthan PUCL has now filed a petition in the Rajasthan High Court, Jaipur.

Both these events—Roop Lal's death sentence commuted to life imprisonment, and the Pakistanis being released from Indian jails and repatriated to Pakistan—would not have been possible but for the efforts made by the Human Rights Commission of Pakistan (through Brigadier Rao Abid) and the People's Union for Civil Liberties (through Justice Sachar).

*

There are hundreds of prisoners like Roop Lal in Indian and Pakistani jails. Many of them, even including PoW's, have been "officially" declared untraceable (read, "dead"). I may refer to one such case. Captain Avinash Kumar Sharma's boat capsized in the Manavvar Tawi river in Jammu on 15 August 1996. The boat had possibly strayed into Pakistani territory and Captain Sharma was arrested by the Pakistani authorities. The family has been making frantic efforts to get news of Captain Sharma. The Pakistani authorities maintain, though not in writing, that they don't know of any Captain Sharma, but according to the Indian Army authorities Sharma is in Pakistani custody—they don't know, however, in which jail he is lodged. What is most distressing is that the Government of India and its officials do not treat such cases with compassion. They hardly ever respond to queries, and even when they do, the process is very slow. The official position is that Captain Sharma is missing but nobody knows where he is. There are hundreds of such armed forces men, including POWs, in jails in India and Pakistan—many of whom do not "exist" officially.

Another lesson that we must draw from the Roop Lal case is that we must not be forced into a situation of hopelessness; relatives of victims and NGOs must persevere with vigour, and relentlessly. Any clue we have must be passed on to the Pakistani NGOs, and vice-versa. We must not give up trying. Second, we in India, while we are moved by the plight of Indian prisoners in Pakistani jails, must not forget the Pakistanis captured by Indian authorities for whatever reason, technical or serious NGOs in India must make efforts to put an end to the suffering of Pakistani prisoners in Indian jails. The "missing" prisoners, including the POWs' relatives, must set up an organization, a platform, in cooperation with NGOs and must pursue the cases with the government, and more particularly with the National Human Rights Commission, and civil liberties' organizations. The NHRC must give the utmost importance to the rescue and release of such prisoners.

Patriotism and war and the glories that go with them have no meaning if the agony of hundreds of fathers, mothers, wives, children is not comprehended. The government must get the unfortunate victims traced and released. If patriotism cannot take care of those who are languishing in jails in foreign countries, its values and meaning will suffer.

Understandably, when a high-profile Air Force Officer, Air Marshal Cariappa (son of late Field Marshal Cariappa), was captured by the Pakistanis, his release had been secured speedily. Less important officers and men get caught in bureaucratic red tape and considerations of reciprocity between the two governments. The human element is rarely at play. This is where the human rights activists have to move in.

[Courtesy: *Mainstream*, Vol. XXXVIII, No. 29, 8 July 2000, pp. 5, 35]

****

CHAPTER 6

The Law of Blasphemy in Pakistan—An Unlawful Law

A Roman Catholic priest committing suicide is an unusual thing. Why did Bishop John Joseph shoot himself to death? Ayub Masih, mentally ill, who was sentenced to death on 27 April 1998 under the Pakistan Penal Code Section 296-C is not the first Christian to be convicted under this unlawful law—indeed, a law against God's law. There have been a number of Christians in Pakistan booked under this Section, including the 11-year-old Salamat Masih. Mention may also be made of the widely publicized case in which the well-known human rights activist and lawyer, Mrs. Asma Jahangir, present Chairperson of Human Rights Commission of Pakistan (HRCP), appeared in the Lahore High Court in defence of the accused Gul Masih, and succeeded in getting his acquittal. Gul Masih had to seek refuge in Germany to escape almost sure death at the hands of the mullahs in Pakistan, and Mrs. Jahangir, after being attacked in the court premises—she narrowly escaped—had to engage Pathan guards for security of life. Mrs. Jahangir declined state security. HRCP has given a detailed account in its annual report of 1997 of the operation of this unlawful law against the Christians [HRCP defines a "mullah" as: "formerly an appellation for an Islamic scholar, now it often refers pejoratively to a semi-literate fanatical campaigner and pronouncer of the orthodox Islamic view in the community."]

The Pakistan government has treated with contempt recommendations made by activists—both from Pakistan and abroad, including Muslim organizations in India—to repeal/ amend the law. Even Mrs. Benazir Bhutto, who had declared in her party's election manifesto that the law of blasphemy would be amended, surrendered—in fact prostrated—before the mullahs. Her law minister introduced a Bill in Parliament in 1993-94, but when the mullahs called on the people to kill the Minister, Mrs. Bhutto lost no time in withdrawing the bill! Even today—after the Bishop's tragic death—the Pakistan government is defiant, and maintains that if the law of blasphemy, which provides for mandatory death penalty (it may be noted that the HRCP is strongly in favour of removing the punishment of death penalty from the statute book) is repealed, the "law of jungle will prevail in the country. One shudders to imagine it."

Even a man of the stature of the Comila and Orangi fame Gandhian, Mr. Akhtar Hameed Khan, a former member of the ICS, was booked under Section 296-C and faced death sentence. He was in his mid-eighties when he was booked, and put to untold miseries and harassment, but he fought the case with great courage.

It is against this background that the Bishop shot himself to death to arouse the conscience of sane people across the world.

The Noxious Law

The law of blasphemy is on the statute book not merely of multi-religious countries where specially the definition of blasphemy needs to be precise and must clearly state the points relating to insult to religions; it is on the statute book of many Western countries. What then is "special" in Pakistan and how is the law different here?

Section 295 of the law of blasphemy appears in Chapter IV of the Penal Code and this Chapter was enacted in 1860, and continues to operate. The Section reads: "Whoever destroys, damages or defiles any place of worship or any object held sacred by any class of persons with the intention of thereby insulting the religion or any class of persons is likely to consider such destruction, damage or defilement as an insult to their religion, shall be punished with imprisonment of either description for a term which may extend to two years, or with fine, or with both." It is clear that it covers the sacred books of all religions.

Section 295-B, inserted by Zia-ul-Haq reads: "Whoever willfully defiles, damages or desecrates a copy of Holy Quran or an extract therefrom or uses it in any derogatory manner or for any unlawful purpose shall be punishable for imprisonment for life." This Section relates to offences against the Holy Quran only, whereas Section 295 relates to sacred books of other religions. The punishment under Section 295-B is imprisonment for life. Which means that until the programme of Islamisation, ruthlessly implemented by Zia-ul-Haq, the punishment relating to all religious books including the Quran was a maximum of two years' imprisonment. Significantly, there had been no report until then of any case of desecration of holy books of any religion, including Islam.

Even a casual reading of the two Sections brings out the most blatant discriminatory character in the law, that is, one law for one, another for another. Furthermore, while Section 295 is precise, there is ambiguity in Section 295-B in that the offence of using the Holy Quran in a derogatory manner is not precise at all and, therefore, can be abused and is being abused. As is well known, this Section as also Section 298-C of Pakistan Penal Code (PPC) have been ruthlessly and cruelly used against the Ahmadia community.

The HRCP notes in its latest 1997 annual report: "There are two sets of laws that are directly discriminatory. One not only declared Ahmadiyas to be non-Muslims, it also went on to prohibit their preaching their faith. Preaching included their speaking about their faith to anyone or handing out any literature relating to it. In practice, this makes it difficult for them to publish their periodicals for the benefit of their own community. The law also forbids their practicing their religion in public nor using any of the forms, symbols or nomenclatures associated with Muslims. They cannot pray in public... These provisions are among the most stringently applied of the laws on the statute book. In fact there is over-zealousness in invoking them." During the period 1984 to 1997, there have been over

3,000 cases against the Ahmadis under the law of blasphemy—the largest number, about 750, being under Section 295-B. These 750 persons have been prosecuted for displaying the *Kalima* – the tent—which says, "there is none worthy of worship except Allah, Muhammad is the Messenger of Allah". As many as 140 Ahmadis were prosecuted for blasphemy under Section 296-C. In 1989, the entire population of Rabwah, the Ahmadiya headquarters in Pakistan, was charged under Section 298-C of Pakistan Penal Code, which is a special anti-Ahmadia law. During 1997, three Ahmadis were killed because of their faith; three others were sentenced to 25 years imprisonment and a Rs 50,000 fine on a charge of blasphemy which was added six years after they were initially charged with preaching Ahmadiyat: 32 were charged under anti-Ahmadiya and blasphemy laws, and 59 cases were registered on religious grounds [Source: HRCP Annual Reports 1996 and 1997].

It needs to be mentioned that the ground was prepared and seeds of Islamization were sown by Zulfiqar Ali Bhutto when he, as President of Pakistan, declared the Ahmediyas a non-Muslim community, thus depriving them of their rights including the use of mosques for *Namaz*. Zia-ul-Haq continued with the Islamization programme in a soil which was already made fertile by Bhutto. Zia said that he had got a direct message from God in this regard!

Section 295-B gives protection to the police to raid people's houses on the pretext that information has been received about the violation of this Section. This is an attack on the privacy of one's home, and contravenes Article 14 of the Pakistan Constitution which states, "the privacy of home shall be inviolable".

Enormous Disparity

Furthermore, as the disparity in the punishment between this Section and Section 295 is enormous, Section 295-B contravenes the provisions of Article 25(1), which states, "All citizens are equal before law and are entitled to equal protection of law".

Let us now turn to Section 295-C, inserted by Zia-ul-Haq, which is directly related to Ayub Masih's conviction and Bishop

Joseph's unusual and unique protest. It reads: "Whoever by words, either spoken or written, or by visible representation, or any imputation, innuendo, or insinuation, directly or indirectly, defiles the sacred name of the Holy Prophet Muhammad (PBUH) shall be punished with death and shall also be liable to fine."

In contrast to ambiguity and arbitrariness of the definition of the crime—there is no ambiguity about the punishment, death sentence is mandatory—mentioned in the Section is obvious. The late Justice Dorab Patel, who was Chief Justice of Pakistan Supreme Court, and later first Chairperson of the HRCP, and an internationally known human rights intellectual-activist, drew attention to this aspect in a speech in Pakistan before a women's gathering in 1993, when he referred to a Christian member of the Pakistan National Assembly saying that Jesus Christ was the son of God. He was denounced by the majority group for having committed blasphemy. Fortunately for him, he could not be prosecuted because he enjoyed immunity by virtue of his being a member of the Assembly. If, however, Justice Dorab added, the Christian member made this comment to a Muslim outside the Assembly, and the Muslim ridiculed Christ, thus insulting Him, the maximum punishment to which the Muslim is liable under Section 298 is only one year's imprisonment. But if, in reply the Christian criticizes the Quranic injunction against the claim of Christ being the Son of God, he would be sentenced to death under the law of the land, that is Section 295-C. Now, this definition is the most disturbing feature.

It is in the context of this arbitrariness that I refer to the HRCP, an NGO, which during the last 7–8 years has consistently and persistently made efforts to see that the two Sections, 295-B and 295-C, are repealed. During the campaign for repeal, Mrs. Asma Jahangir, Chairperson of the HRCP, was threatened with death by the mullahs of Lahore—bumper stickers appeared on buses and cars asking people to kill her.

HRCP Report

The HRCP 1997 report sounds a note of pessimism and sadness in this regard. It comments editorially that instead of providing a healing touch, there have been increasing divisions in society. Religious minorities, women and poor have no hope of redressal of their condition. The policies look calculated to favour the rich and to allow leeway to the fanatics for their physical and verbal *jehad* against their chosen targets. When two minority MNAs complained in the national Assembly of their girls being kidnapped and forcibly converted, when a feudal burnt down the Bheels temple of Devi Mataji to seize the land, or when Roshan Lal and his sister asked the Prime Minister in an open kutchery that their land could not be protected he might send them to India, which was bad enough, but also pervasive official acquiescence in it, which was worse. Persecution of Ahmadias, as in medieval times, public execution of a woman not just in a tribal area but also stoning of another in a village in Punjab, or a high court virtually condoning a father's murdering his daughter, is indicative of how thin the veneer of civilization still wore... There is a drift that seems headed in the direction of further weakening of such of the institutions as still exist, dividing the people, and easing the career of sanctimonious intolerance.

The HRCP and some women's groups, like the well-known Shirkat Gah in Lahore, take the view that horrendous things like increasing intolerance and violence have been happening in the name of Islam, and that it is the task of all right-thinking people in the country to deal with this intolerance effectively, and if they don't stand up and acknowledge this disgraceful happening and close the door on it, the present and future of Pakistan will continue to remain bleak. We in India must also take note of the culture of intolerance that prevails here.

Religious and sectarian intolerance has been on the increase in Pakistan, but not many outside the HRCP and Shirkat Gah have taken it seriously. The silence of Pakistani intellectuals reminds one of their approach and attitude to the 1971 event which led to the break-up of the country. Some kept their lips sealed, and some supported Bhutto and the army regime and their tirade against East Pakistan Bengalees and India. They know now—and privately acknowledge the fact—that if there is one reason which led to the break-up of Pakistan, it was the human rights violations perpetrated by the West Pakistan army and other West Pakistan government agencies in East Pakistan. Let not Pakistani intellectuals keep their lips sealed now. Indeed, intellectuals and opinion-makers all over must stand up and fight the forces of intolerance and fanaticism, wherever they be, including India where the culture of intolerance dominates.

[Courtesy: *University Today,* Vol. XVIII, No.12, 15 June 1998, pp. 9-10]

****

CHAPTER 7

A Tribute to Justice Dorab Patel

The death of one of the best known, most outspoken and fearless human rights activists in this part of the world, gone largely unnoticed in our country, is by far the greatest loss which the human rights movement, not only in Pakistan but also elsewhere, has suffered in recent times. Justice Dorab Patel (who died in Karachi on 15 March 1997 at the age of 72) had shown remarkable judicial independence while delivering the minority judgement in the Zulfiqar Ali Bhutto case during the atrocious and dreaded military regime of Zia-ul-Haq. He resigned as an acting Chief Justice of the Pakistan Supreme Court, after refusing to take an oath of allegiance to the military regime as it violated the country's Constitution. Such men of integrity are disappearing fast from our part of the world.

Justice Patel, in cooperation with an equally upright activist-lawyer, Ms. Asma Jahangir, established the Human Rights Commission of Pakistan (HRCP) in 1987. I.A. Rehman, its wholetime Director, and Aziz Siddiqui, the wholetime editor of the HRCP journal, are two other personalities associated with the movement. Justice Patel as the Honorary Chairperson, and Ms. Jahangir as the Honorary General Secretary, with the active help of Rehman and Siddiqui, have nurtured the HRCP (a non-governmental body) into an institution which should make all freedom-loving Pakistanis proud. The last four annual reports of the HRCP bear testimony to the unique part it has been playing.

One of the first things the HRCP did under Justice Patel's leadership was to organize a regional seminar of SAARC countries on the subject, "Law and Development", in Lahore on 24–27 November 1988. It should be remembered that to start a civil liberties and human rights movement in Pakistan under a much more difficult situation than that in India (because of the continued threat of military dictatorship against a backdrop of Islamisation) was an achievement; what was a greater achievement was that the HRCP invited human rights activists from India and other SAARC countries. Justice Patel played a leading role in that historic event.

Justice Patel came under attack—threats were openly held out to kill him and Ms. Asma Jahangir and her sister, Hina Jilani—from the fanatical mullahs in Pakistan for championing the cause of minorities and defending them in law courts in cases under the Blasphemy Law, the most obnoxious piece of legislation. Justice Patel came down heavily on the government for not prosecuting those who held out assassination threats. He maintained that if the mullahs were allowed to go scotfree, the prospects of democracy in Pakistan would be bleak. He advised the government not to accept dictation from the mullahs; if it did, he maintained, Pakistan will become a theocratic state under the façade of parliamentary democracy.

I may strike a personal note. Whenever I asked him to write for the *PUCL Bulletin* (the monthly journal published by the People's Union for Civil Liberties), he readily agreed. He wrote for us on a number of occasions.

A friend and admirer of the PUCL and many other human rights activists in India, whenever he came to Delhi he would make it a point to meet friends, and it was my unique privilege and pleasure to have arranged get-togethers for him at my place.

Justice Patel's talks and writings were characterized by a "brutal" forthrightness. Sample a few:

1. Pandit Nehru was a thoughtless politician during the freedom struggle (referring to the partition of the country); he became a statesman after the partition.
2. The Congress policy during the Second World War was wrong.
3. Benazir's husband has contributed considerably towards destabilizing the political climate and to her unpopularity.

4. When the mullahs persisted in threatening me on the telephone and the government did not take any action, I started using "four letter" words, and the calls stopped! But Asma is a soft target being a woman, and she could not use the language I did, so they continued to threaten her. Even then she did not accept government security.
5. Human Rights violations committed by India's security forces in Kashmir cannot be condoned.

   And so on.

Justice Patel was intensely committed to friendship between India and Pakistan, and attended the first and second conventions of the Pakistan–India People's Forum for Peace and Democracy held in Delhi and Lahore respectively in 1994 and 1995.

Thoroughly cosmopolitan in outlook, Justice Patel was a force for amity among the peoples of South Asia. How did he opt for Pakistan in 1947? Very simple, he said:

> My father was posted in that part of the country at the time of partition and he stayed on. If he were posted in this part, he might have opted for India. So I stayed there and have served the cause of the people living in Pakistan.

In recognition of his service to the people of Pakistan, the Pakistan Government conferred on him the *Hil-i-Imtiaz* Award in 1995.

Justice Patel, during one of his visits in Delhi, gave me the text of a lecture which he had delivered in Pakistan. This was published in the *PUCL Bulletin* April 1995 issue, under the heading, "The Blasphemy Law in Pakistan Needs To Be Changed: Intellectuals in Pakistan Have Failed." A few excerpts deserve to be quoted to indicate how relevant he will continue to remain, not only for Pakistan but also elsewhere, where intolerance and fanaticism rule supreme:

> I now turn to Section 295-C (of the Blasphemy Law). It reads: 'Whoever by words, either spoken or written, or by visible representation, or by any imputation, innuendo, or institution, directly or indirectly defiles the sacred name of the Holy Prophet

(Peace Be Upon Him) shall be punished with death, and shall also be liable to fine.' ...The words 'by an imputation, innuendo or insinuation, directly or indirectly' make the definition of the crime of blasphemy arbitrary. ...I now turn to a discussion between a Christian and a Muslim about the Christian claim that Christ was the son of God and I am taking this example because I do not accept this claim myself. If a Muslim ridicules the claim with the intention of insulting the Christian, the maximum punishment to which he is liable under Section 298 is only one-year imprisonment, but if a Christian returns the compliment by criticizing the Quranic injunction against the Christian's claim of Christ being the Son of God, he would probably be sentenced to death although he spoke under provocation and without any intention of committing blasphemy.... I am not the only person disturbed by this definition, which clearly violates the guarantee of equality in Article 25 of the Constitution.... In June 1994 the Law Minister announced that the government was amending the Law of Blasphemy. However, the Law Minister's statement led to protests and processions by the religious extremists and to assassination threats against him. The government announced that it was not changing the law... . There is more than one reason for the change in the conduct of the religious extremists in 1992-1994. There is no doubt that religious intolerance has increased but it has been increasing for the last 10 or 15 years.... Why did the majority of our intellectuals remain silent while intellectuals in similar conditions in other countries have protested. The murder of four Turks in Germany by neo-Nazis was denounced by all political parties in Germany and millions of people came out in torchlight procession to denounce the murder... Most of them feel, 'in plain English', that they cannot take the risk of sticking their necks out.... The silence of our intellectuals reminds me of the situation in Germany in the late twenties. The Nazi party had never concealed its worship of violence, and during the election campaign of the last free elections in Germany in the inter-War period, the Nazi party had assassinated some of the leaders of the Socialist and Communist parties and held out assassination threats against other leaders. The good Germans ignored these threats because they believed that Germans were highly educated, and so the Nazi party would be absorbed into the humanistic tradition of Western Europe once it came into power. The false optimism cost millions of lives. The situation in Pakistan is different from Germany. Our danger is the drift to a theocratic state because of the complacency of our intellectuals.... (The fact remains) that a law inconsistent with the Fundamental Rights guaranteed in the Constitution is not being altered because of parties which obtained only five per cent of the votes in the last elections. If a small minority group in Parliament can thus shape the policies of the country, the prospects of democracy are bleak.

[Courtesy: *Mainstream*, Vol. XXXV, No. 20, 26 April 1997, pp. 13-14]

****

CHAPTER 8

Women's Movement in Islamic Countries

Several Islamic countries in recent years have witnessed two simultaneous developments: one, the state's making anti-women laws in the name of Sharia (Muslim Law); and two, articulate and powerful women's movements in the respective countries fighting against such laws. A few examples follow.

Zamfara, one of Nigeria's 30 states, has introduced Sharia (Muslim Law). One of its provisions prohibits women and men from travelling together on public transport. Which means wives and husbands, mothers and grown-up sons cannot travel together! Shiite groups in Zamfara have criticized the Zamfara State—according to them the State does not have the moral or constitutional authority to institute Sharia (Muslim Law) in a secular and multi-religious state like Nigeria. A large number of women from Muslim countries, including Afghanistan, Algeria, Bangladesh, Cameroon, Iran, Malaysia, Nigeria, Pakistan, Palestine, Senegal and Sudan gathered in Nigeria last year and took note of the dangerous consequences of such laws introduced in the name of Sharia. Other countries with sizeable Muslim populations like India, Kenya and South Africa also participated in the protest. The Muslim women gathered in Nigeria declared that the laws are violative of human rights of women even according to the provisions of the Constitution of Nigeria.

"We have already seen this happen in Afghanistan, when in the name of Islam and segregation of the sexes, women and girls no longer have access to education, health care services, job and other means of gaining an economic livelihood or the right to freedom of movement. Similarly, those who claim to be the flag-bearers have attacked girls' right to education and women's rights to mobility in Algeria, Bangladesh and elsewhere. We are alarmed that these abuses are being implemented under the guise of Islam," declared the women's meet; it called upon the Government of Zamfara to protect and ensure the rights of women.

Women in Kuwait are not allowed to vote and hold political office. A bill to give Kuwaiti women this right by 2003 was narrowly defeated in Kuwaiti parliament. However, the fight for this right is continuing. Ali-al-Baghi, a former minister of Kuwait and a supporter of the bill, condemned the "fanatic mentality of Islamist and tribalist members of parliament whose views have held sway". To the charge that allowing women to enter politics would "invite their moral downfall", Ali Baghi said: "All Western women do not work in strip clubs and bars." However, as a result of the introduction of the bill, a woman Under-Secretary has been allowed to perform ministerial duties.

"Women's Rights" is a subject of serious discussion in the Arab countries. In Saudi Arabia, human rights activists have demanded the withdrawal of a law that prohibits women from driving. Women activists' demands in the United Arab Emirates include women's right to become Cabinet Ministers.

There is a fairly strong movement in Bangladesh against the practice of *fatwa* issued by "the half-educated rustic mullahs with virtually no knowledge of Islamic jurisprudence". These mullahs interpret the Quranic injunctions and sunna

> in their own freewheeling way to repress and subjugate the women, taking advantage of their illiteracy ... (and) of the religious sentiment of the simple rural folk.

Fatwas are pronounced on adultery, rape, divorce etc., and "the verdict invariably goes against women".

Bangladesh is not governed by Sharia Law and *fatwa* is strictly prohibited. The National Women's Policy of the present government clearly stipulates:

> that any attempt or step which is contrary to the fundamental rights of women and the law prevalent in the country through the interpretation of injunctions of any religion at local or national level will be strictly dealt with. However, this societal practice of fatwa continues;

at the same time there is, however, a pressing demand from women's groups in Bangladesh to strictly prohibit fatwa. Women's groups are creating awareness among women, specially in rural areas, about this societal violation of women's rights.

One of the Central Asian countries, Turkmenistan (a former Soviet Republic), has abolished the death sentence. "Now in our country neither the government nor anyone else has the right to take away human life," Turkmen President Niyazov told the Khalq Maslakhaty (people's council). Two other Central Asian countries, Kazakhstan and Kyrghyzstan, have suspended executions. It is hoped they too will follow suit and abolish this "unlawful" law of death penalty.

Even in a conservative country like Iran, the women's movement is striving hard to make its presence felt. Ms. Faezale Hashemi, daughter of former President Rafsanjani, "has called for more freedom of dress and behaviour for women in the Islamic society". There is no shame, she said in a meeting, "about a girl proposing marriage to a boy. Why should a girl sit at home and wait for a male suitor to knock on her door one day?" Ms. Hashemi, a reformist and a leading women's rights activist working for equality of women with men in Iran, would not stop her 16-year old daughter "from proposing marriage to a boy". She insists that women must have the freedom to wear clothes of their choice; they must not be compelled to wear black *chador* (or long robe and scarf) which has been the prescribed clothing for women in Iran since the 1979 revolution. Ms. Hashemi, who herself rides a bicycle in public, has demanded that women in Iran be allowed to ride bicycles.

Pakistan had introduced a progressive law, Muslim Family Laws Ordinance 1961 (MFLD), with a view to protecting and promoting human rights of women. This progressive law was challenged in January 2000 in the Federal Shariat Court which directed the President of Pakistan to amend the 1961 MFLO "so as to bring the provisions" into conformity with the injunctions of Islam". One of the best known women's groups in this part of the world, the Shirkat Gah based in Lahore, has recently brought out a *Special Bulletin* in which it has given an account of women's struggle in Pakistan to promote women's rights relating to marriage, child marriage, polygamy, divorce, inheritance, and so on.

The 1961 MFLO prescribed, for example, that every marriage performed under Muslim law be registered; no man, during the subsistence of an existing marriage, shall, except with the prior permission in writing of the Arbitration Council, contract another marriage. The Federal Shariat Court (FSC) upheld some sections of the MFLO, but came down heavily on certain important beneficial provisions for women like divorce, inheritance, etc. Women's and human rights groups like the Shirkat Gah and the Human Rights Commission of Pakistan have issued a number of statements criticizing the FSC. These groups maintain that

> it is not just the MFLO that has suffered over the years, the real victims have been the millions of women whose rights have been undermined by the sustained attack on the MFLO. It is now time to look back at all the recommendations made over the years for strengthening Muslim family law in Pakistan and to move forward to a situation where women's rights within the family are fully legislated and implemented.

[Source materials have been drawn from Lahore-based Shirkat Gah's Netoslieet, Volume XI, No. 4; and its *Special Bulletin*, February 2000 entitled *Women's Rights in Muslim Family Law in Pakistan : 45 years of Recommendations vs the FSC Judgement*. The writer acknowledges his gratitude to Shirkat Gah.]

[Courtesy: *Mainstream*, Vol. XXXVIII, No. 42, 7 October 2000, pp. 9 & 30]

****

CHAPTER 9

Akhtar Hameed Khan

We have reported the valiant efforts made by Pakistani human rights groups to save Akhtar Hameed Khan from the gallows (the last report was published in the June issue of the *PUCL Bulletin*). He has been accused of blasphemy against the Prophet—and the punishment is death, according to the law. The latest report from Farida Shaheed of *Shirkat Gah* of Lahore is a bit encouraging—"at the legal level the situation remains static with the last hearing (9th May) being adjourned. However despite the court's directive Akhtar Hameed Khan has not been arrested", and that all freedom-loving people may send to *Shirkat Gah* copies of their letters of protest addressed to the Pakistan government (address: 14/300 (27-A) Nisar Road, Lahore Cantt).

Who is Akhtar Hameed Khan? I may strike a personal note. In 1959 I went to East Pakistan to see my parents in our village. On my way to my village, I went to Comilla Victoria College where I once wanted to study, but couldn't, thanks to our political leaders of all hues. The college was closed on account of Ramadan. The peon told me that the Principal was in the office. I gave him a piece of paper on which I wrote my name and address. The peon told me that it was not necessary—I should just step in. On my insisting that I would rather have his permission, the peon told me that in that case he would lose his job, for the Principal's instruction was that if he was alone in the office, visitors and students should not be made to wait—and no permission be sought!

As I entered, a tall man in white khadi kurta and pyjama stood up and introduced himself, "Akhtar Hameed Khan". "Are you the famous one?" I asked spontaneously. I was indeed very lucky to have met one exceptional man who had brought philosophy to the poor man's door for practical application (a species which has almost disappeared from the subcontinent). I introduced myself. He asked for tea for me only, for he was observing a fast. Soon it appeared to me that I had perhaps seen this man before, but where? Could it be that he was the same person who was Additional District Magistrate and visited our school—in shorts and a half shirt, walking and eating a banana, for his car had broken down two miles away from the village school. Yes, he was the same person. How come, he gave up the persitigious ICS (did we have anyone in our country?), and got into teaching and voluntary work of village reconstruction? He resigned in 1946 (or 1947?), went to Deoband to study, and then to Aligarh and went through an academic course in Engineering, and joined a lock-maker's concern as a labourer! Later, after Partition he returned to East Pakistan, joined the College and got involved in voluntary work—actively associated himself with all the *Ashrams*, particularly the famous *Abhay Ashrams* of Comilla, which were started by Gandhian workers, but many of whom had left their birthplace.

Anyone concerned with development activities, particularly village reconstruction—a different model centring upon the individual's own initiative without depending on outside agencies, including government—should be knowing this unusual person, with a remarkable personality, who had absolute confidence in man's ability to make his own destiny, and who attracted attention throughout the world for his pioneering work in the field of villege reconstruction. Experts from the West would often come to see the projects that villagers had set up in accordance with his ideals.

In the midst of our talks, when he came to know that I had the privilege of knowing M.N. Roy, he said that he was greatly interested in Roy's theory of party-less politics and democracy, and that he was in contact with some of Roy's radical democrat followers in Dhaka, like my friend Professor Jyotirmay Guha

Thakurta and his wife Basanti (Jyotirmay was the first one in the University to be killed by the Pakistani Army)—Jyotirmay was not an admirer of Sheikh Mujibur Rahman. Basanti and their daughter Meghna, who is now a faculty member in Dhaka University and a well-known social scientist, did not leave Dhaka even after Jyotirmay's death, though the British government offered them asylum in the UK, and that he would like to buy a complete set of Roy's books.

He was frank, forthright but not dogmatic. We talked about many things, including Islam and his somewhat pluralistic views of Islamic philosophy and religion, in which he showed profound learning.

When I expressed my surprise about his changing professions, and particularly giving up the prestigious ICS, he said in a lighthearted manner: "Isn't it nice to look at life from as many angles as possible?" (From then on, I would often quote him in the class room and in later years, also to my children).

As I got up, after about three hours, he asked me to give his regards to Professor Biswas of Meerut College from where, I came to know then, he had done his M.A. in English Literature—he owed a lot, he said, to Professor Biswas, who had taught him English. (On my return, I did convey this to Professor Biswas—tears rolled down his cheeks).

I kept in touch with him till 1963/64. I don't know when he left East Pakistan—perhaps after the 1971 war. If he was compelled by the Bengalees to leave East Pakistan, it has been a great loss for Bangladesh.

Such an unusual man, facing a death sentence on a flimsy charge of what he had written long ago about Islam! It's so sad to think that this earth has no place for good men like Akhtar Hameed Khan, now in his eighties, who has to face such torture. We should however be proud of the fact that Akhtar Hameed Khan has not surrendered and will not prostrate, even if he has to face death. And, that's precisely how one defied death.

News:

HRCP Report Released

Mrs. Asma Jahangir, Secretary General of Human Rights Commission of Pakistan said, while releasing its 1992 report, that " the civil and political rights of the individual came under greater pressure and encouragement of fundamentalism by acts of commission and omission which appeared even more menacing to any progress of women's rights". In its interim report, the HRCP observes that more violations of fundamental rights were made last year in Pakistan that in the previous year.

****

CHAPTER 10

Torture and Media Awareness

Article 5 of the Universal Declaration of Human Rights (UDHR) (1948) states:

> No one shall be subjected to torture or to cruel, inhuman or degrading treatment or punishment.

In pursuance of this, the UN adopted and opened for signature, ratification and accession on 10 December 1984, the Convention Against Torture and Other Cruel, Inhuman or Degrading Treatment or Punishment (Entry into Force, 26 June 1987). Article 2 of the Convention prescribes:

> Each State Party shall take effective legislative, administrative, judicial or other measures to prevent acts of torture in any territory under its jurisdiction.

Another significant step was taken in the UN World Congress on Human Rights (Vienna, 1993) where special attention was drawn to freedom from torture. In spite of the UDHR and the Convention provisions, torture, specially custodial torture, has not declined; in fact, incidents of custodial torture have been on the increase worldwide. (Although India signed the Convention in 1997, it has yet to ratify it; and without ratification the provisions of the Convention remain unenforceable.)

One need hardly emphasize the point that the extreme form of all organised violence—custodial violence falls in this category—is torture, and that it is one of the most cruel and obnoxious forms of human rights violation. The civil society has a special and inescapable responsibility to not only protect tortured victims but also to create a climate of freedom from torture; and without this freedom the foundation of democracy will always remain weak. The civil society, specially the members of the medical profession, have also the responsibility of treating, counselling, and rehabilitating tortured victims. It is in this context that a "Journalist Seminar/Workshop on Media Awareness of Torture Victims and their Rehabilitation" was organised on 18–20 June, 1999 at Timber Trail, Parvanu, Himachal Pradesh, by the Indian Medical Association (IMA) and the Press Institute of India in collaboration with the International Council of Rehabilitation of Torture Victims (IRCT) based in Denmark.

About fifty participants—media persons, medical doctors/physicians, legal practitioners and experts, human rights activists, and members representing the three sponsoring organizations—attended the three-day brainstorming session.

Ajit Bhattacharjee, Director, Press Institute of India, who was scheduled to start off the meet, was not able to attend for some unforeseen circumstances. Veteran journalist G.S. Bhargava did an excellent job, on behalf of the Press Institute, in regulating, and also moderating when necessary, the discussion and interaction. In fact, the intellectual input was provided by him.

Bhargava set the tone by giving a detailed account of newspaper coverage of torture-related human rights issue on the basis of a sample survey conducted by the IMA in April 1999. He drew attention of the participants to

> torture inflicted by agencies of the establishment on the population (like) police violence, police brutalities and interrogations, including investigations.

With regard to media coverage, Bhargava's comments must be taken seriously by journalists, specially by young reporters who are expected to be sensitive:

> The bulk of the media attention is on domestic violence, like dowry deaths or torturing to deaths of brides by their in-laws on the ground of not providing enough dowry. The menace is widespread and so naturally draws more attention but cannot be fitted into the agenda of the Workshop for obvious reasons. Sex-related

> crimes... and the sex angle (catch the attention of the media). So to the extent this reveals media awareness of human rights, it can be less torture-related and more to satisfy reader interest based on several factors, not excluding prurience.

The fact is that our young reporters—at times even senior journalists—do not make any distinction between societal violation of human rights and state violation. Torture belongs to the second category.

Dr. Inge Genefike, Secretary-General of IRCT, in her presentation, appealed to journalists, in the context of media awareness:

> Torture is debilitating for the victims, their families, and society. It breaks down trust, the confidence in fellow human beings. It's the most despicable and destructive of all human interaction. ...As a health professional I have taken the oath of Hippocrates. There is no journalistic equivalent, but as I see it, there are journalistic virtue, journalistic ethics: truthfulness, fairness, exactitude and knowledge. ...You have the responsibility of denouncing torture, raising the public awareness of the problem, raising awareness of the fact that every single individual in this world possesses the right not to be tortured.

Justice Malimath, who recently completed his term of membership of the National Human Rights Commission (NHRC), in his inaugural address gave an outline of what the NHRC has done to improve the situation. Justice Malimath has done pioneering work during his term. It is under his guidance that the NHRC brought out an excellent report on the state of affairs in forensic sciences with a view to streamlining the criminal justice system in our country (this is related to torture); another report that came out under Justice Malimath's guidance relates to mental health—which too relates to torture. It may be noted in this context that until 1982, India did not have any specific mental health policy. The National Mental Health Programme, introduced in 1982, has not been taken seriously by the politicians, policy-makers, bureaucrats, and professionals. Justice Malimath's contribution, specially in the preparation of the two reports, will go a long way in creating awareness about the magnitude of the problem in our country.

A number of members of the IMA, including its President, Dr. V.C. Patel, and General Secretary, Dr. Prem Aggarwal, gave their unstinted support to rehabilitation programmes. The organizational part of the meet was expertly handled by Mrs. Nandini Sahai of the Press Institute, and Dr. Vinay Aggarwal and Dr. Jagdish Sobti of the IMA.

Dr. Pradeep Agrawal of the IMA, in his paper on "Torture Victims and Experience in India" made a specific reference, apropos of rehabilitation of torture victims, to psychological and social treatment, and the need for social counselling. Dr. Agrawal pointed out that India does not have adequate number of trained mental health professionals and rehabilitation centres for torture victims. (I may add that our neighbour, Bangladesh is far more advanced in respect of rehabilitation centres for torture victims.)

As noted earlier, the civil society has a special responsibility in this regard, particularly because most of the torture victims in our country belong to the vulnerable and deprived sections of our country. The NHRC or the judiciary by itself cannot do much—to bring any perceptible change in the situation. It is here that the media can and must play a creative role. This point was emphasized by a number of participants. The general view was that the media has not been giving as much coverage to this aspect as it deserves with a view to bringing about a change in the situation. It was also felt that if NGOs and watchdog organizations go on persisting, fighting and agitating, the media, sooner or later, is bound to take note of the state of human rights in the country. It was also pointed out that of late, a section of the media, for whatever reasons, has started highlighting human rights violations, and that NGOs and activists must pursue their awareness programme with greater vigour. Activists should try to impress upon reporters and senior journalists to introduce a regular civil liberties column, and help reporters in furnishing truthful accounts of human rights violation. In short, it was felt by the participants that human rights activists must have better liason with journalists.

II

It was suggested by this writer that we also need to go into the cultural aspects of the problem, specially in the context of our country. Let us be clear in this regard. We have inherited a culture of violence and intolerance. This finds reflection in the behaviour of our law-enforcing agencies, specially their behaviour with, and treatment of, the deprived and depressed section of our population. (I will illustrate this point a little later.) Let us not forget that for centuries we have not recognized the depressed section of our people even as persons, not to speak of treating them with dignity and respect. Let us not, therefore, romanticize our past. Our first task is to acknowledge the fact that there are horrendous corners which exist in our society; once we accept this fact we will be able to close the doors on that ugly past. We must revive that past which is characterized by humanism, tolerance, and non-violence. Then only we can create new men and new women, and a new society, a kind of society of the Buddha's ideal. (The Buddha's concept of non-violence must not be summarily dismissed as Utopia; it is eminently relevant today, and can be implemented provided we shed a bit of our unnecessary arrogance. Gandhi tried but failed. But this concept, which is our heritage, remains relevant.)

It is in the above context that this writer presented a short paper giving an account of torture in custody—most of the victims belong to the Scheduled Tribes—concentrating on the method and kind of torture inflicted on people by Special Task Force (STF) of Karnataka and Tamil Nadu. A brief summary that follows is based on a fact-finding report conducted by a number of NGOs including the PUCL unit of Karnataka. (The full report has been published in the monthly, *PUCL Bulletin*, June and July 1999 issues.) The governments of Karnataka and Tamil Nadu set up an STF in 1992 to nab the forest brigand and sandalwood smuggler, Veerappan. The STF started combing operations to catch Veerappan. They have not yet succeeded in catching him. In the process they have, however, inflicted indescribable torture on a large number of people on mere suspicion that these people are in league with Veerappan or would not disclose his whereabouts.

The STF detain people illegally for months, and then arrest them (in the past most of them were arrested under TADA). The ostensible charge against them is: they aid Veerappan.

These tribal people are kept in torture camps for months before they are sent to Mysore Jail. (It is sad to note that the Bar Association of Mysore had once decided that no lawyer from outside Karnataka be allowed to represent detenues in courts! And, mind you, they are "officers" of the court!)

The fact-finding team, members of which are distinguished people from Karnataka and Tamil Nadu, met victims who had been released on bail, and video-recorded their versions. They have given an account of the horrendous tortures inflicted on them. I give below a few, by way of illustration.

A woman in the STF's custody, gave birth to a child fathered through rape by the STF personnel. When the woman was having labour pain and was in the process of giving birth to the child, the STF men rejoiced at her discomfiture and added to her pain—they squeezed her breast. (And, we say we Indians worship women as goddesses!) A large number of these tribal women were raped by the STF personnel and made pregnant.

There is one torture camp which is known as "workshop", a place of no return for the victims. They are made to put on clothes like those of the Veerappan gang and shot dead.

Electric shock treatment is very common. Men are forced to place the clips with the electric wires on the genitals and nipples of breasts of women, while women are forced to do the same on the male organ. Horse Shoe method (beating the soles of feet until the lathi breaks); pulling apart the legs; torture with irritants such as chilly powder, salt, etc. applied on delicate parts of the body and on open wounds are routine methods of torture.

Sexual torture: Men and women are compelled to undress and stand naked facing each other for hours; if anyone tries to cover herself/himself with their hands they are kicked and beaten. The STF personnel force children to have sexual intercourse in their presence.

I may refer to one case study—Manjula's cry of agony. Manjula, a young wife, and her husband, Abhay, were detained by the STF personnel. They were tortured, and then handed over to the Superintendent of Police (SP). The SP raped Manjula in her husband's presence. They were then released. Manjula's cry of agony does not end there. Abhay, her husband tells his parents about the rape. Manjula is thrown out of the house.

Can there be a shriller cry of agony than Manjula's?

Let us be honest with ourselves. We are what the great humanist and rationalist, Ishwar Chandra Vidyasagar, exclaimed long ago, in sheer disgust, in the context of widow-remarriage:

> Oh, unfortunate women, what sin have you committed that you should have been born in this blessed country where men are so insensitive!

Has the climate changed?

[Courtesy: *Vidura* (published by Press Institute of India, New Delhi)]

[Courtesy: *Mainstream*, Vol. XXXVII, No. 36, 28 August 1999, pp. 18–20]

****

CHAPTER 11

Police Excesses

THE DEMAND TO GRANT IMMUNITY

The demand for immunity for Punjab police officers guilty of human rights violations may be viewed, among other things, in the background of cases pending before the Apex Court. Let us recapitulate here a few instances of the directives and orders issued by the Supreme Court.

The Court, on 17 April 1995, found five police personnel, including officers, prima facie guilty of gunning down in 1993 a couple in West Bengal who were suspected to be terrorists. The court observed: "Our worst apprehensions have come true. The killings of the couple reveal a state of affairs when human life has virtually no value for officers in uniform, who are supposed to be protectors of human life. We are indeed greatly distressed at the manner in which the incident took place". The court directed that cases be instituted against police officials responsible for the outrage.

In Cold Blood

When the case came up before the court on 1 May 1995, the court, commenting on the callous behaviour of the police, said: "The police kill people in cold blood and then say the judgement is bad. Their attitude appears to be: I accuse, I judge, and I sentence."

In another case of subsequent liquidation of seven members of a family from Bagga village of Amritsar district, the Chief Justice commented on 4 May 1995: "It is a serious matter, people are being killed, their whereabouts and (those of) their dead bodies are not known. And the DGP (K.P.S. Gill) quietly says that the petition has become infructuous. No doubt we will ensure that the law is maintained and its majesty is upheld. But what about the people who are being eliminated in this way? Who will be accountable for that?" When the Additional Solicitor-General, Mr. K.T.S. Tulsi, tried to defend Mr. Gill, the Chief Justice remarked: "You are asking for commendation from this court of police officers who eliminate persons. ... Seven people are dead—killed, and there is an evidence to it. The whole thing is very disturbing. ... I don't think you can assist the court. You are here only to hold brief for the police. ...This is not the case you can defend."

On 15 November 1995, the court issued directives to the CBI to inquire into Mr. Jaswant Singh Kalra's disappearance from Amritsar. Mr. Kalra, a human rights activist, took up the case of cremation by the police of a large number of persons killed in fake encounters as suspected to be terrorists. The court commented that if the allegations are true, they would constitute the "most gory tale of human rights violations", and directed the Punjab government to transfer the police officer, Mr. Ajit Singh Sandhu, from Tarn Taran till the completion of the investigations of the case. According to CBI reports submitted to the Supreme Court later, 2,097 persons were cremated during two years out of which 585 were identified, and 275 partially identified. The rest, 1,238 remain unidentified.

On 29 January 1996, the Supreme Court asked the CBI to prosecute 27 Punjab police personnel, including an IPS officer, Mr. Vivek Misra, who were allegedly involved in the murder of four Sikh youths in Gurdaspur in January 1994.

The recent tirade against human rights activists by "patriotic" quarters, which include the former Director General of Police, Mr. Gill, has also to be viewed against the background given above. (It should be obvious that the attack is against the court also.) The campaign intensified since the alleged suicide by a Punjab police officer, Ajit Singh Sandhu, who had been facing criminal charges. The National Human Rights Commission (NHRC) is investigating the charges under the direction of the Supreme Court. In particular, those relating to 43 cases of elimination ("unceremonious cremation") of people suspected to be terrorists, were under NHRC scrutiny.

Mr. Gill and others like him advocate a policy of bending the law of the land in favour of police officers who "eliminated" terrorists in Punjab by liquidating hundreds of persons, including innocent citizens. According to Mr. Gill and his like, such police officers are being prosecuted, which is tantamount to persecution. Which means that the State and its agencies are permitted to kill people. Terrorism, according to them, cannot be handled in any other way. What then is the difference between the State and the terrorist?

Sanctity

Furthermore, what happens to the sanctity provided by Article 21 of our Constitution ("No person shall be deprived of his life except according to the procedure established by law").

Among those pleading for immunity for police officers found guilty of "bonafide excesses" and for taking a "magnanimous view", is the Director-General of the NHRC, Mr. Sankar Sen, who in an article in *The Statesman* (20-21 June) writes that the acid test should be whether a person acted in bonafides or not.

Apart from other unintended contradictions in the Article, how does one define "bonafide excesses?" Doesn't it sound to be a contradiction in terms? Mr. Sen, while pleading "for a more compassionate view", gives the analogy of the Truth and Reconciliation Commission in South Africa apropos of apartheid, and the Shah Commission. These instances are not relevant in that they did not ask for bending the law nor did they make any appeal to ask for compassion. The inescapable conclusion of Mr. Sen's arguments is that the law should be bent.

In the context of bending the law, we may refer to a Supreme Court judgement on 5 February 1997 (in a case relating to fake encounters in Manipur brought before the Court by the People's Union for Civil Liberties in a writ petition): "It is true that Manipur is a disturbed area, that there appears to be a good amount of terrorist activity affecting public order and, may be, even security of that State. ... The present case appears to be one where two people along with some others were just seized from a hut, taken to a long distance away in a truck and shot there. This type of activity cannot certainly be countenanced by the courts even in the case of disturbed areas. ... 'Administrative liquidation' was certainly not a course open to them."

Deaths

In another case relating to "encounter" deaths in Andhra Pradesh, the NHRC itself observed: "the hardships of the State, in our view, cannot take away or abridge the guarantee under Article 21 of the Constitution or Article 6 of the Covenant (International Covenant on Civil and Political Rights), and apply it as a cover against the fundamental right".

It may also be noted that even political leaders in Punjab, including those of the CPI, who are known for their outright anti-Khalistan stand, assert that police officers in Punjab have liquidated not only terrorists and their families but also innocent people.

It is hoped that people like Mr Gill will give thought to the question of rule of law and human rights, keeping in mind that our officers and men should not act at the cost of India forfeiting the right to occupy her rightful place in the comity of civilized nations governed by the rule of law. The common man and woman expect Mr. Sen and the NHRC to devise ways and means to create conditions in which respect for human rights and the rule of law is realizable and in which the law-enforcing agencies will treat the common man and woman—victims of abuses—with "magnanimity" and compassion. One of the ways to achieve this, as this writer has written on a number of occasions and spoken to police officers in police and administrative academies while lecturing there on human rights and the rule of law, is increasing interaction between social activists and the police. This might inculcate in the police a culture conducive to respect for human rights and the rule of law. This should be done, not by trading charges or suspecting motives mutually, but through discussion of specific instances of violations by the police, like the ones mentioned earlier.

[Courtesy: *The Statesman*, Saturday, 5 July 1997]

****

CHAPTER 12

Emergency: Looking Back

On June 25, the country observes the twenty-second anniversary of the imposition of the 1975 Emergency.

Two historic events took place in 1975: one, the Allahabad High Court on 12 June held Prime Minister Indira Gandhi guilty of corrupt electoral practices; two, all Opposition political party leaders announced in a public meeting on 25 June that Mrs. Gandhi should not continue as Prime Minister, and if she did not quit they would start a civil disobedience movement from 29 June. The consequence of these events is well known: internal Emergency was imposed on midnight, 25-26 June and thousands of people, including Opposition leaders were arrested and put in jail, and all the important Fundamental Rights were suspended. The Emergency waged war upon democracy. There were violations of all standards of morality, justice and freedom. The authorities were ordered to sign blank arrest warrants and they did—to send people to jail. The excesses that were committed were not accidental, but were the logical and deliberate acts of a policy. The object of this policy was destruction of all that is fine and valuable in human culture, and triumph of the strong.

It is essential to refresh our memory, specially in two contexts.

One, the nightmarish experience of the Emergency in which one could be detained without any reason given to him/her and without being told why he/she was being detained, and how people fought to uphold the democratic values enshrined in our Constitution, and defied the unlawful laws of the Emergency regime.

Two, to recollect how senior political leaders had sent letters of apology to Mrs. Indira Gandhi, how some "celebrities" lodged in jail had made frantic efforts to establish contact with her emissaries to be released without loss of faith, and how some wonted liberals and even the Rashtriya Swamsevak Sangh (RSS) had hailed Sanjay Gandhi as the new "star" on the horizon. (These were all detailed, for the first time, in a book, *Five-Headed Monster—A Factual Narrative of the Genesis of the Janata Party*, by Brahm Dutt, published in 1978.)[2] It should also not be forgotten that Vinoba Bhave had hailed the "new-found discipline" during the Emergency without dwelling on its other aspects.

Recalling the Emergency and the subsequent political practice during the last two decades and more, the common man feels let down and betrayed by persons in whom our people reposed faith and hope. The central issue of ridding the system of tendencies and forces which made the Emergency possible, has been overshadowed by personal greed, lust for power, and unprincipled conduct of our politicians. It is painful to recollect how people connected with managing the Emergency, and indulging in unlawful acts and infringement of civil liberties and total curbing of the freedom of expression, found berths in subsequent non-Congress governments. One such "celebrity"—one of the most obnoxious in Mrs. Gandhi's Emergency Cabinet—managed to hold senior ministerial positions in almost all the Ministries from 1980 onwards, both Congress and non-Congress!

I may dwell on another personality who was most prominent among the opponents of the Emergency and a VVIP in the Janata Party. At a wedding reception in New Delhi a couple of years ago, we were shocked to see not less than 50 or so armed and unarmed policemen providing "security" to an expected guest. They looked at us as though we were potential or actual enemies of the country, pointing their armament at all and sundry. Then entered this VVIP—he continues to remain a VVIP—visibly enjoying the *bandobast*, with gun-toting cops all around A pretty disgusting sight! We, the ordinary human mortals, watched him as he emerged like a divinely appointed hereditary ruler who considers all citizens as enemies. The same

VVIP at another function declared that in no other country do people talk so much about human rights as in India. Yes, because we continue to be victims of fraud, deceit, and being treated like cattle. No wonder, he continues to claim that he is the only person who is competent to become the Prime Minister of the country!

A quick look at the role of academics and intellectuals during the Emergency. This writer (during the latter part of the Emergency) was advised by the Vice-Chancellor, the Dean of Colleges, faculty members, and professors of Delhi University on the Governing Body of the college where he was working, to do tight-rope walking by not criticising the Emergency and yet retaining freedom of action! It was depressing to see academics holding high offices cringe before small-time Congressmen, addressing them as "Sir" and "Madam". It is impossible not to derive a measure of amusement and even malicious satisfaction to see the same persons fawning upon RSS leaders after the post-Emergency regime came to power and wooing them.

Professor Nurul Hasan, the Minister of Education in Mrs. Gandhi's Emergency Cabinet, addressed a students' function. Speaking on the occasion, this writer delved into the philosophy of the Renaissance, questioning, scepticism, and related issues, like "what concerns all must be solved by all" as enunciated by a King of England in the Middle Ages, and so on. Professor Hasan didn't spare this writer! He debunked the theory of perpetual enquiry. He was at his "Marxist" best in demolishing my expiation on scepticism and questioning—but didn't utter the word 'democracy' even once. Well, one must remember, perhaps that's how our scholars prosper in all seasons!

We may also recollect how feigned ideological and political differences were used as a cover for ego-centricism and quest for self-aggrandizement to wreck a pro-democracy coalition (the Janata Party Government formed in 1977) within two years of its formation, dashing, in the process, the hopes of the people for a democratic system. It was this lack of character and commitment to basic values among a large number of political parties which had first enabled Mrs. Indira Gandhi and an upstart like Sanjay Gandhi not only to ride to unquestioned authority and strike at the roots of the system but also to get away with it. This aspect of want of moral fibre must not be lost sight of while analyzing the roots of the Emergency. Contrary to what some well-meaning liberals maintain, the Emergency was not an aberration. We must take note of increasing corruption, manipulative politics, and other evils in the system which have been systematically eroding the values of democracy and destroying it.

We must also remember that the factors which led to the imposition of Emergency, namely, degeneration of public life, diabolical scramble for power, and erosion of democratic practice, have remained unaffected. In fact, the situation in some respects has become desperate. (What happened to the United Front Government sometime back, and what is happening now to the Janata Dal President's election, for example, are pointers to this.)

We must go to the roots and explain the rise of a totalitarian government in June 1975. One wonders, in this context, if the Congress-led, nationalist movement had taught our people the philosophy which goes into the making of a civilized and democratic society. Furthermore, political leaders and social activists must not hesitate to take note of the fact that some ingredients of fascism are ingrained in our culture, and Mrs. Gandhi gave it a practical shape.

We will have learnt the lessons of the Emergency if we accept the fact that it is the fundamental lack of commitment to values of freedom and democracy, of tolerance, of dissent, and of the capacity to look beyond one's immediate interests which had made the intellectuals, with a few honourable exceptions, accept the Emergency and abide by its soul-destroying demands. Unless our intellectuals and politicians are able to mend their thinking and approach, and their mindset, and stand up for basic principles, the democracy we fought for in 1975–77 will be a chimera.

NOTES

1. Brahm Dutt was a leader of Charan Singh's political party, the Bharatiya Lok Dal. During the Emergency he spent 19 months in jail. On his release from jail he dissociated himself from Charan Singh on the issue of the RSS. He was opposed to the RSS and its association with the Janata Party. On this issue he left the BLD: Later he joined the Congress and served as a Minister in UP, and in the Union Government under both Indira Gandhi and Rajiv Gandhi. He was a witness and participant in a long series of discussions and negotiations which slowly led to the formation of the Janata Party, which he calls a "Five-Headed Monster". He writes:

   > There are lessons to be drawn from the account I have presented. I have left to it the readers, by and large, to draw them. Nor have I endeavoured to cast the horoscope of the newly born Janata Party, beyond indicating that what was born under forced labours was not a normal baby. And it is a fact of Nature that monsters don't usually survive.

   Brahm Dutt had made a further prophecy in the book:

   > In the present circumstances (written on July 20, 1978), I feel that we may have to face a mid-term poll of the Lok Sabha in 1980, if not before....The real contest, therefore, will be between the Congress-I and the scattered fragments of the Janata Party. The many-headed monster faces annihilation as a result of various heads trying to devour each other. The beginning of the end is discernible already.

   P.V. Narasimha Rao once told this writer that Mrs. Gandhi had asked all Congress MPs and legislators to read Brahm Dutt's book.

[Courtesy: *Mainstream*, Vol. XXXV, No. 28,
21 June 1997, pp. 7–8]

****

CHAPTER 13

Humanists and Human Rights Under Attack

When Bangladesh came into existence, this writer was at the University of Leeds, UK. There was a number of students from East Pakistan. They organized a function to celebrate the occasion. This writer was also invited to speak. I expressed the hope that the new South Asian country with its background of Buddhism and humanism, and tolerance as represented by poets like Kazi Nazrul Islam and the Baul singers (both Hindus and Muslims) would be different for the better for India and Sri Lanka. The recent happenings in Bangladesh have belied that hope. Evils like religious intolerance and majority communalism have found a fertile soil in Bangladesh too. It all began with the driving away of the Buddhists from the Chittagong Hill Tract.

It is sad that humanism and a tolerant culture, which Bangladesh could be proud of, are under attack. The people who represent humanism and tolerance have been under the threat of being eliminated. They are the Bauls whose main task has been preaching religious tolerance and equality among men and between man and woman. They sing songs of humanity between men and women. Bauls do not observe asceticism nor do they believe in celibacy. Love, they maintain, helps them to attain divine love and harmony between material and spiritual needs. To quote one such song, "That is why, brother, I became a mad cap Baul. No master I obey nor injunction or custom. Man-made distinctions have no hold on me. Now I rejoice in songs of hearts for ever and I dance with each and all. That is why, brother, I became a mad cap Baul." One of the most famous Bauls, Fakir Shah Lalon sang thus, "Everyone asks Lalon what is your religion. Lalon says I know not my religion. If a male is circumcised you know he is a Musalman, but how do you identify the religion of a female? A Brahmin male is identified by his *paita* (sacred thread), but how would you identify a Brahmin female? One holds rosary in his hands, the other wears *tasbir* in his neck, that is how one's religion is known, but at the moment of birth and death, do these signs remain? People everywhere talk and gossip about religious differences. Lalon says I have dropped all polemics about religion in the free market. That is why I became a mad cap Baul."

The Baul movement in Bengal is well known for its simplicity, directness and for preaching and practising tolerance, love and friendliness.

These are the people (humanists) who are now under attack by the fundamentalists and Mullahs in Bangladesh.

These Mullahs have also started a movement to introduce a Blasphemy Law, which would liquidate the Bauls and all other progressive and humanist forces.

The syncretic and humanist tradition in the South Asian society and social thought is remarkably portrayed in the following poem of Kazi Nazrul Islam:

"I sing the song of equality where all barriers have crumbled, all differences have faded and Hindus, Buddhists, Muslims and Christians have come together and mingled. I sing the song of equality." (Quoted from this writer's essay 'Human Rights Education: India's Heritage' published in *Human Rights of Dalits: Societal Violations* edited by R.M. Pal and G.S. Bhargava, Gyan Publishing House, New Delhi)

These humanists, predominantly Muslims in some villages in the border districts of Bangladesh, have been declared outcasts by a *fatwa* of the Mullahs (fundamentalists who have reached a consensus on the social boycott of the Bauls). Ali Bux, a victim of this social boycott, said (report published in *The Statesman* of 10 January 2005): "We cannot buy anything from the grocery shops or other stalls of the market. The big farmers who own shallow land and deep tubewells refuse to irrigate our farmland. The sanctions would be withdrawn only if we plead guilty to the charges leveled against us (under the Pakistani Blasphemy Law they would be sentenced to mandatory death sentence) before the Maulana, but we have not committed any offence." These Muslim Bauls, about 20 Baul families at Chhabitola, Durlaverpara and Dagapara villages in Naoda Block, predominantly Muslims, had their houses blackened when they became Bauls and joined the Baul Fakirshah of Murshidabad.

[Courtesy: *Mainstream,* Vol. XLIII, No. 17,
16 April 2005, p. 14]

****

CHAPTER 14

Human Rights and Nuclear Explosions at Pokhran

There was a time when men like Bertrand Russell and Albert Einstein raised their voice with regard to the human rights violation aspect of nuclear weapons while leading a movement against the manufacture of nuclear bombs and nuclear tests, and for destruction of the arsenal in possession of the nuclear power countries. There has not been any such movement in recent years, and basic questions apropos of nuclear explosions have paled into insignificance, except that a few governments having stockpiles of nuclear weapons have been making a lot of noise about non-proliferation, CTBT, and so on. Regrettably, the United Nations Organization (UNO) too has been totally ineffective with regard to the elimination of the evil.

Human rights violations—reminiscent of Hiroshima and Nagasaki perpetrated by the USA— and nuclear weapons (the bomb), which have the capacity to wipe out all life from the earth, are intimately connected with one another. Opinion-makers, political formations and their leaders, intellectuals, and the media, while almost wholeheartedly welcoming the explosions and tests at Pokhran in May 1998, have not referred, or have chosen not to refer, to this aspect of the explosions. I happened to raise this with two friends—one a Gandhian intellectual and social scientist, another a radical humanist; they sidetracked the issue by just saying: "Who is America to dictate?" True, the nuclear states have been following double standards. But, can this be a justification for not taking into account some basic questions/problems while carrying out nuclear tests and explosions? I did not pursue the point with these two friends, for reports indicate clearly that the entire middle class and the elite—do the rest, the vast majority count for anything?—in our country have decided to rationalize the irrational and put such questions under the carpet, for these are uncomfortable.

What we have been witnessing since the explosions is either condemnation of India by the nuclear states and funding agencies and governments on the one hand, and on the other "national celebrations" on a gigantic scale with sounds of crackers, *mridangas, dhols* renting the air, and lighting all around—like celebrating Diwali—organized by the BJP and the RSS.

We have had a lot of "sombre" and "thoughtful" outpourings too! A national daily, *The Hindustan Times*, in a front-page editorial, while warmly welcoming the explosions, advised Pakistan

> not to maintain parity with India... in its obsessive desire... for the effect of any such move can only impose a heavy and perhaps unbearable burden on its less than robust economy.

Our own economy is so "robust"! Never mind, we haven't been able to implement the operative part of Nehru's "tryst with destiny" speech—we are behind the poorest of poor countries with regard to elementary education, for example! In any case, we have the bomb now, so why bother! Our supercillious attitude has done immense damage to India—for centuries. Can't we take the ground realities into account for a change and accept these with a sense of humility, again, for a change?

The *Economist* of London sums up the mood in India succinctly:

> The yield of India's five nuclear explosions this week past runs into megations of national pride. Euphoric citizens embraced each other on the streets. Triumphalism filled the newspapers. We've shown we're a full blooded nuclear power; we can stand up to America and give China and Pakistan a bloody nose. Economic sanctions? Who cares, national pride can't be counted in dollars. And remember, nothing much happened to China, despite

> Tiananmen Square. So hold firm, keep your spirits up and celebrate.

The following report in *The Statesman* of 16 May, quoting the BJP Vice-President summarizes the plan for celebrations:

> All the BJP party offices including the national headquarters of the BJP would be illuminated with candle light. The saffron forces would celebrate the 'nuclear explosions at Pokhran—a day of national pride'. The celebrations would be carried out throughout the country. Apart from bursting crackers, dancing to the rhythm of dhols and mridangas, the BJP would also take out rallies to remind the fellow countrymen of how the Vajpayee Government made India proud by carrying out nuclear tests. ....Partymen would also illuminate the BJP offices with deepmala—candle lights—to mark the occasion. Rallies and meetings would be organised to speak of the BJP Government's major achievement within 50 days of coming to power.

And the celebrations, as outlined above by the party, did take place in all the wards of Delhi. Sweets too were distributed! At the time of writing this, "celebrations" are spreading far and wide in the country. In these celebrations, the Prime Minister was hailed as a bold leader who had changed the face of India. Even the "social justice" political formations and leaders are terribly excited over the explosions. Let it not be forgotten that *chauvinism and cultural nationalism are heady wines.*

Interestingly, even a Shankaracharya, the God's man, has hailed the tests!

A Gandhian, holding a very high office in the country—he was also a civil liberties activist in the PUCL—has hailed the explosion on the authority of Gandhiji—why can't our politicians spare Gandhi's soul to rest in peace—saying:

> even a great apostle of truth like Mahatma Gandhi was not averse to the idea of sending the army to defend the borders of the country; and for India, a nuclear weapon could be a rightful one on the peace table!

We have also heard Prime Minister Vajpayee affirm that although

> we do not want to use such weapons against anyone, (we) would

> not hesitate to do so should the contingencies of our security so enjoin us.

If it is a bit vague, let us hear his Home Minister, Advani, who thundered from a high pedestal and made things "transparent";

> Pakistani should realize (now that the explosions have taken place) the change in the geostrategic situation in the region and the world,

and that Pakistan should now take note of the "qualitatively new stage" with regard to relations between the two countries specially with a view to finding a lasting solution to the Kashmir problem. The theory of "self-defence" and "deterrence" advanced by a host of liberal intellectuals and columnists in favour of the explosions is not relevant any longer—Advani has made that fairly clear. A columnist comments that Advani's statement with regard to Pakistan gives the impression that "India is a bit of a war-monger". In any case, it is most unfortunate that the peace prospects between the two countries have now become bleak.

As is clear now, George Fernandes, Vajpayee's Defence Minister, had prepared the ground by announcing that China is our number one enemy. (Actually George said "number one potential threat" not "number one enemy"—Editor.) The "secret service revelation" came at a time when, by all reckonings, it was clear that threats to India's security from China are much less now—indeed, have almost totally disappeared. As Amulya Ganguly writes (*HT*, 18 May)"

> China may be unwilling to recognize Sikkim and Arunachal Pradesh as parts of India, but India, too, has allowed the Tibetan government-in-exile to function from its territory. Pakistan does continue to send terrorists across the border in Kashmir and other parts of India, but terrorism is a fact of life in today's world. No one flourishes a nuclear bomb for that.

In the context of the Baja's exercise of the nuclear option, Ganguly adds:

> Pakistan, too, will have to respond; otherwise its rulers will be

> seen to be lacking in spirit. In the process, an entirely avoidable atmosphere of conflict—in which China, too, will be drawn in—will be created in South Asia.

In this atmosphere and climate—of "national pride", jingoism, chauvinism, cultural nationalism and, above all, intoxication—it is not possible to have any rational discourse and dialogue on the subject. It is not surprising, therefore, that basic questions relating to nuclear weapons and explosions have not been raised, not even including the Left parties and organizations who have protested against the explosions. Although the Left parties have said that the explosions "will not benefit Indians who have more serious problems about their livelihood to deal with", their main complaint is that

> the BJP-led government has taken this drastic decision on its own without even caring to discuss with the national political parties.

and the Prime Minister should not have written to the US President regarding the explosions. The veteran Communist leader, Hiren Mukherjee, has this to say about his colleagues:

> I do not know how credence can be placed in the political 'luminaries' striding the stage. Even the Left where I have belonged all my life and shall belong till my last breath, suffers from a kind of ideological debilitation it has not yet sought earnestly to overcome.

At some stage, questions like the following will have to be raised: radiation effect, if any, due to the explosions (has any- one heard of any investigation carried out in the Pokhran area after the 1974 test?), the all-important question of elimination of nuclear weapons with a view to saving the world from a nuclear holocaust (can we be sure that we do not have political rulers who have not been intoxicated by heady wines and who may not use the bomb?); the question of social justice in a country like India, which has the largest number of illiterate people and the largest number of non-schoolgoing children, consequently the largest child labour force, in the world; economic and social development; and, above all, the moral aspect of possessing nuclear weapons; and so on.

Let me quote Hiren Mukherjee again (*The Statesman*, 18 May):

> In Mumbai, a talented cartoonist turned mob-mover, Bal Thackeray by name, acts as if it is his will that rules India. His strength is due no doubt to whatever 'charisma' he and his likes in history—who are better, not named—, no doubt possess or demented mobs would not do their evil bidding. ....One is treated to the 'sublime' sight of the Shiv Sena chieftain laying down the law so that, very recently, a musical performance by a distinguished Pakistani artiste, invited specially for the occasion, was rudely broken up, the police and the administration in Mumbai just demonstratively looking the other way. ....This extraordinary impudence is tolerated, and Mumbai, where this worthy operates, dares not stage even a cricket match with Pakistan. ...The law of the land is thus flouted with impunity.

Is the bomb safe in such a man's hands?

Let us remember that Pakistan—the present Indian Government has decided to "fix-up" this country— was not defeated in 1971 by India; it was defeated by its own Army and other government agencies for violation of human rights of its own people in the then East Pakistan. One hopes, our intoxicated leaders will learn a lesson in relation to our own country. It is hoped the questions raised above and a number of other basic questions including the relevance of nuclear weapons in matters relating to security, deterrence, etc. will be taken up by human rights/civil liberties intellectuals and activists. I would conclude this brief essay—ramblings, properly speaking—by quoting a young columnist, Siddharth Varadarajan, *TOI* 16 May:

> If India stops aggressively campaigning for the elimination of nuclear weapons in exchange for a place at the nuclear apartheid table, it will not only be universally condemned by all right-thinking people, but will also help to condemn the world to the possibility of a nuclear holocaust.

[Courtesy: *Mainstream*, Vol. XXXVI, No. 23, 30 May 1998, pp. 6-7 & 12]

****

CHAPTER 15

Affirmative Action in Danger

THREAT TO THE FIFTH SCHEDULE OF THE CONSTITUTION

The founding fathers of our Constitution were indeed thoughtful and wise in making provision for affirmative action for and by the weaker sections of our people like the Scheduled Castes, Scheduled Tribes, women, children and the minorities. The political rulers continued with this policy until new fangled "ideas/ideologies" like globalization-liberalisation-privatization started the process of doing away with policies relating to affirmative action—in the beginning surreptitiously, and now openly with a spirit of defiance.

One of the latest attempts relates to the Fifth Schedule of the Constitution which is now under grave threat.

The Fifth Schedule provides protection to the Adivasi people who live in the Scheduled Areas. The Constitutional provisions (Fifth Schedule and Article 244) empower the Governor of a State to regulate and make regulations for the Scheduled Areas and for Adivasis to ensure that what rightfully belongs to the Adivasis (tribals) is not taken away by any means. Under these provisions, tribal lands are not transferable. Regulations are framed under this schedule "to prevent the exploitation of tribals by non-tribals and alienation of agricultural lands being passed on to non-tribals". The Union Government is now actively engaged in amending the Fifth Schedule with a view to giving effect to transfer of tribal lands to non-tribals and corporates.

Once this becomes law, it is almost certain that a very large number of Adivasis will be wiped out.

It is in this context that we may refer to the 1997 Supreme Court judgement. Samatha, an NGO working in the East Godavari district of Andhra Pradesh filed a case against the Andhra Pradesh Government which had leased tribal lands to private mining companies in the Scheduled Areas. The salient point of the judgement (by Justice Ramaswamy and Justice Saghir Ahmed forming the majority with Justice Pattanaik dissenting) are:

> As per the 73rd Amendment Act, 1992, "every Gram Sabha shall be competent to safeguard under clause (m) (II) the power to prevent alienation of land in the Scheduled Areas and to take appropriate action to restore any unlawful alienation of land of a Scheduled Tribe. Minerals are to be exploited by tribals themselves either individually or through cooperative societies with financial assistance of the State.... Transfer of land in the Scheduled Areas by way of lease to non-tribals, corporation etc., stands prohibited.... Renewal of lease is fresh grant of lease and therefore any transfer stands prohibited..... Transfer of mining lease to non-tribals, company, corporation, aggregate or partnership firm etc., is unconstitutional, void and inoperative.... Conference of all Chief Ministers, Ministers holding the Ministry concerned and Prime Minister and Central Ministers concerned should take a policy decision for a consistent scheme throughout the country in respect of tribals' lands." Which means the government cannot transfer land to non-tribals and also that all lands held by industries in tribal areas are illegal.

What happened after this landmark judgment is a sordid tale. The Andhra Pradesh Government as also the Union Government, instead of respecting the orders of the Supreme Court, resorted to acts some of which can be termed as diabolical. First, both these governments approached the Supreme Court with a plea to modify the Samatha order; the Court, however, dismissed the petitions of both the governments.

Meanwhile, a new development took place—the BALCO (Bharat Aluminium Company Limited) disinvestment process.

This too created a controversy on the Fifth Schedule and the Samatha judgement. This case is now before the Supreme Court. It is through this case, the government hopes, that the Samatha judgement will be reopened, reviewed, and reversed.

What is depressing to note is that instead of welcoming the Samatha judgement, the Union Government wants to get over it, and refers the case to the Attorney General, Soli Sorabjee. The Ministry concerned also issues a secret note about the judgement. Sorabjee agrees to give his opinion—obviously forgetting that he had appeared for the Samatha and obtained the stay order which in turn made the judgement possible. Was it ethical for the Attorney General to render advice to the government since he himself had appeared to oppose the government in the case?

Sorabjee advised the government that the Fifth Schedule can be amended to counter the adverse effect of the Samatha judgement. The Ministry welcomed Sorabjee's advice. Also, Sorabjee added, the Supreme Court can consider its previous judgement if a pending case on a similar issue is brought before it. (As referred to earlier, the BALCO case is before the Supreme Court, and this is being used by the government to amend the Fifth Schedule). Arun Shourie, the Minister for Disinvestment, issued a statement on 1 May 2001 that the government wants to review the Samatha judgement.

The secret note for the Committee of Secretaries regarding amendment of the Fifth Schedule to the Constitution of India in the light of the Samatha judgement, states, inter alia:

> The impasse created by the Samatha judgement can perhaps be resolved only through an amendment of the Fifth Schedule to the Constitution as opined by the Attorney General. One way could be to add the following explanation after paragraph 5(2) in the Fifth Schedule: The regulations framed under paragraph 5(2) shall not prohibit or restrict the transfer of land by members of the Scheduled Tribe to the government or allotment by government of the land to a non-tribal for undertaking non-agricultural operations including reconnaissance or prospecting or mining operation under the provisions of MHDR Act 1957.

The secret note adds:

> It could never have been the intention of the framers of the Constitution that no economic activity should take place in the Scheduled Areas or that tribals should always remain isolated from the mainstream of society....

Yes, our Constitution-makers did want the tribals to come out and enjoy the fruits of independent India's development and progress. But, have they during the last 54 years of independence? We may recall what Dr. Ambedkar had said:

> Civilising the aborigines means adopting them as our own, living in their midst and cultivating fellow feeling, in short loving them.

What, instead, we have done during these 54 years is to increasingly deprive them even of their Constitutional rights, and that in the name of development!

One fails to understand why the government, instead of implementing the order of the Supreme Court, has resorted to efforts to get the judgement reversed. The government should have convened a conference of ministers, as directed by the Supreme Court, to take a policy decision in the matter which could then apply to the States and Union Territories.

It is very sad indeed that our government has treated the Samatha judgement with contempt. It is in the context of these developments that President Narayanan's address be read:

> Let it not be said of India that this great Republic in a hurry to develop itself is devastating the green mother earth and uprooting our tribal population.

Apart from the legal aspects, the government's attitude towards the Adivasis is one of contempt for human rights, for uprooting the Adivasis and depriving them of their means of livelihood. In short, the government seems to be determined to undo the provisions relating to affirmative action if they come in the way of their policy of globalization-liberalization-privatization.

[Courtesy: *Mainstream,* Vol. XXXIX, No. 38,
8 September 2001, pp. 7-8]

****

II. Dalits, Reservation & Caste

CHAPTER 16

Caste Iron

A PHILOSOPHICAL REORIENTATION IS NEEDED

In 1992 I shared a platform in Delhi with Swami Agnivesh and Justice Krishna Iyer. Both of them delivered emotional speeches on the horrendous crimes committed against Scheduled Castes and Tribes by upper-caste Hindus. Justice Iyer recommended that there must be more judges—at least 50 per cent—from SC/ST communities so that they could get justice. Swami Agnivesh was very angry and suggested that SC/STs must be given firearms so that they could teach a lesson to the upper castes!

If Constitutional provisions alone were the remedies, I suggested, the incidence of such crimes would not have increased; and taking to arms, of course, should be summarily dismissed. We might pause, I added, to look at the system that has sanctioned the degradation of the SC/STs. And is it possible to reform the caste system, which mainly prevents the achievement of social justice, human rights and equality of opportunity? Swami Agnivesh now agrees that without dismantling the system it is not possible to make headway.

Let us note the approach of a humanist and liberal, Nissim Ezekiel, who is well-known in the English-speaking world as an outstanding Indo-Anglian writer, critic and academic of our time.

Hierarchy

I had written a brief editorial note in the *PUCL Bulletin* on the subject, suggesting that without demolishing the impregnable walls erected by the system "lock, stock and barrel, respect for rights and liberties, will remain a distant goal. Nothing short of a philosophical revolution can bring a change, and for that we need to have iconoclasts not status quoists and constitutional experts".

Nissim Ezekiel wrote in reply to this proposition that he did not support the status quoists and agreed that a philosophical revolution was necessary. But this revolution would have to face the obstacles posed by a multi-cultural and multi-lingual society. Thus, while the philosophical revolution was necessary, it was not desirable to wait for it. In this context, Constitutional experts and liberal reforms are still needed for validating social change, in the direction of the ultimate goals. "If, on the other hand," he continued, "we dismiss such a proposition as a shameful compromise, we have to, as the *PUCL Bulletin* editor does, consider it impossible 'to reform Hindu society so far as the caste system is concerned' ...All I am drawing attention to, and even insisting on, is the need for a strategy which will help us spread our ideas without creating more enemies than friends... ." Nissim Ezekiel represents genuine liberals and secular humanists in the country, who do not want India to fall apart, whose appeal to reason is founded on robust optimism, and who hope that those who violate human rights, instead of demanding a national debate on conversion, a non-issue, will join the debate on the caste system. If, however, past history is any indication, Mr. Ezekiel's appeal to reason is unlikely to influence the dominant majority.

Let us first look at the intellectual, moral, and religious support that has been given to the caste system, *varna-vyavastha* with a view to examining it in relation to the provisions of the Universal Declaration of Human Rights (UDHR). In the *Gita*, usually referred to as the guide to the Hindu way of life, Lord Krishna tells Arjuna: "The work of Brahmins, Kshetriyas, Vaishayas, and Shudras are different. ... The work of the Shudra is service. They all attain perfection when they find joy in their work ... Greater is thine own work, even if this is humble, than the work of another, even if this be great. When a man does the work God gives him, no sin can touch this man."

Discrimination

The *Rigveda* describes how the gods created the Brahmin, the Kshatriya, the Vaishya and the Shudra respectively from the head, arms, thighs, and feet of the *Purusa*, the cosmic man respectively "for the sake of the prosperity of the world". Brahma assigned separate duties and occupations to them in order to "protect" this universe—the first three for teaching, protecting citizens, trading and moneylending respectively, and the last for serving the first three without being critical of them.

The Shudras are described as *varnasankara* born out of the intermixture of the "pure varnas" and they are outside the system. They are not recognized even as persons by Manu—who decreed that a Brahmin's penance for killing an animal or a Shudra would be the same; in fact, killing a cow is more heinous than killing a Shudra.

The first two Articles of the UDHR make it clear that freedom, equality, and fraternity are the very basis of human rights. "All human beings are born free and equal in dignity and rights" (Article 1). "Everyone is entitled to all the rights and freedoms without distinction of any kind, such as race, colour, sex, language, religion, political or other opinion, national or social origin, birth ..." (Article 2).

It is obvious that the caste system is inconsistent with the provisions of the UDHR: our system gives different status to different persons on the basis of birth. Denial of education to some people, including women, violates Article 26(1), according to which, "everyone has the right to education..." . Theoretically, the caste system requires a person to join the occupation of the caste to which he is born—this violates Article 23(1) which prescribes that everyone has the right to choose his occupation, to just and favourable condition of work and protection against unemployment. Circumscription of the freedom to choose a spouse within the caste system is a violation of Article 16(1). Our system does not permit certain sections of the people to enter temples, to learn Sanskrit, to read religious books, to be priests. This is in contradiction with Article 18, "Everyone has the right to freedom of thought", etc. Dalits are forced to live on the outskirts of villages, a violation of Article 13(1).

Failure

A *begdar* (labourer), generally of the lower caste, according to the laws of Manu, is obliged to work without payment. If a Brahmin forces a twice-born to work for him, he is to be punished, but if a Brahmin forces a Shudra to work for him, with or without payment, he is not to be punished. Clearly, the upholders of the caste system use the authority of scriptures to persuade the oppressed and the exploited to reconcile their lot to suffering and poverty, by piously performing their allotted occupation and gaining an otherworldly reward. Social hierarchies exist in other societies also, but scripturally maintained hierarchy is unique to Hindu society.

There are a number of well-meaning liberals—Gandhians, radical humanists and human rights activists—who are ashamed of the fact that this kind of discrimination exists in our society. These well-intentioned people, who cherish the true values of democracy, suggest that there should be a vigorous reformist movement, along with Constitutional movements and provisions, to eradicate the evils of the system. All attempts to reform the Brahmanical religion—even to make it a non-Sanskritic religion—including religious and social reformist movements, have failed. The Buddha, Nanak, Kabir and their disciples made brave, but futile, attempts. Under the British rule Raja Rammohun Roy, Ishwar Chandra Vidyasagar and other reformers also tried to reform Hindu society, but no "fundamental" change was wrought. Only a philosophical revolution can bring such change.

[Courtesy: *Statesman*, 10 April 1999]

###################

Fali S. Nariman's comments on the above article:

My dear Mr. Pal,

Congratulations on the article in today's 'Statesman'.

I recall that when Justice D.P. Madon became Chief Justice of Bombay and had an occasion to look into the files he told me later in Delhi (when he was elevated to the Supreme Court) how unjust he found some of the administrative orders of his predecessors who belonged to the "scripturally sanctioned hierarchy": many District Judges though able and fit to be appointed to the High Court had been overlooked ("deliberately" Madon said), and had retired. In his short tenure as Chief Justice, Madon tried to rectify the wrong; by promoting some capable District Judges still in service and not belonging to the "preferred" classes: they made good judges: Justice Daud is one example, I recall, and Justice Suresh another. But for Madon they would have all retired as District Judges!

With warm regards,

Yours sincerely,
Sd/-
[Fali S. Nariman]"

****

CHAPTER 17

Reconversion 'Movement' with a Vengeance

June 2, 2000 was a historic and glorious day for the Hindu middle class—a reconversion 'movement' with a vengeance was started on that day. It was a day of celebrations. It was on this day that 72 tribal Christians of Manoharpur village, Keonjhar district of Orissa [where Graham Staines and his two sons were burnt alive, allegedly by Dara Singh (now in custody)] were converted to Hinduism by the Shankaracharya of Puri, Swami Nischalananda Saraswati. The leaders of the "movement" were, however, confronted with a serious problem. Where are the 72 reconverts to be placed in the caste hierarchy? Where do they, now Hindus, go to worship? The temple priests of the Jagannath temple will, of course, not allow these tribals to enter. The reconverts have no access to any Hindu temple; they have been made to settle for worshipping in an old tribal temple in the village where the people worship a tribal god. According to a report by Poornima Joshi of *The Hindustan Times* (11 June 2000), "they have to donate 20 kg of rice, a pig, a goat, a chicken, and some money", and then only would they be permitted to worship there.

It is in this context we are reminded of Gandhiji's temple entry movement which, regrettably, fizzled out not long after the movement was started—the upper castes, the twice-born, and even many of his freedom-fighter colleagues were hostile to the movement. Many attribute the failure of the movement to India's being under foreign rule at that time. (In fact, even

Gandhiji said on a number of occasions that the problems arising out of the divinely ordained hierarchical system, and the Hindu–Muslim question would be solved once the British leave the country.) Let us, therefore, remind ourselves of what happened in independent India which had adopted a Constitution abolishing all discrimination, and that too to the most trusted disciple of Gandhiji, Vinoba Bhave. He led a procession of lower caste people and proceeded to enter a Hindu temple in Orissa. The priests (the Pandas) made a lathicharge on the processionists in which Vinoba Bhave was seriously injured. He and the processionists made a quick retreat. Vinoba Bhave had learnt a lesson—he made no further attempt! Let us, therefore, be clear: the evil cannot be eradicated without demolishing the hierarchical system lock, stock and barrel.

The Pandas of Orissa did not find it necessary to offer any explanation for the illegal action—it was higher right, they asserted, to protect Hinduism and to maintain the sanctity and purity of temples. This time the Puri Shankaracharya's secretariat has advanced sophisticated arguments, following India's age-old culture-rationalizing the irrational, quibbling, and practising intellectual dishonesty:

> As far as the entry of reconverts into prominent temples is concerned, well, people cannot go anywhere they alike. Can you enter an operation theatre even if you want to? Similarly, there are restrictions at all religious places. People have to comply with them. As for not allowing them to marry into the 'original' Hindu families, the tribals anyway wed only within their community.

The message is clear. The Shankaracharya has found a way out: keep the reconverts at the bottom of the system. The Shankaracharya has now embarked on the task of building "special" temples having the Swastika symbol for Christians and Muslims who, according to him, have responded to his call for reconversion to Hinduism. These "special" temples will obviate any confrontation between the upper-caste Hindus ("original Hindus") who will not in any case step into these "special" temples, and the reconverts. Furthermore, the "special" temples will strengthen the institution of caste. The promoters and protectors of Hinduism will ensure that only people at the bottom, people who have been recognized as persons for centuries, use these "special" temples.

What is most objectionable and disgusting in the reconversion "movement" is the effort of the guardians of Hinduism (the Brahminical religion) to rationalize the caste system, the ugly cultural heritage of India. The treatment meted out to a large section of our people including the 72 tribals is the reality, the obnoxious reality, of our present-day culture. There has hardly been any attempt to analyze the reasons for the victimization of the poor tribals and brainwashing them into accepting their victimization. One hopes India revolts against "foulness, falseness, hypocrisy, that vitiate Indian social life and block the road to progress". Will our intellectuals, too, join the revolt against what the promoters of the Hindu faith, in the name of Hinduizing, have started doing, and usher in a philosophical revolution or a cultural renaissance to bring about a social change in India where social justice and social democracy will take firm roots?

[Courtesy: *Mainstream,* Vol. XXXVIII, No. 30, 15 July 2000, p. 9]

****

CHAPTER 18

Academics Renew Anti-Reservation Stir

The anti-reservation (in effect, anti-affirmative action) agitation in 1990 had found active promoters in newspapers and periodicals, as also university, college and school students and academics, particularly in Delhi and other parts of north India. It became a mini industry. It was stopped mercifully for a brief period in 1993, after the Supreme Court judgement upholding the government action on the Mandal Commission recommendations. Now, once again, it has surfaced, in a fairly big way, in Delhi University.

Anguish and pain prevent one from giving a detailed description of the raw materials of this "industry". However, a summary account of the finished products is necessary for an analysis of the background of the current revival of the anti-reservation stir among academics of Delhi University.

The V.P. Singh Government's decision in 1990 to implement the Mandal Commission's recommendations had brought about a situation in Delhi University in which any discussion on the assumption that a coin has two sides became impossible. At a meeting of academics and students of the university, an invited speaker was not allowed to have his say in support of reservation. The editor of a national daily went to the extent of exhorting students to take to the streets and they did. This was despite the fact that no political party had opposed the recommendations.

Colleges and faculty members of the university held meetings to voice their opinion on a directive issued by the then Vice-Chancellor who, despite claiming to be a human rights intellectual, had expressed reservations about affirmative action, albeit in a language of honey and sophistry. The decision was already written on the walls: it would be disastrous for the country; it would give rise to casteism, and so on. This writer was present at a meeting where faculty members were asked if they had read the Mandal recommendations; no, they had not and yet stuck to their "identities". The Delhi University Teachers' Association (DUTA) took up Mandal on the trade union level and waged a regular warfare. This writer is unable to recollect any occasion during his long association with the university when the DUTA or any other teachers' organization had taken up an issue of social justice and waged war against the inequities in our society. But when it came to opposition to reservation, the inhibition ceased.

The verdict given by many editors, distinguished columnists, and academics in 1990 may be summarized thus: The government has created a situation in which there would be caste war; the administration will collapse; if the stir continues, India will not survive; V.P. Singh has embarked on the task of dividing the country as did Jinnah, and he is another Hitler in the making, and therefore he must go—and he went. History was created by the festival of fireworks being celebrated not on Diwali day, but on the night of V.P. Singh's resignation, with crackers bursting throughout the night while the light kept burning.

It is against this background that the recent stir in Delhi University, mostly by teachers owing allegiance to the BJP and the Congress Party, against reservation of teaching positions for the Scheduled Castes and Scheduled Tribes (SC/ST) should be viewed. The other dominant group in the university led by the CPM, though not against affirmative action, is however conspicuous by its silence, for fear of being thrown out of power in the next DUTA elections. Clearly, social justice and affirmative action to eradicate inequities are not on the agenda.

It may be recalled that the university took the decision (which is now part of a University Ordinance) in April 1996 that 22.5 per cent of teaching and non-teaching positions in the university and its colleges be reserved for SC/STs. It is painful to recollect in this context that at a meeting of the Academic Council of the university, to discuss the item on the agenda on two or three occasions earlier—some faculty members had gone to the extent of saying:

> Mother goddess Saraswati's clothes will be desecrated if the policy of reservation is adopted. (literal translation of what was said in Hindi)

It is equally painful that no one present at the meeting thought of reminding them of what Abraham Lincoln had said in the context of slavery; it is dangerous to nurture a society and nation of half-slaves and half-free.

During the period April to October 1996, hardly any effort was made to make the university decision of reservation effective. It is in the light of this non-implementation of the law that the University Grants Commission (UGC), reportedly under pressure from the concerned Parliamentary Committee, issued a letter on October 29, 1996, asking the university authorities to launch a special recruitment drive to fill the teaching and non-teaching positions reserved for SC/STs.

It is significant that although the UGC took the decision to write to the university on July 31, 1996, it prevaricated for four long months to communicate the decision to the university; in fact the letter has not yet reached the university (on November 12 at the time of writing this note). The contents of the letter were, however, made known to the leaders of anti-reservation teachers on or about October 29, 1996!

One of the arguments advanced by teachers, including well-known "Marxist" and "progressive" faculty members, is that academic standards will suffer if SC/ST teachers are appointed. "Implementation of the UGC decision would result in collapse of standards of instruction and research activities in the university system," they announced majestically, and warned that if the UGC "does not withdraw its letter, there would be intense unrest on the campus". No one, however, has said a word about the increasingly and alarmingly falling standards in spite of the fact that the academic community has always been dominated and controlled by the upper and forward castes.

The fact remains—it should be obvious to all thoughtful men and women—that the upper and forward castes are bent on maintaining the status quo; they are determined to resist, whenever the situation demands, any struggle for social justice and affirmative action. The north Indian educated middle classes (whom Rajni Kothari calls "the lumpenised middle class") feel threatened, not because they would be deprived of jobs, but because their caste identities would be at stake. One may recall in this context that a large number of banners was put up in Delhi in 1990, mostly in women's colleges, to assert their identity.

We are not particularly concerned with the question of reservation and politics involved in the controversy. We do feel concerned, however, about the fact that a large number of communities in our country have had their social status fixed for all time to come. This fact, too, has been summarily dismissed by anti-reservation faculty members of Delhi University. You refuse to accept the given social status, you are dubbed a casteist! These scholars do not accept the fact that every human being, given favourable conditions, is capable of, is capable of developing unlimited powers of intellect and will; that those conditions have not yet been created for those who deserve them the most.

It is a great pity that universities which ought to be centres for initiating movements for progress have embarked on the dangerous path of leading us to the dark age of history.

[Courtesy: *Mainstream*, Vol. XXXIV, No. 52,
30 November 1996, p. 10]

****

CHAPTER 19

President of India under Attack

President K.R. Narayanan has been under attack for some years now from the middle class. His crime? He has not accepted the advice given by this class to keep his lips sealed. Why should he speak against criminalization of electoral politics? Why should he express his anguish over non-implementation of social justice programmes like compulsory basic education, uplift of the marginalized sections of our people, like the Dalits and Tribals? And why should he express his concern about the absence of social democracy in our country?

The President's Republic Day-eve address this year has angered and upset a section of the intelligentsia—it is no longer any veiled criticism. This time the attack is virulent. Quite a few national dailies have attacked him in a 'forthright' manner. Some have gone to the extent of declaring that Narayanan is not fit to hold the high position. One columnist has characterized Narayanan's view as 'classic Arundhati Roy-style, *jholawalla* stuff'. Note the language of the chief editor of a national daily:

> It is not for me to try and fathom from where the President gets his advice; he is free to consult whom he chooses and as often as he wishes ... The Head of State can never forget his position and his authority; the licence to an ordinary citizen to be irresponsible is not available to him, ideally even after he demits office next year.

This gentleman is very angry that the President feels that there should be more judges from SC/STs and from women. He is not willing to accept the fact that Narayanan is an intellectual like some of his predecessors, Dr. Rajendra Prasad,

Dr. Radhakrishnan, Dr. Zakir Husain.

What has the President said that has made our "opinion-makers" angry? He has drawn our attention to the political, social and economic rights of the people, universal adult franchise; that the people as a whole must be involved in the decision-making process, we must have faith in the common man and woman, we should abolish illiteracy and poverty; and that we are widening the existing inequalities and creating new inequalities resulting in the SC/STs' increasing sufferings, and so on. Referring to how large projects are uprooting the tribals, the President said:

> The development path we have adopted is hurting them and threatening their very existence.

He recommends an enlightened development policy, and during that the planners should take the tribals into confidence, and explain the benefits of the projects and consult them in regard to *"the protection of their livelihood and their unique cultures"*. (emphasis added)

What has unnerved the intelligentsia is his reference to the question of "stability", to which Prime Minister Vajpayee referred some time ago. The Prime Minister maintains that there should be a fixed term for Parliament to ensure stability. Narayanan is opposed to this proposal:

> The founding fathers had the wisdom and foresight not to overemphasise the importance of stability and uniformity in the political system. As Dr. Ambedkar explained in the Constituent Assembly, they preferred responsibility to stability.

The President has also noted that the governance of this vast country is not to be kept in the hands of the elite class but the people as a whole. I have no means to know what the President had in mind when he said this. I may, however, refer to a document prepared and circulated by the RSS, *Constitution of Bharat* (now an ABVP publication), which, it is said, is meant for discussion in the Constitution Review Commission. The salient features of the document are as follows:

> The Parliament will consist of the President, the Vice-President, the Guru Sabha and the Lok Sabha. The educated and enlightened will elect the members of the Guru Sabha. Primary school teachers will have one vote each, middle school teachers will have two, Professors in a recognised college/university will have thirty votes each, persons who have received awards will have one hundred votes each. Legislations will be introduced in the Guru Sabha. The Guru Sabha will decide the policies of the State. It will never be dissolved. The Lok Sabha of 550 members (to be elected for a period of five years by direct elections) has only one function: of monitoring the implementation of the policies decided by the Guru Sabha. The opinion of the Lok Sabha will not be binding on the Guru Sabha. There will be a Raksha Sabha. It will make the defence budget; the Lok Sabha and the Guru Sabha cannot discuss the defence budget.

Did Narayanan have this obnoxious document in mind?

Note, the uneducated people have no voting right for electing the Guru Sabha members. And who are uneducated? The SC/STs, women and the minorities. Why are they debarred? Are Vajpayee and his RSS scared of the "uneducated" people, the common man and woman? Note also that under this Constitution India shall no longer be a Union of States; "Bharat shall be a union of the citizens". Furthermore, the provisions of Article 25 (Freedom of Conscience and Religion) have been changed. The *Constitution of Bharat* has dispensed with the present provision of "throwing open of Hindu religious institutions of a public character to all classes of Hindus." Also, a social justice provision in Part IV of the Constitution (Directive Principles) has been done away with; the *Constitution of Bharat* merely states:

> The Directive Principles of State Policy will be decided by the Guru Sabha from time to time and the same will be binding on every wing of the State.

It is hardly necessary to add that the cause of Dalits, and other marginalized sections, and issues like eradication of poverty, health care, compulsory basic education have been done away with by the RSS.

Is it not the duty of the President of India to draw our

attention to the dangers involved in the whole exercise of reviewing and examination of the Constitution? If he did not, he would not be worth his salt. The deprived sections—the majority of the Indian community—will remain beholden to him for raising these questions.

I may add a few words about the Constitution Review Commission. When the National Commission to Review the Working of the Constitution was appointed by the present BJP-led government, the Opposition parties were not consulted. The President was not taken into confidence. It was a simple government resolution which announced the constitution of the Commission. Justice M.N. Venkatachaliah, the former Chairperson of the National Human Rights Commission, was appointed the NCRWC Chairperson by the government. [Let me add a personal note. I came to know Justice Venkatachaliah when he was the Chairperson of the NHGRC—I was impressed by his concern about human rights violations and his commitment to the rule of law, to compulsory basic education and so on. We shared a number of platforms. I have had occasion to make critical comments about the NHRC; Justice Venkatachaliah always took my criticism in the right spirit. I trust he will take my views regarding the Review Commission and his being the Chairperson in the spirit I make them. I was dismayed when he accepted the position (of the Chairperson of the Review Commission), even if on no salary or a salary of Re 1. The government does take care of his other expenses. The 1993 Human Rights Act says that the Chairperson and members of the NHRC cannot accept government assignments after they retire/resign from the NHRC. But some of them became Governors of States. Some of his colleagues whisper that he should not have accepted the position.]

I may quote what F.S. Nariman, the noted jurist, said in his M.N. Roy Memorial lecture in March 2000:

> It could have been ascertained whether (or not) the 'commitment' of the major political partner in the coalition government, the BJP, expressed in its own political document of 1998 for the elections held in that year, to the concept of One Nation, One People, and

> One Culture was the real motivating factor for setting up a commission to review the Constitution; if it was, then (more importantly) whether cultural and educational rights of sections of citizens and of minorities (guaranteed by Articles 29 and 30) were proposed to be altered or done away with... In its manifesto of 1991, the party (BJP) proclaimed its clear intention to set up 'a system will give us a more stable government than the present parliamentary system'?

Regarding inviting suggestions, Nariman said:

> Inviting suggestions as to what parts of the Constitution should be reviewed without even defining those parts is an invitation to anarchy.

Our "opinion-makers" have attacked the President for committing "improprieties, if not excesses" in giving expression to his views which are critical of the Prime Minister and the government's views. In the past too, there were occasions when the President gave expression to his own views—President Rajendra Prasad differed from Pandit Nehru on some aspects of the Hindu Code Bill. The press and the intelligentsia did not then use the kind of language against Dr. Rajendra Prasad as they have done against Narayanan. It would be most unfortunate if it is because Narayanan does not belong, by birth, to the order to which Dr. Rajendra Prasad belonged, and to which all his critics belong.

[Courtesy: *Mainstream*, Vol. XXXIX, No. 8,
10 February 2001, pp. 11-12, 19]

****

Justice V.S. Malimath
Former Chief Justice
Karnataka and Kerala High Court
Former Member, National Human Rights Commission
Chairman, Criminal Justice System Reforms Committee

Shantiniketan
Palace Loop Road
Vasantha Nagar
Bangalore-560 052

22/5/2001

Dear Sri Pal,

Thank you for a copy of your article 'President of India under Attack' in the *Mainstream* issue of 10-2-2001. I was quite impressed by your candid and forthright views. It has the stamp of R.M. Pal's sincerity, courage of conviction and transparent concern for public good. I shall preserve your article.

With Pranams,

Sincerely Yours,
Sd/-

To

Sri R.M. Pal
M-35, Greater Kailash-I
New Delhi-110 048

****

CHAPTER 20

Human Rights of Dalits on the Agenda of the UN

REMEMBERING M.N. ROY AND HIS HERESY

The following article has been written on the occasion of M.N. Roy's one hundred and sixteenth birthday, which falls on 21 March 2001.

Most of what M.N. Roy wrote in jail (1931–36) remains eminently relevant today in the context of the societal violation of human rights. One hardly comes across any other political figure among non-Dalit intellectuals and politicians who came down so heavily and comprehensively on the ugly aspects of our past, like the caste system (which he called an "ugly relic of the past"), the Brahmanical religion, the law of *Karma*, transmigration of soul, and so on, and fought for social justice and social democracy. It is through my study of Roy's sociological and philosophical writings that I studied Phule, Periyar and Ambedkar's writings, specially those related to the divinely ordained hierarchical system (Roy calls the caste regulations "shackles of antiquated social cause") which, if not demolished, will remain a hindrance to the realization of social justice and growth of social democracy in India.

Our ancient philosophers and law-givers gave an intellectual, moral and theoretical justification for the case system, for example,

> *Karma* is not a mechanical principle, but a spiritual necessity. It is the embodiment of the mind and will of God is its supervisor. Justice is an attribute of God.

Roy maintained that fatalism and blind faith have killed in the bulk of the Indian people the incentive for knowledge and progress.

> The root of this evil can be traced to the doctrine of the transmigration of soul.... It is time to realize that the present inebriation offered a solace to proud intellectuals with inferiority complex. The legacy of that psychological aggressiveness is not an asset, but a liability. A critical examination of what is cherished by India's cultural heritage will enable the Indian people to cut off the chilly grip of a dead past. It will embolden them to face the ugly realities of a living present and look forward to a better, brighter and pleasanter future (1950, Introduction to *India's Message*, second revised edition).

Referring to the hierarchical system, Roy wrote:

> Social privileges are due to the Brahmin traditionally. ...All others are placed lower to him in the social scale by Providential Ordinance, as the Gita teaches... The only thing any reasonable person will find objectionable is the effort of the modern Hindu intellectuals to rationalize the custom. (1932–36)

The essay, "Why Men are Hanged" (1932–36), indicates Roy's concern for the marginalized, the deprived sections of our people. He makes an earnest plea for the elimination of such conditions which not only victimize the poor but also brainwash them into accepting their victimization as pre-ordained by the laws of *Karma*. In the essay, "Crime and Punishment"? (1932–36), Roy makes no secret of his distrust of the penalizing powers of the government. In "Crime and *Karma*" (1932–36) Roy writes:

> Regarded as a determine law the doctrine of *Karma* renders the ideal of freedom unattainable. Consequently, it militates against the higher ideal of *niskam karma*. But there is some sense in the apparent madness. The two seemingly contradictory ideals supplement each other for forging the chain of social slavery for the masses. The doctrine teaches everyone to be reconciled to his faith.

Roy maintains that every human being, given favourable conditions, is capable of developing unlimited powers of intellect and will. Regrettably, as we know, the favourable conditions have not been created for a particular section of our people who have not been treated even as persons for centuries.

Roy called upon young India

> to revolt against the foulness, falseness, hypocrisy, that vitiate Indian social life and block the road to progress. (1950)

Roy's commitment was not merely to freedom and truth, but was also, most importantly, to social justice.

There are now signs of revolt against the "ugly relic". Discrimination against, and human rights violation of, Dalits are now on the agenda of the UN. The UN Committee on the Elimination of Racial Discrimination in its meeting held on 7 and 8 August 1996 considered the question of discrimination against SC/STs and made the following observations:

> The Committee expresses its appreciation for the opportunity to resume its dialogue with the State party (Government of India) on the basis of tenth to fourteenth periodic reports. It regrets the brevity of the report, all the more so since ten years have passed since the previous report was submitted. It also regrets that the report does not provide concrete information on the implementation of the Convention in practice; it furthermore regrets that the report and the delegation claim that the situation of the SC/STs does not fall within the scope of the Convention.

The Committee also noted that

> the system of castes and the climate of violence ... impede the full implementation of the Convention by the State party.

The Committee added that the term "descent" mentioned in Article 1 of the International Convention on the Elimination of all Forms of Racial Discrimination does not refer to race only, and that "the situation of SC/STs falls within the scope of the Convention." The Committee then made a number of recommendations, including the following:

> The Committee recommends a continuing campaign ... (which) should be aimed at eliminating the institutionalized thinking of the high-caste and low-caste mentality.

It recommended that the Government of India's next periodic report, due on January 1998, be "a comprehensive report". [The government has not yet submitted the report. Nor has it or the National Human Rights Commission (NHRC) taken any action to "eliminate the institutionalized thinking of the high-caste and low-caste mentality."]

It is in the above context that we may take note of a Conference "Occupation and Descent-Based Discrimination Against Dalits" held on 1–4 March, 2001 at New Delhi (organized in preparation of the UN World Conference Against Racism, South Africa September 2001). The Conference was organized by the National Campaign of Dalit Rights, India, jointly with national, regional and international organizations. Over two hundred human rights activists from India and across the world, including members of South Africa and Sri Lanka Human Rights Commissions, attended the Conference.

The highlights of the Conference were testimonies given by a number of victims of human rights violation. To mention a couple of them: a Dalit bridegroom was thrashed and humiliated by upper caste people just because the groom was riding on horseback in a procession. The Dalit woman, Ms. Shakinben Senma's testimony:

> They say that the caste system was done away with 50 years ago. But in our village, Dalit women cannot wear *ghagras* (traditional skirts) with embroidered borders or carry metal pitchers for fetching water. The Dalit men cannot wear footwear or tuck in their shirts in the presence of the upper castes. No *shehnai-dhol* (wedding music) at a Dalit marriage.

Shakinben became the first woman from the Dalit community to be unanimously elected a Sarpanch—but she had to pay a heavy price. Her husband became the target of a murderous attack by the upper castes. Shakinben found him lying in a pool of blood in their field.

> The attackers broke his legs, smashed his chest and repeatedly hit him in the abdomen with a metal pipe and a sickle.

There was the testimony relating to three Dalit husbands—their wives belong to upper caste families—who were "tonsured, stripped naked and even paraded naked around the temple". One of them was jailed.

What is significant in all these cases of torture is that none of them surrendered before the perpetrators of human rights violations; they revolted; in the words of Roy, "against the foulness, falseness, hypocrisy that vitiate Indian social life", and they are determined to remove all barriers that "block the road to progress".

Well-known Dalit intellectual activists, like Ruth Manorama, Martin Macwan, N. Paul Divakar, Bishop Azaria, Henry Tiphagne, Yogesh Varhade and others pointedly referred to the fact that India supports the UN World Conference Against Racism, Racial Discrimination, Xenophobia and Related Intolerance (WCAR); but what India is opposed to is the inclusion of caste discrimination in the agenda of the WCAR.

One fails to understand why India has been resolutely persisting in keeping the question of caste, which is the primary source of human rights violation of Dalits, under the carpet. The Government of Nepal in its report to the UN Sub-Committee has accepted the fact of discrimination on the basis of caste.

It was intriguing to know that the NHRC, which was invited, chose not to attend the Delhi Conference. We were also disturbed to know that the Government of India refused to give visa to a number of delegates from Europe.

What is important in the context of societal violation of human rights of SC/STs is that the NHRC, NCW, SC/ST Commission and NGOs must rise to the occasion and declare that they do not accept the commonly held belief that caste hierarchy and the social system based on it have been beneficial or benevolent. They must start a movement with a view to demolishing the structure of hierarchy so that there is no discrimination and human rights violation on this score. Such a movement, as M.N. Roy pointed out in his writings, will have formidable foes: the vested interests in perpetuating and glorifying the system; philosophers and social anthropologists who sing its praise and give intellectual, moral and religious support to the caste system. The fact, however, remains, to quote Roy again, that without such a movement our society cannot be rendered purposive and placed on the road to progress.

We have always maintained that the problem of caste cannot be solved overnight for the walls raised by the system have stood rock-like for centuries. What we suggest is that there ought to be a clear-cut recognition of the fact by the NHRC and social activists that caste divides, that it gives rise to divisiveness and dissension, that it is a major source of human rights violations, and that unless "the ugly relics of the past" are done away with and we close the doors to our horrendous past, social justice will remain a distant goal. Therefore, the system under which "some are less equal than others", a phrase used by the NHRC, must be demolished. It is here that the NHRC appears paralyzed.

[Courtesy: *Mainstream,* Vol. XXXIX, No. 14, 24 March 2001, pp. 23–25]

****

CHAPTER 21

Durban: A Victims' Conference

The following piece is by a participant at the NGO Forum of the UN-sponsored World Conference Against Racism (WCAR) that recently took place in Durban (South Africa).

Ms. Mary Robinson, the UN High Commissioner for Human Rights and Secretary-General of the Durban Conference—the UN World Conference Against Racism, Racial Discrimination, Xenophobia and Related Intolerance (WCAR)—that took place from 27 August to 7 September 2001, observed in the context of the Conference:

> In different parts of the world, people are hurting because of problems of inequality or injustice and are pressing their case at this Conference.

Romans, Palestinians, Dalits, Africans and African descendants, indigenous peoples, Burako people of Japan (there were about 5000 delegates at the NGO meet of the UN gathering—the two main groups being the Dalit Caucus and the Palestine Caucus), all victims of one kind of discrimination or another, gathered at Durban to participate in the NGO Forum which was inaugurated by Ms. Robinson. UN Secretary-General Kofi Annan addressed a special session of the NGO Forum.

I will limit myself to the NGO Forum of the Conference (for the Governments' Forum and its deliberations were guided more by politics and economic interest than by any concern for human rights). Ms. Robinson rightly urged on the NGOs:

> I want to assure you that my wish is for NGOs to participate to the maximum extent possible over the coming two weeks. I regard

> this Forum as an integral part of the World Conference.... Even though it has been a difficult road to Durban, I feel it has been worth it. Worth it for the victims who suffer daily for the impact of discrimination. Worth it because we must never forget that those victims are looking to Durban to see real improvements in their lives.

As I sat through her speech I felt the human warmth, the human concern, her concern for the victims that ran through the words that she spoke. She made it plain that it was a Victims' Conference and that horrendous practices cannot be eliminated without the active cooperation of the civil society. She participated in a number of seminars organized at the Conference venue and in all presentations she gave the utmost importance to this aspect. Kofi Annan, the UN Secretary-General, while addressing the NGO Forum, also referred to this aspect. He maintained:

> No UN Conference is complete without its NGO Forum.

[However, at question hour time, while reacting to an observation made by a member of the Indian Dalit Caucus, Kofi Annan got a bit irritated. His response to the observation—response of a rather bureaucratic nature—was not liked by a section of the Caucus who raised their voice. He cut them short—curtly. It was quite obvious that he forgot, for a moment at least, that he was addressing the victims who had gone to Durban for justice, and that it was a Victims' Conference. Quite unlike Ms Robinson. I for one expected a rational and humane handling by the top executive of the UN of the passionate and sensitive reaction on the part of the victims.]

If the proceedings at the Governmental Conference, and the manner in which the Conference came to an end, are any indication, both Ms. Robinson and Kofi Annan's assertions and wish have been belied. The NGO Forum and their recommendations were not taken seriously by the Conference. Both of them, for example, referred to work and descent-based discrimination in South Asia, but the Conference did not include it in the Declaration.

I may refer specifically to the question of caste and descent-based discrimination and the NGO Forum's Declaration and Action Plan on this subject. The Declaration states that caste discrimination is one of the most horrendous forms of discrimination. The Programme of Action also refers to this aspect. I give below a few salient parts of the Declaration and programme of Action:

Caste and Discrimination Based on Work and Descent

Work and descent-based discrimination, including caste discrimination and untouchability, being a historically entrenched, false ideological construct sanctioned by religion and culture, which is hereditary in nature and affects over 300 million people in the Asia Pacific and African regions at the personal, social and structural levels, irrespective of their religious affiliation.

The practice of untouchability is rooted in the caste system.

The system of "hidden apartheid" based on caste practices of distinction, exclusion and restrictions denies Dalits' enjoyment of their economic, social, political, cultural and religious rights, exposing them to all forms of violence and manifests itself in the segregation of housing settlements and cemeteries, segregation in tea stalls ("two-cup" system), denial of access to common drinking water, restaurants, places of worship, restrictions on marriage and other insidious measures, all of which inhibit their development as equals.

Caste discrimination and 'untouchability' practised against generations of Dalits for centuries together amounts to systemic 'generational and cultural Daliticide', which is the mass-scale destruction of their individual and collective identity, dignity and self-respect for generations through cultural methods and practices.

Any action or even any sign of an attempt to act by Dalits either individually or collectively to assert their rights is met with extreme measures of violence, such as burning or destruction of their homes, property and crops, social boycott, rape or gang-rape of Dalit women and murder by dominant caste individuals or groups, police or the bureaucracy, and that in such instances the State often acts with impunity and in connivance with these perpetrators.

Work and descent-based discrimination against the Buraku people of Japan has existed for over 400 years and continues to be experienced today by over three million people in relation to marriage, employment and education, with new forms of discrimination emerging such as discriminatory propaganda and incitement to discrimination against them, especially on the Internet.

Enact suitable legislation to recognize and eradicate discrimination based on work and descent, including caste discrimination and untouchability against Dalits, Buraku people and other affected communities, in those countries where such legislation does not exist. Declare work and descent-based discrimination, including caste discrimination and untouchability, as Crimes against Humanity and enact and enforce legislation to guarantee the right to life and security, particularly the women and children of these communities.

Undertake a survey of the situation of the Buraku people in Japan to ascertain the nature and extent of the discrimination they continue to face despite the enactment of temporary "Special Measures" by the Government of Japan, and take all necessary legal, administrative and other measures to eradicate discrimination.

Allocate adequate funds to guarantee the enjoyment of their rights to livelihood, land, education, housing, potable drinking water, sanitation, health and employment opportunities, with special emphasis on their women, and establish effective monitoring mechanisms to ensure full and proper utilization of available funds.

The United Nations to ensure the implementation by the States of all relevant recommendations and resolutions of the UN human rights treaty monitoring bodies and of the UN Sub-Commission on the Promotion of Human Rights, and immediately appoint a UN Special Rapporteur to study the question of work and descent based discrimination, including caste discrimination and untouchability, against these communities in different parts of the world.

The Dalit Caucus at Durban made its presence felt in a very big way. The Government of India and its bureaucrats got so shaken that its leader was led to make irresponsible statements, like:

> In the run up to the world conference, there has been propaganda, highly exaggerated and misleading often based on anecdotal evidence, regarding caste based discrimination in India.

Thanks to the government and its bureaucrats' thoughtless action generated by panic, this subject has now been internationalized for all time to come. I have referred to the mindset of the people who are opposed to caste-based discrimination being on the WCAR agenda in the next section.

I may mention here some of the observations made by the National Campaign for Dalit Human Rights and National Federation of Dalit Women, who formed the Dalit Caucus:

> The Dalits are oppressed, suppressed and dehumanized people. India is creating an image as a nuclear power and a global economy that produces technocrats and computer geniuses and our protests and demonstrations in Durban are aimed at shattering this one-sided image of a country with a social shame.... Dalits are compelled into dehumanishing jobs like manual scavenging and garbage picking and pushed by the grueling cycle of generational poverty and landlessness and hunger, into lifelong indebtedness. During the monsoon, women carry feces in bamboo baskets and it drips on their heads and bodies. Is this not racial discrimination?

The Dalit Caucus in Durban led by devoted activists like Martin Macwan, Henry Tiphagne, Paul Divakar, Professor Kancha Illiah, Professor Chalam, Professor and Mrs. Thorat, Ms. Ruth Manorama, Dr. Aloysius, Ms. Jyoti Raj, Mimroth, John Vincent Manoharan, Bishop Azaria, Henry Thiagaraj and many others—they were actively helped by the International Dalit Liberation Movement and the US/Canada-based Ambedkar Centre for Justice and Peace—made tremendous efforts to bring to light the ground realities, and they succeeded to a considerable extent. One hopes the struggle for establishing a caste-less society in India will go on with greater vigour.

Prior to the Conference a number of social anthropologists

produced "learned treatises" and "Ph.D thesis" in newspaper articles of a thousand words with journalistic flourish—a remarkable achievement indeed—that race and caste are not the same thing and hence caste-based discrimination should not be allowed to be placed on the agenda of the Conference Against Racism at Durban. They were and are reluctant to come down heavily on the ugly relics of our past. Relying on the writers of such treatises, the Government of India was determined to see that caste-based discrimination is not included in the agenda of the WCAR—and it succeeded. In fact the government made it a prestige issue—the government spent an enormous amount, running into crores, in sending GONGOs (government organized non-governmental organizations) to canvas for its non-inclusion in the agenda. One cannot think of a more irrational and arrogant decision.

The government, our establishment intellectuals and GONGOs were opposed to its inclusion ostensibly on two grounds: one, that caste discrimination is not racial discrimination; two, that international agencies must not be allowed to fight human rights abuses caused by our hierarchical system, and that it is an internal issue and it should not be internationalized. (The fact, however, remains it was already partially internationalized as we will see later and now completely, as mentioned earlier.)

First, the question is not whether caste and race are the same thing; the system, however, had a racial origin: in its association of castes and colour. Note, for example, an important verse in the *Mahabharata:* Bhirgu explains the nature of castes to Bharadvaja:

> Brahmins are fair, Kshatriyas are reddish, Vaishyas are yellowish, and the Sudras are black. *(Shanti Parva)*

The question before us is: does caste discrimination fall under the Convention on Racial Discrimination? What the government has done is to conceal under the carpet decisions and recommendations made by a number of UN committees. The proposition that caste discrimination does not fall within racial discrimination was responded to by the International

Convention on the Elimination of all Forms of Racial Discrimination (ICERD) in 1996: The term "descent" mentioned in Article 1 of the ICERD does not refer to race only, and it "affirms that the situation of SC/STs falls within the scope of the Convention". Various other UN bodies have affirmed the existence of discrimination towards SCs (Dalits). The UN Human Rights Committee had this to say in 1997:

> The Committee notes with concern that, despite measures taken by the Government, members of SCs.... continue to endure severe social discrimination and to suffer disproportionately from many violations of their rights under the Covenant, *inter alia,* inter-caste violence, bonded labour and discrimination of all kinds. It regrets that the *de facto* perpetuation of the caste system entrenches social differences and contributes to these violations.

The CEDAW observed in 2001 that it

> is concerned with the continuing discrimination, including violence suffered by women of the Dalit community, despite the passage of SC/STs. (Prevention of Atrocities Act 1989)

Interestingly, in 1965 when the Convention on the Elimination of all forms of Racial Discrimination was being debated, it was the Government of India which urged on the Drafting Committee at the UN that descent-based discrimination be included in Article 1 of the Convention. This is in accordance with, the government argued, protective discrimination and affirmative action provisions in our Constitution. One fails to understand why from 1996 onwards the government has been opposed to its own earlier position!

The second proposition is that caste is an internal matter. It has been an "internal matter" for centuries until the world was reduced to a big village after World War II and the UN came into existence, and now UN Conventions are expected to be respected by all countries. Furthermore, so far as the hierarchical system and its resultant societal violations of human rights are concerned, we know that even the efforts to make Hinduism a non-Sanskritic religion have failed. Buddha, Nanak, Kabir and many others made brave but futile efforts. During the British regime, a number of rationalists, humanists and reformists fought relentlessly. But the system exists, the unbreakable walls have not been demolished. It is only appropriate, therefore, that a world body like the UN takes up the challenge and in cooperation with the NGOs, the NHRC and social activists in India succeed in eradicating the evils of the system.

Our government maintains, and rightly, that since Independence, a number of Constitutional provisions and other legal measures have been adopted to remove caste-based discrimination. Our government, however, has accepted the practice of discrimination towards the Dalits before a CERD meeting in 1996 by saying "that a practice that is so old cannot be eliminated rapidly". It was, therefore, in the interest of the government that if the subject was included in the agenda it would have got an opportunity of telling the world that the government has been taking all progressive measures to eradicate caste-based discrimination.

In the light of the above, one fails to understand why the government, and specially its bureaucrats, should have opposed the inclusion of the subject. In fact the government should have respected the opinion of the National Human Rights Commission, which recommended its inclusion on the agenda—the Commission made a statement to this effect in one of the plenary sessions of the Governmental Conference. One cannot think of any other reason except a special kind of arrogance ingrained in our culture which makes the Government of India persist in keeping the question of caste under the carpet, and oppose its inclusion in the agenda of the WCAR.

Where do we go from the Conference? We must rise to the occasion and declare that India does not accept the commonly held belief that caste hierarchy and the social system based on it have been beneficial or benevolent. With growing awakening among the Dalits, who constitute a sizable section of our population, and the Dalits' persisting alienation from the mainstream, if caste identity remains intact, the very concept of integration, assimilation, patriotism—in short, pride in being an Indian, pride in being involved in nation-building—will be undercut. Making the dominant section respond to the welfare of our people and our society is a veritable challenge because they continue to assume innate superiority that they being clever, intelligent, educated, cultured and refined deserve what they have. They want the others to take shelter under their dominance and seek sustenance at their mercy. In such a social atmosphere, developing the culture and values of human rights and non-discrimination will remain a distant goal. These values cannot be legislated but activists have the mandate to put the issue in the proper perspective both before the government and the human society ignoring geographical boundary.

[Courtesy: *Mainstream*, Vol. XXXIX, No. 40,
22 September 2001, pp. 6–8, 22]

****

III. Hindutva & Communalism

CHAPTER 22

Hindutvavad and Communalism

The thirst of kindred blood, my sons, detest, nor turn your force against your country's breast.

—Dryden

This writer quoted the above lines in an article, "Mischiefs of Party Spirit" in the Independence Day issue of *Mainstream* (15 August 1998), in the context of dissension and divisiveness that prevails in the country, and dangerous consequences that may follow.

Is there anyone in the BJP/RSS—now ruling the country—who will listen to this wise saying, and also tell the "Fuhrer of Maharashtra" that the *fatwa* issued by him, and accepted by his puppet Chief Minister, to reject the Srikrishna Commission Report on the 1992-93 communal riots in Bombay (now renamed Mumbai) is fraught with dangerous consequences for the country? Will the Home Minister, L.K. Advani (who says it is the prerogative of the Maharashtra Government to reject the Report thereby implicitly endorsing the action), take a sober and responsible view so that the country does not fall apart?

Communalism of any variety, as history tells us, gives rise to dissension, division, and then disintegration, apart from the worst form of human rights violation. Majoritarian communalism is more heinous.

How can a man like Atal Behari Vajpayee associate himself with someone who is a law unto himself, Bal Thackeray? He boldly declared, after the Report was tabled in the Maharashtra Assembly, that he had written inflammatory articles in his paper,

Samna; and what is more, that it was the right thing. And then came a smearing, even if disgraceful, attack on Justice Srikrishna, a practising and devout Hindu, dubbing him as pro-Muslim and anti-Hindu. All these, to put it mildly, are alarming—their only result being to create dissension and division and alienating the minorities from the mainstream. (Incidentally, this is not the first time that Bal Thackeray has attacked the judges.)

Everything Bal Thackeray has done and said is cancerous; and since he is not intellectually equipped to comprehend that he is contributing towards the disintegration of the country, there must be other sane elements, specially the law courts, to prevent him from engulfing the country in lawlessness. The minimum that Prime Minister Vajpayee must do is to see that the Report is accepted by the Maharashtra Government and the guilty brought to book. (The Prime Minister should know that even now the executioners of Hitler's orders are being brought to book and their victims are receiving compensation from the Government of Germany.)

The Srikrishna Commission has found the Shiv Sena guilty:

> Shiv Sena and Sainiks took the lead in organizing attacks on Muslims and their properties under the guidance of several leaders of Shiv Sena from the levels of Shakha Pramukh to the Shiv Sena Pramukh Bal Thackeray who like a veteran general commanded his loyal Shiv Sainiks in organized attacks on Muslims.

The Commission has also found a section of the police guilty:

> The police firing resulted in the death of a large number of Muslims as compared to Hindus. ... The built-in bias of the police force against Muslims became pronounced. ... The Commission has also come down heavily on the then Congress Chief Minister.

The culture and climate of anti-minoritism, resulting in increasing intolerance, appears to have found a fertile soil elsewhere also in our country, namely, neighbouring Gujarat. Those who plant the seeds couldn't care less about their fruits for the country at large. They have taken the law into their hands with the administration looking the other way. What is happening in Gujarat is unspeakably obnoxious. Even the

Hindutvavadi Chief Minister was constrained to criticize his followers for the recent organized violent attacks on Christians and Muslims. He said:

> I endorse whatever the Director General of Police had said about the activities of the VHP and Bajrang Dal workers.

The DGP had held these two formations responsible for the violent incidents against the Christians and Muslims and said that

> the VHP and Bajrang Dal workers are taking the law into their own hands, which could disturb the peace in the State.

What are the activities referred to here?

Schools run by Christians and even Churches have been under attack and copies of the *Bible* burnt publicly in Gujarat for some time now. The provocation is that Hindu children are converted to Christianity in a "clandestine" manner. If it were true, Hindu parents would have certainly made complaints to the police. There has not been any such complaint.

The charge against the Muslims is that Hindu girls are being forced to marry Muslim boys. And who is to decide whether it is out of free choice or under compulsion? Certainly not the law–enforcing agencies/courts, or the parents, or even the girls themselves, but the *Hindutvavadi* forces, whose word is final! (A corollary of this will be that adult girls and women will have no right to choose their husbands.)

Look at the logic of the *Hindutvavadi* forces: If a Muslim girl elopes with a Hindu boy, she has done this at her own free will in order to get away from the rigours of Islamic practices; if, however, a Hindu girl elopes with a Muslim boy, it is for "forced conversion".

In one case, in a village two Hindu girls eloped with Muslim boys; the *Hindutvavadi* cadres attacked and burnt all Muslim shops and houses, and all the 69 Muslim families were forced to leave the village.

Vajpayee and Advani have repeatedly declared from the house-tops that they and their *Hindutvavadi* followers are true "patriots". The recent happenings in Maharashtra and Gujarat speak a different language—*Hindutvavadis* are the potential destroyers of the country. One hopes, however, that Vajpayee raises himself above narrow party politics. The RSS and other *Hindutvavadi* ideologues and activists may not know, but Vajpayee surely appreciates the fact that the minorities in our country cannot be thrown into the Arabian Sea—they are part and parcel of what is known as Indian culture and Indian civilization, and their contributions have been no less significant than that of the dominant community. Let them not be treated like second class citizens as fancied by the unruly *Hindutvavadis*; they must have all the rights they are entitled to.

[Courtesy: *Mainstream*, 12 September 1998, pp. 15-16]

****

CHAPTER 23

Hindutvavadis' Intolerance of Minorities

CHRISTIANS UNDER ATTACK

The rape of four nuns in Jhabua (Madhya Pradesh) is a criminal and inhuman act—it is a blot on our culture. What is equally criminal and disgusting is its justification— unspeakably obnoxious—by the *Hindutvavadi* leaders who maintain that Christian missionaries represent "anti-national forces working against Hindu interests in the country", and that the gang-rape was "a reaction to these anti-national activities". Which means, plain and simple, that if those who are not "patriotic", from the point of view of the *Hindutvavadis*, it is perfectly permissible to rape their women. (It is high time patriotism is defined—a civilized nation cannot permit criminal acts in the name of "patriotism". It is also time to remember Dr. Johnson, who said: "Patriotism is the last resort of a scoundrel.") This justification reminds one of what happened in Surat during the communal riots after the demolition of the Babri Masjid—a large number of Muslim women were raped.

Many like us expected the de facto ruler of the country and the most important *Hindutvavadi* ideologue, L.K. Advani, to condemn this justification in a forthright manner.

Instead, he has tried to wriggle out of this justification by saying that the BJP section of the *Hindutvavadis* are not involved in this justification. This is quibbling, to put it mildly. As is well known/the Vishwa Hindu Parishad (VHP), Bajrang Dal, RSS,

Shiv Sainiks are all integral parts of the family, the Sangh Parivar, and Advani presides over its political wing.

Advani did the same with regard to the Shiv Sena-BJP Government's rejection of the Srikrishna Commission Report on the 1992-93 communal riots in Bombay. It is the prerogative of the Maharashtra Government to reject the report, he said. Doesn't this statement amount to endorsing the action of the State Government? And, is it a responsible view?

The justification referred to above reflects the *Hindutvavadis* as being intolerant of minorities, political reaction, and social/religious barbarism—all these directly related to the philosophy and practice of fascism.

It may be added that the gang-rape of the nuns in Jhabua, it appears, is part of a large plan to terrorize the Christian minority all over the country—attack on schools run by Christians and burning of copies of the *Bible* in Gujarat; attack in a convent in Jhabua; a convent looted in Baghpat in UP; a church attacked and desecrated in Meerut in UP; a woman raped in a convent in Bandel in West Bengal.

To give a couple of instances of this philosophy and mindset. The other day the fuehrer of Maharashtra, Bal Thackeray, who has been indicted by the Shrikrishna Commission, thundered, while addressing a Dussehra rally in Mumbai: "Dare arrest me and the entire city will be in flames." When the *Hindutvavadis* came to power in 1995, the fuehrer's first *fatwa* was that the "foreign nationals" and Pakistanis and Bangladeshis be identified. "These 42,000 managed to have voting rights in the last elections, but this will not do," he had thundered then. The reference was to the Supreme Court judgement restoring the rights of Muslims to vote whose names were arbitrarily removed from the electoral rolls. This mindset is built on their being intolerant of minorities— the sole objective being destruction of the weak and assertion of the strong; and this is exactly what the practitioners of Fascism in Germany and Italy did.

In the context of rights of minorities, the *Hindutvavadis* need to be told about the UN General Assembly Declaration (Resolution 47/135, 11 December 1992). Article 1 prescribes that states shall protect the cultural, religious and linguistic identity of minorities within their territories and shall encourage conditions of the promotion of that identity; and that persons belonging to minorities have the right to establish and maintain their own associations; and the states shall take measures to see that the minorities' human rights are protected.

"The culture and climate of anti-minoritism, resulting in increasing intolerance, appears to have found a fertile soil in our country", I wrote in an article, 'Hindutvavad and Communalism' (*Mainstream*, 12 September 1998); adding: "Those who plant the seeds couldn't care less about their fruits for the country." They are also sowing the seeds of disintegration by giving rise to dissension and divisiveness.

It is very depressing and distressing that human rights groups and activists are not as outraged by such a culture of intolerance, and practices of tyranny and oppression.

[Courtesy: *Mainstream*, Vol. XXXVI, No. 42,
10 October 1998, pp. 3-4]

****

CHAPTER 24

Communalism

Societal violation of human rights (like that caused by communal violence, and violation of human rights of Dalits, minorities, women and children) has not received due attention from the middle class-dominated civil society and opinion-makers, and not even from the National Human Rights Commission (NHRC); it does not appear to be on the government's agenda.

During the freedom struggle two leaders—Mahatma Gandhi and M.N. Roy—took serious note of communalism and the Hindu–Muslim question. Almost all other leaders under the Congress umbrella, including Jawaharlal Nehru, maintained that once the British left, this problem (as also the question of human rights violation caused by the hierarchical system) would be solved in no time. Gandhiji, however, often said, in most unambiguous terms, that unless these two evils (communalism and untouchability) are done away with, India has no right to independence from British Raj. Ultimately he fell a victim to an intolerant cult—nationalism. Gandhiji was a religious man, and he had the same respect for other religions that he had for his own, Hinduism. And he wanted the Hindus, as also other Indians, to follow his example and solve the Hindu–Muslim question. Regrettably, this approach has not helped in combating communalism.

Roy wrote a book, while in jail in 1930–36, *Historical Role of Islam*, with a view to solving the Hindu–Muslim question. He wrote:

> Although Islam came to India after it had played out its progressive role, and its leadership had been wrested from the

> learned and cultured Arabs, the revolutionary principles of the days of its origin and ascendancy were still inscribed on its flag.

A critical study of history would reveal that

> Brahmanical orthodoxy having overwhelmed the Buddhist revolution, India of the eleventh and twelfth centuries must have been infested with multitudes of persecuted heretics who would eagerly welcome the message of Islam.

Roy maintained that we must be clear as to the causes of the Muslim conquest of India so that we get rid

> of the prejudice that makes the orthodox Hindu look upon his Muslim neighbour as an inferior being. Unless a radical change of attitude is brought about by a sober sense of history, the communal question will never be solved.

Addressing the Muslims, Roy wrote:

> Few Muslims of our days may be conscious of the glorious part played on the stage of history by the faith they profess.

Roy, therefore, urged both Hindus and Muslims to revive the positive aspects and creative heritage of Islamic culture. "Indians, both Hindus and Muslims," Roy concluded, "could profitably draw inspiration from [the] knowledge of Islam's contribution to human culture and a proper appreciation of the historical value of that contribution would shock the Hindus out of their arrogant self-satisfaction, and cure the narrow-mindedness of the Muslims of our day by bringing them face to face with the true spirit of the faith they profess."

Gandhi's approach minus the mystique and Roy's scientific approach to a solution of the problem must be taken seriously by our government and opinion-makers.

The Massacre of Sikhs in 1984—General Aurora's Affidavit

It is in the above context that we refer to the 1984 pogrom when more than three thousand Sikhs were brutally killed in Delhi alone. "Who are the Guilty"? has not yet been answered. The rulers and their officials have adopted diabolical methods to see that the guilty are not punished. The government has now instituted another inquiry commission to go into the cruel killings with a view to identifying the guilty. A number of people have submitted sworn affidavits to the commission. The affidavit submitted by Lt. Gen. (retd.) J.S. Aurora, hero of the Bangladesh war in 1971, is significant in that it indicates quite clearly that the government was not interested in "protecting lives and property of innocent Sikhs". The government allowed the communal riots to go on. We give below a summary of what General Aurora stated in his affidavit dated 21 September 2000.

> We [Gen. Aurora, Air Chief Marshal Arjun Singh, Brig. Sukhjit Singh—all retired at that time, and Patwant Singh] issued a joint statement on 31 October 1984 at 3.30 p.m. condemning the attempt on the life of the Prime Minister of India. We could make out that a highly volatile situation was fast developing, which if not controlled and timely action not taken, it could flare up beyond all proportions and which could cause immense harm to the Sikhs and their families. We agreed to call upon President Zail Singh. In our meeting with him on 1 November 1984 we expressed our concern on the large scale violence and looting which had erupted consequent to the killing of Prime Minister, Mrs Indira Gandhi, and requested him to use his good offices to stop the bloodshed and destruction of properties. The President said, 'I do not have powers to intervene.' We were amazed to hear the said remark. On our insistence he agreed to speak to the Prime Minister later. We had also requested him to use the electronic media to stop the mob frenzy and save innocent Sikhs but he never did so. On our inquiries whether the Army was being called to restore law and order and normalcy, he said, 'I am not in contact with the Home Minister, Shri Narasimha Rao', and he asked me to speak to him on the phone. I telephoned Mr Rao from Rashtrapati Bhawan but was told that he was not available. Later on when we tried to fix a meeting with him, we were told that he was busy in some other meeting at his residence. We then barged into his house without appointment at about 3 p.m. and were surprised to see that there was no meeting in progress. The situation there looked very normal and did not reflect that half the city was in flames and murders were taking place over widespread areas. Was the Army being called? He said, 'It will be here in the evening'. To our suggestions about coordination between police and Army as was done in 1947 at the Viceroy's house, the Home Minister casually replied, 'We will see when the Army arrives.' He did not seem to be concerned at all about the Sikhs being butchered. We had also

> noticed that he did not make any attempt or effort either to call the GOC of the Delhi Area or to contact him. The Home Minister was grossly negligent in his approach to the events which clearly reflected his connivance with the perpetrators of the heinous crimes being committed against the Sikhs with impunity. On 2 November the Area Commander told us that no control room (as suggested by us to the Home Minister) had been set up. After about a week when we met the Lt. Governor of Delhi and asked him to take action against the guilty we were shocked when the L.G. mentioned that the police could not control the violence because for forty-eight hours they were stunned as two of their own policemen had committed the heinous crime of murdering the Prime Minister. It was apparent that the government was not at all interested in protecting the lives and property of the innocent Sikhs.

General Aurora's account is reminiscent of the Dark Ages. And, yet Pandit Nehru was so confident that this evil would disappear automatically once the British left.

Demolition of Babri Masjid

A number of civil society groups and activists hold meetings and demonstrations on 6 December every year to condemn the demolition of the Masjid and subsequent communal riots. Last year (A.D. 2000) too meetings were held. This time the Opposition parties in Parliament raised questions apropos of the demolition. The Opposition parties demanded the resignation of three Union Ministers against whom cases are pending in a court of law, on the charge that they were responsible for the demolition. All informed peoples including those in the *Sangh Parivar*, know who were responsible for the demolition of the Masjid. The leaders of the *Parivar* appear to have been trapped now. They want to get away from this situation. The RSS chief has come out with the "revelation" that a bomb explosion brought the Masjid down! Earlier it was claimed by some *Hindutvavadi* leaders that the Masjid had fallen down on its own! Note also the Prime Minister's statement, "the entire nation wants the Ram temple at Ayodhya" although he later said it was a slip of tongue! We should be grateful for small mercies: the equally guilty Narasimha Rao, the Prime

Minister on 6 December 1992, has not come out with any new theory! (He has conveniently forgotten his promise made on 6 December 1992 that the Masjid would be rebuilt.)

Hindutvavadi leaders like the RSS chief have perfected and legitimized the art of doublespeak and the language of deceipt, utter lies and hypocrisy, like George Orwell's (*The Animal Farm*) four-legged dictator who quietly changed the original thesis of the revolution, "four legs good, two legs bad" to "four legs good, two legs better"; and from "all animals are equal" to "all animals are equal but some are more equal than others". The mindset behind this kind of deceit and lies is that if one goes on repeating a lie, like the sheep on Orwell's animal farm chanting regularly the revised versions who begin to believe that these are the true lessons, the lie will become truth! Hitler's propaganda chief, Goebbels, in Nazi Germany had perfected this art: go on repeating a lie, it will be accepted as truth.

If there is one thing that has been made clear by *1984 Delhi (1992 Ayodhya)* as also by *1992-93 Mumbai* and many other communal riots during the last 53 years, it is that there is no place for political freedom, civil liberties, and tolerance in our country—these values have been made irrelevant by political reaction and social/religious barbarism. In all these communal riots—the Muslims, the Sikhs, and now the Christians are victims—there are violations of all standards of morality, justice and freedom. (The RSS chief has declared that he will tolerate only a *swadeshi* church for Christians. Encouraged by such arrogant announcements, assaults on Christians, rape of Christian women including nuns, destruction of churches, have been on the increase.) Acts of barbarism are committed, and justified, in the name of faith, thus placing a premium on ignorance and making the masses easy of exploitation.

[Courtesy: *Mainstream*, Vol. XXXIX, No. 16,
7 April 2001, pp.11-12]

****

CHAPTER 25

Objectionable Nonsense

The National Council of Educational Research and Training (NCERT) (a Government of India establishment) stated, around 1994, in their guidelines to human rights education that their textbooks on different subjects had been written keeping in mind the values of human rights. In those days the NCERT made efforts to maintain its autonomy. It affirmed:

> The basic approach which has been followed as one of integrating various aspects and dimensions of human rights are integrally connected with various other issues which are among major concerns of school curriculum as a whole as well as of the curricula in various school subjects. They cannot be seen as being apart from issues relating to secularism, national integration, gender bias, protection of the environment and many others which are among the major concerns of curriculum in languages/literary social sciences, sciences and other subjects... All subjects should be taught in such a manner as to foster the spirit of scientific humanism.

The point of departure today is scientific humanism —scientific humanism and Hinduization on the authority of the Brahmanical religion are contradiction in terms.

The Educational Policy of 1986 of the Government of India (revised in 1992) laid stress on the national curriculum with a common code as a basis for building the National System of Education. It laid emphasis "on the combative role of education in eliminating obscurantism, religious fanaticism and violence, superstition and fatalism". These principles were sought to be reflected, in varying degrees, in the subject courses and teaching materials, particularly textbooks, prepared at the national level by the NCERT for school curriculum. Textbooks were written to provide

> a critical understanding of Indian society through the ages with some focus on the position of women, the inequalities created by the caste system and various barbarous practices which arose during various periods and of attempts by reformers in various periods to bring about a more human social order.

My purpose is not to analyze textbooks or whether these are in conformity with the above stated principles.

What is relevant is to note that now the NCERT under a new Director, who is ideologically close to the BJP and its *Hindutva* philosophy, has surrendered its autonomy to the government and questioned the guidelines referred to above; as a first step he deleted certain portions from a few textbooks, and as a second step the Director and the NCERT (obviously under instructions from the political masters) have decided to do away with the present textbooks and write new ones. It is obvious that the main aim is to Hinduize education and history. Given the social philosophy of the RSS and the *Hindutvavadis*, this is understandable.

What one cannot understand is the over-enthusiasm of the BJP stalwarts in conceiving of the entire history of India as a saga of Hindu resistance against foreigners, as asserted by V.D. Savarkar in his *Six Glorious Epochs of Indian History*.

The main aim of the *Hindutvavadis* is to write off the "presence" of Islam and its contribution. The fact also remains that all the formations around the BJP are bent on establishing a Hindu state in India. Their political ideology is, therefore, based on their own (mis)interpretation of history. Their method is simple: If you do not accept our interpretation of history you are a distorter of Indian history.

Why should the ideologues of the RSS be scared of studying Islam and its contribution to human culture? Is it because that a "proper appreciation of the historical value of the contribution would shock the Hindus out of their arrogant self-satisfaction"?

I may quote, in this context, what Rammohun Roy said:

> I myself have read all the Koran again and again; and has that made me a Musalman? Nay, I have studied the whole Bible, and you know I am not a Christian. Why then do you fear to read it? Read it and judge for yourself.

There is another problem which the BJP formations do not take into account or prefer to brush off under the carpet. When their political leaders want us to say: "Announce with pride that you are Hindus," what Hinduism are they referring to—the Brahmanical religion with the impregnable walls that have been created by the caste system, or the non-Sanskritic Hinduism which made valiant efforts, but regrettably did not succeed, in the medieval period (that is, during Muslim rule), to demolish this ugly relic of our past? If it is the Brahmanical religion—they obviously refer to this religion—no thoughtful Hindu has any reason to be proud of this religion which has kept a particular section of our population in perpetual bondage, in fact, have not even recognized them as persons for centuries.

The BJP Prime Minister and his men and women are angry at the conversion of Hindus to other religions; they are not concerned with the obnoxious, divinely ordained hierarchical system. Indeed, they glorify this system. The upholders of the system, on the authority of scriptures, seek to persuade the poor, the depressed, the oppressed, and the exploited to reconcile their lot to suffering, sacrifice, love and voluntary poverty—all that signifies complete surrender and the absence of the spirit of revolt.

India, however, has a great and glorious past; regrettably the BJP and the formations around it are bent on keeping that past buried. We have a past which, if revived, will help India coming to the inheritance of the blessings of, modern civilization. It is in this context that our historians must give an account of the non-Sanskritic tradition—the Buddhist period (interest in man and woman, man and woman not in God's image but in their own image, their affairs on this earth unlike interest in gods and goddesses and good life in heaven after death), non-Vedic sects like the Nath, Yoga, Siddacara, the medieval period (Bhakti and Sufi movements), the advent of

Islam which led to a series of responses. Also an analysis of the Muslim conquest of India is of practical value today, and will help Indians, both Hindus and Muslims, appreciate the positive results of the Muslim conquest of India. This is necessary for a solution of the communal question—communalism which has found a fertile soil in our country.

Our historians must give their attention to these historical facts. It is these facts that the BJP and its formations—now through the present RSS-oriented management of the NCERT—want to remove from history books. The NCERT's action in rewriting history reminds one of Pakistan's methodology of distorting history. A history textbook for junior college students in Pakistan teaches the following:

> As a result of Akbar's liberal policy the very existence of true Islam in South Asia was threatened. Those who opposed these policies were either murdered or exiled. All these contributing immensely to the resolution of the Hindu nationalists. Imagine their pleasure at the Muslim adoption of Hindu dress and customs.

Fundamentalists across the world speak the same language!

It is in the above context that we may view the recent deletions from the NCERT textbooks. But before I do that, let me refer to a couple of horrendous and dangerous "gems" in textbooks brought out by some States in India. A textbook of Uttar Pradesh has this:

> Hindus had to give away their daughters in marriage very early for fear of the Muslims.
>
> The purdah system and child marriages became common because of the bad character of the Muslim rulers.

A textbook of Madhya Pradesh informs us: "Ancient India was a Hindu Rashtra" and "Mughal intolerance led to the rise of Hindu nationalism". These "gems" may be kept in mind while noting the deletion of the "objectionable paragraphs". (There is some mystery about these deletions. Since the government and NCERT have decided to remove these textbooks and get new ones prepared to replace them in the coming academic session beginning April 2002, why did the government and NCERT delete the portions in indecent haste? The books are ready but the authorities would not disclose the identity of the authors!)

Since the "objectionable" materials are historical truth, they stand in the way of the *Hindutvavadis* reviving an imaginary glorious past of 5,000 years which is supposed to have been written in golden letters and also making the Brahmanical religion firmly rooted.

Let us now give a quick look at the deleted portions—the Central Board of Secondary Education (CBSE) has already issued instructions to schools that these portions must not be taught, and there must not be any discussion on these aspects:

- For special guests, beef was served as a mark of honour. In ancient times people took beef.
- Archaeological evidence should be considered far more important than long family trees given in the *Puranas*. The Puranic tradition could be used to date Rama of Ayodhya around 2000 B.C. but extensive excavation in Ayodhya do not show any settlement around that date. Similarly, the earlier inscriptions and sculptural pieces found in Mathura between 200 B.C. and A.D. 300 do not attest to Krishna's presence.
- Cattle wealth slowly decimated because cows and bullocks were killed in numerous Vedic sacrifices.
- The Brahmanical reaction began as a result of the policy of Ashoka. He prohibited killing of animals and birds and derided superfluous rituals performed by women. This naturally affected the income of the Brahmanas. They were not satisfied with his tolerant policy. They wanted a policy that would favour them and uphold the existing interests and privileges.
- In course of time, *varnas* or social classes or *jatis* or castes were made hereditary by law and religion. All these were done to ensure that Vaishyas produce and pay taxes and Shudras serve as labourers so that Brahmanas act as priests and Kshatriyas as rulers. What was done by slaves and other producing sections in Greece and Rome under the threat of whip was done by the Vaishyas and Shudras out of conviction formed through Brahmanical indoctrination and the *varna* system.

- Jats founded their state at Bharatpur from where they conducted plundering raids in the regions around and participated in court intrigues at Delhi.
- In 1675, Guru Teg Bahadur was arrested and executed. The official explanation for this, as given in some later Persian sources, is that after his return from Assam, the Guru, in association with one Hafiz Adam, resorted to plundering and raping, laying waste the whole province of Punjab. According to Sikh tradition, the execution was due to the intrigues of some members of his family who disputed his succession and by others who had joined him. But we are also told that Aurangzeb was annoyed because the Guru had converted a few Muslims to Sikhism.

The deletions are objectionable, both on legal ethical and historical grounds. As has been pointed out by a number of historians, including the authors of the textbooks under reference, the NCERT and CBSE have no power to make any changes without the permission of the authors. The NCERT Director and the Union Minister of Human Resource Development, who is also an important RSS ideologue, maintain that they have deleted the portions after having discussion with historians but they will not identify those "historians", and that they have done so after consulting the religious leaders. A sad day for our young students! The Minister has gone to the extent of asserting that it is not necessary to consult historians—"who are they to be consulted?"—he thundered arrogantly. The Minister also asserted:

> After the war of independence there should be a second war for the country's cultural freedom.

He has left us in no doubt about his intention— to wage war on those who do not accept his interpretation of the cultural history of India.

So far as historical truth/evidence is concerned, historians have asserted that the deleted potions are based on historical evidence. I may refer to a couple of these subjects.

Eating of beef in ancient India is a well-established fact; and our children must know facts about our past. It is a stated policy of the BJP to impose, as enunciated in one of its election manifestoes, a "complete ban on the slaughter of cows, calves, bulls and bullocks". The BJP and its guiding spirit, the RSS, are of the view that beef is the food of Muslims and Christians, and that in pre-Muslim India people did not eat beef, and therefore this food culture must be made to disappear from a Hindu India. They want to usher in this "cultural freedom". Incidentally, how many of us are aware of the fact that a very large number of Indians—Dalits, Tribals, very Backward Castes as also Muslims—have no other option, for economic reason, but to eat beef food (which includes buffalo food)? Also, do we know that a vegetarian meal is a luxury which only the rich and well-to-do can afford? Why should we gloss over the fact that the deprived and poor sections of our people do respect and care for their cattle, but do not accept the "sacred" theory?

The attack on culture and cultural habits of a section of our people, in the name of "cultural freedom" is a dangerous game—it is communalism, plain and simple. Today Hinduism is in danger in the hands of the *Hindutvavadis*—let us be sure, the real enemy of Hinduism is the *Hindutvavadi.*

The Minister, as an ideological defender and follower of the Brahmanical religion, has deleted references to *varnas*/the caste system. What does he want to achieve by expunging historical facts? Will this deletion do away with the fact that, according to the caste system, all human beings are not born free and equal in dignity and rights? Does the Minister want that the outside world must not know this fact? (He forgets that thanks to him and his government, the issue of caste has been internationalized at the Durban Conference!) Our students must know that caste divides and gives rise to divisiveness and dissension; that the system has erected impregnable walls between groups of human beings; that it has ordained that social hierarchy is to be determined by birth; that under this system one must find joy only in the work that has been allotted to him/her by birth and if you act against this injunction you are committing a sin and you must be punished; that you must accept the theory of Karma and must not revolt against a system which, as I mentioned earlier, does not recognize a section of our people even as persons. These are dark and horrendous corners in our social life. If our students are not made aware of these corners, how will they close the doors on these corners and build up a new society of new men and women?

I have a number of friends—secular liberals—who, though they are generally opposed to the RSS approach to education (curriculum of Shishu Mandirs), take objection to archaeological evidence as against mythological evidence—that is, writings related to our great ancient literature like the *Ramayan*, the *Mahabharata*, the *Puranas* etc. They suggest, by implication, that whatever Tulsidas has written about Rama in his *Ramayana* is the gospel truth or that our cultural heritage is based on his story of Rama. These liberal friends do not take into account other versions of the *Ramayana*. One of the heroes of the Bengalis of my generation was Michael Madhusudan Dutta (and I guess he still remains a hero), the first modern poet of India, who used uncomplimentary epithets for Rama—thank God, my friends have not read Michael's comments on Rama! It is very difficult to generalize—which myths are part and parcel of Hinduism and Hindu culture. In any case, in such matters we have no other option but to rely heavily on the language of reason. Here, too, we could learn from Rammohun Roy. He quotes Vashishtha approvingly:

> If a child says something reasonable it should be accepted, but if Brahma himself says something unreasonable it should be discarded as a piece of straw.

Archaeological/historical evidence cannot be sacrificed at the alter of unreason and myths.

As to deletion of references to Sikhs, Jats, Guru Teg Bahadur, these are for direct political advantage—the BJP as also the Congress want their votes!

Looked at from any angle—historical evidence, right to discussion and enquiry, freedom of speech, function of education and acquiring of knowledge, the right to question unreason—the BJP Government's act of deletions and removal of the present history textbooks with a view to deliberately distorting history, through its agencies, the NCERT and CBSE, is an objectionable nonsense.

[Courtesy: *Mainstream*, 22 December 2001
(Annual 2001), pp. 39–41, 50]

****

CHAPTER 26

The Communal Virus Will Destroy the Country

SEARING CRIES OF AGONY IN GUJARAT

I may be forgiven for quoting from what I wrote, under the heading "Human Rights Trodden Under Foot", after the demolition of the Babri Masjid:

> If there is one thing which has been made clear by Ayodhya on December 6, 1992 is that those who cherish political freedom and civil liberties have been made irrelevant, at least for the time being, by political reaction and social/religious barbarism. There has been violation of all standards of morality, justice and freedom; everything has been done in the name of faith—divine sanctions. Acts of barbarism and violence have been committed and justified in the name of faith, thus placing premium on ignorance and making the masses easy of exploitation. Religious sentiment has come very handy. The perpetrators of violence in Ayodhya have sought to prove, indeed they have succeeded in doing so, that manmade laws have no validity. They (the *Hindutvavadis)* have waged war upon all that is fine and valuable in human culture. What we have witnessed in Ayodhya is an appeal to violence, to emotion, to passion. And this kind of appeal inevitably leads to cruelty, madness, and gangsterism.

The massacres in Gujarat starting from 27 February—and continuing at the time of writing this (3 March 2002)—are a reaffirmation of the above: appeal to violence, to emotion, to passion leading to cruelty, madness, and gangsterism. People like this writer have been made irrelevant, even though we, I have always believed with good reason, are in a majority. The reason why our voice is not heard/felt is because the sane elements, the majority, are silent in that they are not organized, are not united. What prevents, for example, the sane and rational elements, all the political formations which profess to be secular and do not subscribe to anti-minorityism, from giving a call—to hold huge public meetings across the country and to come down heavily on cruelty, madness, and gangsterism?

I suggest our liberals do not have the courage. Otherwise, how could they digest what a "secular liberal"—he calls himself so—an editor of one of the largest circulated English dailies, and that too a supporter of the Congress party, said (in a signed article), namely, that the "secular establishment" has ignored the brutal and cruel attack on *kar sevaks* (who returned from Ayodhya) at Godhra station in Gujarat on 27 February. This "gentleman" is angry that while we condemn majority communalism, we do not take note of minority communalism that resulted in the killings at Godhra. (An opinion-maker like him ought to know that in all countries it is majority communalism that breeds minority communalism.) He is also angry that in all civilized societies minorities are treated with consideration and that they deserve protection. He asserts that this kind of attitude is "counter-productive" and must be condemned. This kind of attitude will lead Hindus to believe, this "gentleman" further asserts, that "their suffering is of no consequence and will be tempted to see the building of a building at Ayodhya as an expression of Hindu pride in the face of secular indifference." (No wonder the *Hindutvavadis* have found in him their own ideologue, dear to their heart—in all debates and discussions they fly the article.) What is most insulting is that the author claims to be a secular person. No civilized and thoughtful person would like to get mixed up with such "secular" persons. You don't need any mad gangster to destroy this country nor do you need any enemy from outside the country—liberal editors and opinion-makers like him have succeeded in creating a climate of dissension and divisiveness—sure elements to destroy a country. I am surprised that the "liberal" press has not thought it fit to censor him. If thoughtful people in the press are worth their salt, people like him must be made to quit this noble profession. He is an insult to the profession. Let him be in the business of showmanship. [Is he not the same person who used his "press freedom" to attack the Chairperson of the Press Council of India (a retired Supreme Court Judge) because the verdict given by the Council had gone against the editor?]

Let us recapitulate the facts. The *kar sevaks* are attacked a short distance away from Godhra station. Fifty-seven of them are burnt alive. All thoughtful sections of our people immediately reacted to this cruel and inhuman killing by condemning the massacre. Human rights organizations like the People's Union for Civil Liberties condemned the incident. (This writer, the President of the Delhi PUCL, issued a statement condemning the massacre. Whatever the provocation, the killings stand condemned, we said and urged the Union Government to take all steps to see that the communal conflagration does not spread, and that *kar sevaks* are not allowed to go to Ayodhya. We urged the government to set up a high-level judicial commission so that the miscreants could be brought to book and punished. We also called upon the people to remain peaceful.) Muslim organizations throughout the country have condemned the killings at Godhra as "barbaric and brutal". And yet the editor referred to above insinuates that "secular establishments resort to blaming the victims". He, plain and simple, has made an appeal to violence, to emotion, to passion with a view to committing acts of cruelty, madness, and gangsterism.

The horrendous outrage at Godhra gave rise to massacres and killings of Muslims in a number of cities including Ahmedabad. Since the 27 February evening and 28 February morning, the killings have gone on unabated and till 3 March at the time of writing this the death toll is over 500.

The BJP-RSS rulers of Gujarat have not even regretted that over 500 people have been brutally killed in different parts of Gujarat—mobs continue to be on a killing spree in villages—many of them burnt alive. The refrain of the rulers, including Chief Minister Narendra Modi, is that these killings are a natural outcome of the killings at Godhra. Narendra Modi—he is also a well-known RSS leader—instead of reassuring the people of Gujarat that he is responsible for their safety and security, maintains by way of justification that what is happening is that "every action has an equal and opposite reaction". "The five crore people of Gujarat have shown remarkable restraint under grave provocation," Modi says with great satisfaction. Incidentally, it is now known that he did not cooperate with the Army in bringing the riots under control. What has happened in Gujarat is reminiscent of the tragic happenings in Delhi in 1984—the authorities' refusal to call the Army at the appropriate time. The editor, to whom I have referred above, is not concerned with this aspect of the tragic happenings. His soul cries out only for the *kar sevaks*—that the country may disintegrate because of them and because of communal disharmony and killings, is not his concern.

Let me quote a few headlines in some national dailies (of 3 March) to indicate the seriousness of the situation: 29 burned to death in Mehsana massacres; Riot toll nears 300; No let-up in Gujarat violence; Gujarat looks like a ghost State; No tall man around, only struggle for power; Blame it on Newton's law: Modi; Riot after riot, police play a negative role; Gujarat : Liberal but never secular; Lunacy Abounds—Police lose morale and courage (en editorial); Delay in Army development made the difference; Mayhem in presence of an inert police and on.

Let us go back a little. After the attack on the Sabarmati Express train some distance away from Godhra station on 27 February, the VHP gave a call for a bandh. The President of the Gujarat BJP announced his support to the bandh—thus directing the BJP Government not to take any action against the bandh. On 28 February Muslims in Ahmedabad and other cities came under attack; and the police turned their face. It is because of this—police inaction and complicity under instructions from their political bosses—that many people like the former Congress MP Ehsan Jaffri, were burnt alive in the presence of the police force. Let us hear his wife:

> My husband called the Police Commissioner, his party President Amarsingh Chaudhary and scores of leaders. For almost three hours he continued to make frantic phone calls, pleading for help. At one time he even cried on the phone to save so many lives. But no one, not a single leader, not one policeman came to our rescue. When I came down (from the upper floor) it was all over. I could not believe my eyes. I could not find my husband's body. My neighbours were unrecognizable too. The police are not helping us nor am I allowed to go home to look for his body. I think I will go mad.

Hundreds and thousands of such cries of agony from both Muslims and Hindus are heard every day—can there be anything more searing than such cries? We have seen images of agony on the TV screen—heart-rending accounts and cries for help. Is it because of this that the Gujarat Government has banned the transmission of Star News in Gujarat? The Star News, especially its correspondent Rajdeep Sardesai, must be congratulated for bringing to us, to all sensitive people, reports and agonizing visuals. He has contributed immensely towards bringing back sanity—we may remember the colour TV's contribution to bring an end to the Vietnam War, under pressure from American citizens, especially parents and wives of the US soldiers.

Let us make a confession: we Indians have every reason to be ashamed of ourselves. If we cannot eliminate the cancerous virus of communalism, we have no right to be called civilized. Also, let us remember that this virus, if not eliminated, will break the country.

[Courtesy: *Mainstream*, Vol. XL, No.13,
16 March 2002, pp. 7–8]

****

IV. M.N. Roy, Gandhi and Partition

CHAPTER 27

M.N. Roy

UNCOMPROMISING ANTI-FASCIST AND RADICAL PHILOSOPHER

This article was written to mark M.N. Roy's 111th birth anniversary on 21 March, 1997.

Activist, intellectual and social philosopher, M.N. Roy was an unusual person. He remained a radical throughout his life—as an ardent nationalist, communist, radical humanist propounding partyless direct democracy. He had to swim against the current in every phase of his many-splendoured career, and as a result "failed" as a practical party politician. Anyone familiar with his works would not fail to come to the conclusion that he was not cut out for party politics. It is surprising that his political party colleagues did not feel that way.

In this article, I propose to deal with two most important aspects—the first leading to the second. One, his uncompromising fight for human freedom and fight against Fascism—paradoxically this was his "unmaking" as a party politician. The other, his commitment to democracy, and urge for freedom which eventually culminated in propounding the philosophy of radical humanism.

These were complemented by his devotion to truth. The philosophy of radical humanism led Roy to the conclusion that party politics is inconsistent with the ideal of democracy and that this is bound to degenerate into power politics. Roy dwelt at length, in his lectures and articles during the period 1947–53 (he died on 25 January, 1954), on the subject of an alternative system of political practice and economic development based on decentralization of power. The second part of this article will give a summary of this alternative system of politics and economic management.

Roy is not widely read. Not many Indians knew, or know even today—particularly those who think that he was wrong in his thesis about the anti-Fascist character of the Second World War—that Roy was an uncompromising opponent of Fascism and wrote a book in jail during 1933–36 (he was in jail in 1931–36), *Fascism : Its Philosophy, Profession, and Practice,* first published in 1938, in which he made an "enquiry into the monstrosity (of Fascism) of our time". He maintained that those who say that Fascism has no philosophy were totally wrong.

> The philosophy of Fascist dictatorship can be traced through Schopenhauer whose disciple, Nietzsche was the father of Fascism. The Fascist movement suppresses with violence the revolt of the slaves of Capitalism. The State must have the courage to break its own laws. (Goebbles). ...'Let it be written on our epitaph : we have been hard, we have been ruthless, but we have been good Germans. (Hitler).' ...The moral sanction for such arbitrary, absolutely unrestricted power on earth can be derived (from a force) which is not bound by the laws of nature, yet is the sovereign principle of power governing the destiny of man. That is the philosophy of Fascism, the quintessence of which is the cult of superman.

He appealed, in this book, to

> Those Indian nationalists who can think, who are not simply swayed by prejudice, or who are not conscious reactionaries—potential Fascists—themselves.

In a letter to Ellen Gottschalk (his future wife) in Germany, Roy wrote from jail in 1936, at the critical moment of the civil war in Spain, the outcome of which tragedy greatly determined the subsequent events in Europe:

> I am terribly worried. How could the Bhumians be such confounded fools? Don't they see that the noose is ruthlessly closing on their own accursed necks, with the aid, and connivance of the democratic powers, for the pleasure of whom they are selling

> their soul, and themselves assisting the rape of democracy? The French Republic is doomed, unless some miracle happens.

How prophetic—with remarkable accuracy he looked ahead. Four years later, France fell.

In October 1939—until Hitler invaded France in April 1940, Roy termed the war in Europe a "phoney war"—Roy came to the conclusion that a triumph of Fascism in Europe will mean a serious setback for the forces of revolution throughout the world and will constitute a great menace. Therefore fighters for freedom, democracy and progress, without desiring the victory of imperialist powers, must not act in such a way as may contribute to the imminent victory of Fascism. He maintained that an Anglo-Franco-Soviet anti-aggression pact would have prevented the German invasion of Poland, and Europe might have been spared the ordeal. If England and France were genuine in stopping the victorious march of Fascism, Roy said, they should abandon the anti-Soviet policy and resume negotiations with Soviet Russia.

Roy wrote in an article, a few days before the fall of France:

> The birth of Fascism twenty years ago sounded the death knell of democracy. As a matter of fact, the ugly child of Fascism, to grow up into the present bloody monster, was conceived in the womb of parliamentary democracy, and carefully, though covertly, nurtured on her lap. 'The creator of (both parliamentary democracy and Fascism) is capitalism. ...Fascism is the illicit love of parliamentary democracy. Passion persuaded her to allow the paramour to enter her house and ravage her.

When Hitler invaded France, Roy declared that the war had become an anti-Fascist war, and called upon the people to mobilize themselves for the decisive struggle for freedom

> By availing themselves of an opportunity which may be presented before long by the possible development of the international situation.

He also gave a call to all fighters for freedom and democracy to prevent the reorganisation of the forces of international counter-revolution under the domination of Nazi Germany.

The Congress Working Committee passed a resolution at this stage of the war (June 1940), expressing sorrow over

> the misfortunes that have befallen the people of France.

The resolution did not categorically condemn Fascism even though the Congress had, on a number of occasions earlier, declared itself against Fascism. Roy maintained that this declaration had no meaning if it shirked the responsibility of fighting Fascism. He was forthright in his views:

> The proper approach to the complex problems of the new situation is conditional upon a clear understanding of the issues involved in the European struggle. For one thing, it is not a European struggle. It is a struggle involving the entire world. It is a struggle for the future of entire humanity. It is a fight neither against Nazi Germany nor against Fascist Italy. Fascism or Hitlerism is a sinister force which today operates on the international scale. It proposes to destroy all the achievements of modern civilisation, and threatens human liberty throughout the world. Our attitude in connection with the present European conflict must be determined by this consideration of the fundamental issues involved.

He therefore maintained that resistance to India's participation in the war was an ill-conceived policy. He appealed to the Congress to return to office (Congress-led governments in the provinces had resigned earlier on the war issue) and in cooperation with other popular organizations pledged to national freedom, participate in the war for world freedom and thus contribute to the cause of her own freedom. He appealed to the Congress to capture the control of the government and then to organize a National Militia. He asked the Congress to seek the cooperation of the Muslim League and other organizations to protect the poor people from the obligation of shouldering all the burdens of India's participation in the war.

On 14 July, 1940, on the 151st anniversary of the French Revolution, Roy called upon the members of his group in the Congress—the League of Radical Congressmen, to adopt the Jacobin Cap as its emblem, to be worn as a badge by all its members. The emblem will be

> the token of their determination to defend and promote human liberty and progress against the Fascist onslaught, no matter from where it comes.

At this stage of the war, Roy thought that Hitler could not be defeated without Soviet Russia's help:

> Barring the eventuality of Russian intervention on the basis of a realignment of international forces, there is little chance of Europe being liberated in the near future from the Fascist stranglehold.

He did not think that British imperialism would liquidate itself and India would attain her freedom by fluke. Before England was attacked, there was the possibility of imperialist powers and Hitler signing a peace treaty on the basis of redivision of the world and sharing the world. Roy warned that

> People should ponder over the possibility of British imperialism continuing in India with the visibly Fascist warpaint. Imperialism is bad. But will it be better when the British Empire will be administered by out and out Fascism?

He submitted a resolution—he was a member of the AICC—to the meeting of the AICC held at Poona on 27 July 1940:

> The AICC resolves that the people of India should actively participate in the struggle against Fascism in every way available to them. That will not be helping Imperialism, because the cooperation of India will strengthen the position of the genuinely anti-Fascist elements in England and enable the masses of the British people to prevent the liquidation of the struggle against Fascism under the influence of more reactionary forces who still wield considerable power in the British ruling circles.

Disciplinary action was taken in September 1940 against Roy by the UPPCC on the ground of his advocacy for active participation in an anti-Fascist war. Roy wrote in protest to Maulana Azad, the President of the Congress, which said, inter alia:

> I have done nothing worse than recommend an alternative policy for the Congress. The action against me having been arbitrary, unfair and unjust, for the sake of our organisation, it should be rectified. If that is not done, I shall have no other alternative than to resign my membership of the Congress. ...The will of the Indian

> people to gain national freedom will be quickened by the consciousness that they are voluntarily participating in the historic fight against the mortal enemy of all freedom. I shall do my best to awaken that consciousness which will absolve the Indian people from the shame of the Congress attitude amounting to an encouragement and indirect help to Fascism. If I cannot do that as a Congressman I shall do it as an Indian whose love for freedom cannot be subordinated to any dictation.

In December 1942, Roy told his colleagues in the Radical Democratic Party (the party was formed in December 1940) in its All-India Conference—Central Executive Council meeting—that the war was going to end in 1944 when the Fascist Powers will be defeated, that Indian freedom fighters must bear in mind that 1943 or 1944 cannot be 1939, and that whatever be in the mind of a Churchill or a Roosevelt, none will be able to bring the world back to 1939. Roy made the further prophecy that

> Japan will be defeated. While the Soviet Union will be very exhausted after this war (having defeated the Fascist Powers comprehensively), and the USA will emerge as a formidable military power and economic force, Britain will be seriously weakened in every respect.

He added that, in view of the fact that British imperialism will have no power to retain India, transfer of power was inevitable. He therefore asked his colleagues to prepare the ground for reconstructing Indian economy on a very largely non-capitalist basis. He said:

> Capitalist methods of production, that is to say, introduction of the mechanical means of production, will be welcome; but the capitalist mode of production, that is, production exclusively for profit will be under control.

He wanted reconstruction of the economy with a view to eliminating poverty. (At this point of time, Roy charged the British of digging Indian democracy down with themselves. The British Government, according to him, never cared for India, their relations being always with the Indian upper classes. Blood, after all, is thicker than water, he maintained.)

From December 1942 onwards, Roy looked ahead and concentrated on preparing plans for free India. He always maintained that the problem of India is essentially the problem of her economic and social backwardness. He, therefore, appealed to all freedom-loving people and the government—in view of the fact that after the certain defeat of the Axis Powers British imperialism was bound to be liquidated—to set their mind on promoting the welfare of the people.

During this period, he also exhaustively dealt with the concepts of nationalism, freedom and democracy. He subjected the concept of nationalism to a thorough analysis and discarded it as an antiquated cult. He analysed the concept of formal democracy and maintained that formal democracy will not mean freedom for the Indian people. All these culminated in the People's Plan for Economic Development of India and Draft Constitution of Free India (1944). It would be of interest to human rights activists that the Plan gave the utmost importance to food, clothing, shelter, health, and free compulsory primary secular education. That the Plan was taken very seriously is indicated by the fact that within two months of its publication in 1944, the first edition of 5,000 copies was sold out and a second edition was brought out in October. In the Foreword to the Plan, Roy wrote:

> (in the social sector) the most elementary requirements of the people—food, clothing, shelter, health, and education— (must be provided). ....The plan aims at financing itself. Wealth is created by labour. Therefore, a substantial increase in national income can be expected to take place in that sector of the national economy where the largest volume of labour is performed. In our country, that sector is agriculture. Rationalisation and modernisation of agriculture, therefore, are placed in the forefront of the plan.

The Draft Constitution of Free India was released in 1944. The Draft presented a picture of Roy's conception of organized democracy based on a network of People's Committees. In his introductory note to the Draft, Roy observed:

> The *Draft* visualises organised Democracy as the source of all constitutional authority—the instrument for the exercise of popular sovereignty. The experience of history is that an atomised

> individual voter cannot make democracy prevail. The structure of the basis of the State which will be established by this Constitution will be a source of political education for the people. It, therefore, eliminates the objection to universal suffrage in a vast country like India with largely illiterate people. Organised democracy will also eliminate the difficulties of holding elections in a vast country. (It may be remembered that Roy was a Marxist/Communist at that time.)

Roy tried to solve the problem, namely, that economic equality is not possible in the absence of political democracy, in these two documents. The ideas were further expanded and elaborated upon in his philosophy of radical humanism which he propounded in 1946. In a lecture at Calcutta University on 31 January 1947 Roy said:

> Radical humanism incorporated the positive contents of Marxism freed from the fallacies of its theory of revolution, from its postulation of dictatorship and from its greatest and basic fallacy of dismissing the freedom of the individual as a meaningless obstruction. In politics, radical humanism points out that democracy can be possible, that economic planning is reconciliable with the freedom of the individual; that is to say, radical humanism tries to present itself as a philosophy which covers the entire field of human existence from abstract thought to social and political reconstruction.

A radical democratic state which he visualized would on one side eliminate the inadequacies of formal parliamentary democracy and, on the other, beware of the dangers of dictatorship of any class or elite.

Throughout the period 1947–53 (Roy died on 25 January 1954), he went round the country, lectured at various universities, and study camps on this alternative system of politics and economics. I give below a very brief summary of what he spoke and wrote during this period:

Decentralisation: The state has become an engine of coercion. But the point is that it is so not because of power as such, but because of concentration of power. So, ultimately, the problem of democratic political practice is that of decentralization. The desired decentralization of power is conditional upon the disappearance of the instrument of centralization. It must be replaced by another instrument which can guarantee that the sovereignty of the people will always remain with the people. In this context, we must have confidence in our people. It is true that the common people in our country are illiterate.

> Yet, is it not a fact that left to themselves, even the most ignorant peasants can manage their affairs better than our present government? The distrust for the ability of the common people to think for themselves and take care of themselves is only a pretext for seizing power in their name and abusing that power to suppress their liberty.

Direct Democracy: Delegation of power is a negation of democracy, because it can never establish a government of the people and by the people. It can, under the best of circumstances, only establish a government for the people, which, again in the best of cases, may be a benevolent dictatorship. We must practice direct democracy in smaller social groups. Voters can organise themselves on a local scale into People's Committees, and function as local republics, in which direct-democracy is possible. On this basis a complete constitutional scheme can be visualised. In the new society of decentralised democracy, the state will be coterminous with society. Every citizen will be consulted. This process itself is the best education for citizens.

The only objection to this plan may be the question of time. Assuming it will take fifty years or even a hundred years—the question is irrelevant. For; what is the alternative? That is the relevant question.

Party System breeds Corruption: The best of men are corrupted by the party system. The period of office is limited. As within a few years none can bring heaven on earth, the first concern of politicians in power is to have a second, a third and more terms in power.

> The most skilful and resourceful party may be perpetually in power. The approximation to the ideal of the party system is attained by winning the next elections; and to do so, greater demagogy is practised. To compete with demagogues in a system which puts a premium on dishonesty, a politician must come down to this level if he wants to succeed. Thus, practically nobody

> engaged in politics as it is practised today, can remain entirely untouched by its corrupt atmosphere. The 'sea-green incorruptible' have always been a fiction; personalities are built up by propaganda. Robespierre was an upright man—stern, ascetic, completely dedicated to a cause; yet, his virtue turned out to be the pretext for abominable vices. (Furthermore) the necessity of rigging elections is inherent in the party system under formal parliamentarism. When a party or a coalition of parties, not sure of the support of the electorate, cannot avoid an election, they can amend the electoral law while still in power, so as to prejudice the chances of the opposition. ...(Power) politics is not only a scramble for power, but a competition in all manner of questionable practices.

A New Approach to Economic Management: The concept of cooperative economy—in a cooperative economy, the means of production will neither be controlled by the old capitalist mode nor by the other pressed by various shades of socialist and communist opinion; they would belong to the workers themselves. Cooperative economy is superior to both capitalism and state ownership.

The democratic reconstruction of the economic life of a country as vast as India cannot happen by way of an imposition from above. Most well-intentioned people have usually ignored one important aspect in this context:

> The fundamental problem of Indian economy is not an economic problem properly; it is the problem of population. The rapid rate at which the Indian population is growing is bound to make all economic problems more complicated. If we persist in finding a solution in either of the old ways, which were conceived in conditions where the population problem was not so acute or non-existent, we shall not succeed. Both these methods have failed elsewhere. The method of concentrating on rapid industrialisation by building up heavy industries as a means to raise the standard of living of the people is obviously not suitable to India. ...We must therefore naturally begin with the main sector of Indian economy, which is agriculture.

In the past, very largely for political considerations, it was held as an article of faith that an agrarian country is bound to be poor. In order to get rid of the evils of poverty, the country must be industrialised and agriculture mechanised. Unfortunately, that obsession is still persisting and prevents us from making a fresh, realistic approach to our problems. Even America was a predominantly agricultural country until fifty years ago, and even today the value of American agricultural production is no less than that of its industrial production.

> To produce food for the people is the most elementary human activity. The reorganisation and development of agriculture as the foundation of a healthy rational modern economy stands a greater chance than any other method to succeed in removing the poverty of the Indian people.

In almost every speech during this period, Roy emphasized, over and over again, the primary needs of the people: food, shelter, health, and free secular education.

The new approach to economic management must be based on reorganization from below—through cooperative self-help which presupposes a certain democratic spirit, the confidence that the affairs of the people, in their own localities.

> That is how the humanist economic approach is linked up with that of building up a democratic state in India. The initiative has to come from the peasants themselves, and cooperative organisations should never go to an extent beyond what they are voluntarily prepared for.

Roy said often:

> Our own backwardness may prove to be a blessing in disguise. We have no false conventions to overcome. We begin from scratch. The peculiar conditions of our life do not allow us to travel the beaten track. But to make good use of this blessing in disguise, we must find an entirely new approach to the whole problem of democracy, in its political operation as well as in its application to economic problems.

Let me conclude this essay with a reference to his emphasis on the need for morality in politics: all thinking people complain about the absence of morality in public life, and are looking for ways and means to introduce decency and morality in public life and politics. Morality has disappeared, Roy often said and wrote during this period, because it is forgotten or ignored that only individuals can be moral; and that morality is an attribute of men, and men have been lost in the masses. In the mass, men's reason and conscience are submerged and suspended. Masses respond more easily to emotional appeals, because men merge into masses on their lowest common denominator, and then the level of the politicians adjusts itself to this mentality.

[Courtesy: *Mainstream*, Vol. XXXV, No. 15,
22 March 1997, pp. 31–35]

****

CHAPTER 28

Life of an Iconoclast

Two days after M.N. Roy passed away on 25 January 1954, *The Statesman* wrote in a lead editorial that only a romantic novelist would be able to write his biography. A large number of articles and books have been written, covering the period up to 1929, in Roy's life. They were mostly by Europeans, Americans, Mexicans, and Chinese. British Intelligence officers serving in British India have also written about him fairly extensively, from the beginning of his political career up to the period 1930, when he was arrested. They also dwelt on the period after his return to India, detailing his participation in Congress activities, attending meetings including attendance at the Karachi Congress, which gave a socially radical turn to Congress politics; organization of a group by Roy when he was in detention, and his smuggling out literature from jail were highlighted by the Intelligence officers. The purpose of recalling these incidents while writing about Professor Sibnarayan Ray's seminal biography of Roy, *In Freedom's Quest: Life of M.N. Roy,* which covers the period up to 1922, is to fill the gaps in the narrative. Similarly, Professor Ray's account of the last phase 1948–54 in the Introduction to the work has to be supplemented. The idea is to keep the record straight for the benefit of researchers, although my additions are far from exhaustive.

Roy's flair for dynamism, both in physical movement and mental progress comes out loud and clear in Professor Ray's biography as also in other writings about his early life. Son of a poor village priest without formal education, already an iconoclast at heart, he became a revolutionary to be reckoned within no time, travelled to the far-off lands to get arms and ammunition to liberate India through an armed struggle, got back to India eluding British Intelligence, went to the USA, Mexico, Europe, Moscow, and then to Central Asia, again to organize an armed attack on the British in India to liberate the country. In the process he founded the emigre Communist Party of India at Tashkent in 1920 (having founded earlier the first Communist Party outside Russia in Mexico in 1919). A worthy biographer of such a life has to blend history, romance, and art; he has to have the imagination of a romantic novelist but certainly not the fantasy of a thriller writer.

Some of the writers have tried to give a "romantic" touch by stressing that a number of revolutionary women in and around the Comintern were in love with Roy, or that he was a magnet of attraction for women in those days. Most of the women were attracted by his intellectual brilliance as much as his physical personality—over six feet tall, broad shoulders and a winsome visage. The veteran Communist (CPI-M), late Muzaffar Ahmad, who was one of those who wrote about Roy, mentions three women and complains that Roy had ignored in his Memoirs his first wife Evelyn Roy, who contributed considerably towards the growth of the communist movement in India. (Sibnarayan Ray dedicates his book to the memory of these three women, "who at one stage or another in the stormy career of Roy shared fully in his great quest and in the hazards and glories, achievements and setbacks, revolutionary activities and reflections: Evelyn Trent, Louise Geissler, Ellen Gottschalk".)

*

During the years I spent with Roy, staying in the Roy household, I had the privilege of receiving a large number of visitors at his Dehra Dun residence. They included Roy's old friends of the early Bengal period, the Comintern period, and the post-Radical Democratic Party period, from 1948 until his death, like Ruth Fisher, a well-known Comintern leader, later a rabid anti-communist and anti-Stalinist, and Phillip Price, a British Labour MP who was with the Comintern in Moscow in the 1920s; and Dr. Shyama Prasad Mookherjee, a great admirer of Roy, in spite of Roy being an uncompromising critic of the Brahmanical religion. Dr. Mookherjee had just founded the Jana Sangh and was its President. Dr. Mookherjee greeted Roy in the traditional Bengali way by touching Roy's feet. Among the other visitors were Bhupati Majumdar, an old colleague in the Bengal revolutionary days and at that time the Minister of Home Affairs in West Bengal; Surendra Mohan Ghose (Madhu-da), a Rajya Sabha MP at that time, an old revolutionary colleague of Roy; Suresh Majumdar of *Ananda Bazar Patrika*; Jayaprakash Narayan (JP); and Prime Minister Jawaharlal Nehru. A number of Indian armed forces officers, both serving and retired, like General Rudra, and General Habibullah, at that time the Commandant of the Indian Military Academy at Dehra Dun (Habibullah was a Marxist but became a great admirer of Roy), and many Indian and foreign scholars of repute visited him.

I took Mr. and Mrs. Price round for sight-seeing in Dehra Dun and had plenty of opportunities to talk about Roy. Although Mr. Price was rather reticent and at times tended to ignore my questions, occasionally he yielded to my 'obstinacy'. The result was his acknowledgement that Roy was one of the most outstanding theoreticians in the Communist International. Mr. Price added that many of Roy's colleagues thought that Roy was arrogant, but he did not find him so. Did he antagonize his colleagues? No, but he was uncompromising and ruthlessly logical. Roy perhaps did not realize, Mr. Price mentioned, that the communist methodology did not allow dissent. Mr. Price also added that women were attracted towards Roy. Ruth Fisher, during her brief stay at Dehra Dun, would often have a dig at Roy's weakness for Stalin. Most of the time she talked about the "evils" of communism. Roy was, however, pleasant with her, without getting into any serious discussion with her—so very unlike Roy.

A very beautiful Austrian woman, Mrs. Mady Uttam Singh, later Mrs. Martyn (she married the Head Master of the Doon School after Mr. Uttam Singh's death) was a close friend of Mrs. Roy. (Mr. Martyn and Mr. Gibson of the Doon School were frequent visitors to the Roy household. On a number of occasions they invited Roy to give talks to students and faculty members.) Mrs. Uttam Singh's short stories appeared in

The Illustrated Weekly of India. Mr. and Mrs. Uttam Singh were frequent visitors. She would often talk against communism. That was the fashion in those days—rabid anti-communism and blind pro-Americanism. One day she complained to me that Roy did not take her seriously and that he responded only to intellectuals!

Apropos of Roy's attitude to communism and Soviet Russia, quite a few senior colleagues of his—leaders of the erstwhile Radical Democratic Party—fell out with him on that count. Roy had been very close to them. But on the issue of American attack on Korea, he was again his own uncompromising self—he came down heavily on the US action. His colleagues, who out and out shared the American way of thinking, being viciously anti-communist, were very uncomfortable with Roy's stand. At a personal level, however, they maintained contact and would visit him from time to time. Their argument was that it was not possible for India to remain neutral in the face of the "grave danger" posed by communism. One of them asked: "If you have to choose between communism and fascism, what would you choose?" Roy's response was that there was nothing to choose between two irrational political practices. Pressed hard, Roy said that if he had to choose he would choose communism. But Roy was always kind and considerate to them, treating them with affection. However, he felt lonely, with many of his former colleagues parting company from him intellectually.

Bhupati Majumdar's visit, referred to earlier, was a disaster. Roy flared up at Majumdar's justifying police resorting to killing citizens of newly independent India. Majumdar added that he would not hesitate to order more shooting at protesters and dissenters. Mrs. Roy took charge of the situation!

Dr. Shyama Prasad Mookherjee's visit was very pleasant. He dropped in about dinner time. Most of the time Roy and Mookherjee conversed in Bengali. Mrs. Roy on this occasion did not mind! He was accompanied by a local leader, Haradhan Banerjee, an old revolutionary. Dr. Mookherjee came to Dehra Dun to attend and lead a Jana Sangh rally. That was after his famous speech in Parliament in which he said: "It is not the birthright of the Prime Minister to lose his temper." While greeting him, Roy approvingly reminded him of the quip. All the three, Bhupati Majumdar, Dr. Mookherjee and Suresh Majumdar dropped in without any prior notice. Suresh Majumdar's visit was also pleasant. Roy cracked jokes at Majumdar's cost, mostly centering on the latter's miserliness! Majumdar was very happy.

JP came to discuss Roy's political philosophy of party-less democracy and politics. He had written earlier to say that he would be coming. Roy was much too ill at that time.

Pandit Nehru also came unannounced to see an ailing Roy. But we had come to know of the Prime Minister's impending visit when the police came to make security arrangements. Mrs. Roy was adamant that she would not allow any security forces to enter the premises. It was finally arranged that a couple of policemen would keep watch from tree tops! The Prime Minister was accompanied by only one senior police officer of the rank of Inspector General. Contrast that with what happens today!

Apropos of Prime Minister Nehru's visit, I may mention a couple of events. When JP realized that Roy was dangerously ill at the time, he was very angry that the government did not even inquire about Roy's illness, not to speak of arranging for his treatment, and informed President Rajendra Prasad with whom he stayed on his return to Delhi from Dehra Dun. Prompt came a letter from Pandit Nehru to Mrs. Roy, "Dear Mrs. Roy, I was distressed..." etc., asking her to let him know about Roy's condition and arrangements for his treatment. The letter remained unanswered in spite of my reminding her. After a few days came in another letter, "Dear Ellen,..." etc. She was hurt that Pandit Nehru, who had known her intimately in the good old days, wrote to her a formal letter, "Dear Mrs. Roy".

After saying good-bye to Roy—"get well soon"— Nehru came out and asked Mrs. Roy about their future plans of literary and scholarly work. Roy had received a number of invitations from US universities to lecture, but the US Government would not give him a visa. (Roy was in the bad books of both the US and Soviet governments. He was disillusioned with Soviet communism and policy; at the same time he was very critical of US foreign policy and wanted India to steer clear of both the superpowers, Soviet Russia and the USA.) Ultimately, the US Government agreed to give him a visa, but Roy could not avail of Nehru's help—he died.

It may also be mentioned that Dr Rajendra Prasad felt concerned and offered state help for Roy's treatment. It was however not necessary, as the arrangements for treatment at Dehra Dun were adequate.

*

After Roy's death, Mrs. Roy visited Delhi on a couple of occasions in connection with research projects to be undertaken by the Indian Renaissance Institute which Roy had established at Dehra Dun, and stayed with Mrs. Indira Gandhi at the Prime Minister's residence. Mrs. Gandhi also visited Mrs. Roy at Dehra Dun. On one occasion I received her. Mrs. Gandhi had to wait because Mrs. Roy was having a bath. To while away the time, Mrs. Gandhi wanted to visit the garden. She asked a lot of questions about the garden. I showed her round the garden. "What a friendly garden", she commented. It was a pleasure talking to her—very refined and unassuming. (How could such a refined person become an authoritarian ruler against whom we had to wage war!) Mrs. Gandhi used to visit Dehra Dun to meet her sons. I must record here that in spite of our total opposition to her Emergency, she responded very warmly to a communication—she was the Prime Minister then—regarding a proposal to celebrate Roy's centenary. The matter was not, however, pursued with her. (Subsequently, much later, we came to know that Indira Gandhi had sent the letter to the Ministry of Culture and the officer concerned, who was close to Roy's political party, the Radical Democratic Party, did not forward the letter, out of sheer fear because we were politically opposed to the Prime Minister!)

I may mention another incident. Mrs. Roy maintained an excellent garden—Nehru during his visit spent quite some time going round the garden, *The Statesman* sent its photographer to Dehra Dun, at least on two occasions, to take photographs of the garden which appeared in the paper. There was acute shortage of canal water at Dehra Dun. I suggested to Mrs. Roy that she should write to the UP Irrigation Minister, Mohan Lal Gautam, a well-known socialist before he decided to remain in the Congress party. She reluctantly wrote to him. (They had known each other very well and worked together in 1937-39.) There was no response to the letter. After about a month, an office assistant acknowledged the receipt of the letter! I must add that it is the Mohanlal Gautams who are true representatives of Indian culture and tradition, not Jawaharlal Nehrus, Acharya Narendra Devs and JPs!

The Statesman editorial did not refer to women's attraction for Roy; it referred to his odyssey in three continents. But isolated accent on the odyssey dimension can distort the picture. A book written by a *London Times* correspondent, Peter Hopkirk (*Setting the East Ablaze: Lenin's Dream of an Empire in Asia*, 1986), is in the style of a "thriller". The hero of this thriller is one Colonel Bailey, a British spy; and the principal "villain" is M.N. Roy, for Roy undertook the task of liberating India from British imperialism through an armed insurrection. I will refer, later, to what this bitterly anti-Bolshevik writes about his "villain"—it is interesting in the context of the Indian Communists' thoughtless, irrational and, at times uncivilized, attacks on M.N. Roy.

Let me give a couple of instances of the Communists' inability to rise above petty politics and to get rid of old prejudices. I have also formed the impression, from my interaction with a number of Communists with whom I have worked in different capacities—some of them are my good friends—that Communists (of all hues), by and large, cannot stand an intellectual, even a Communist intellectual, and they are not farsighted enough to see beyond the text. In any case, none of them has read anything written by Roy of the 'beyond communism' phase. And, quite a few would not even like to be reminded that Roy's *India in Transition*, written in 1921-22, which is a classic, was their Bible.

This section of Communists and their "intellectuals", however, refers to Roy only when they have to defend Stalin, even though they have disowned the role of their fight against Fascism during the Second World War, and have done "*prayaschitta*" for their "sin" of not being with those nationalist forces in India who gave direct and indirect support to Fascism during the War. They now owe allegiance, with a vengeance, to those whom they had debunked as nationalists, counter-revolutionaries and reactionaries! This new-found loyalty should not, however, be a compelling reason to cease to acknowledge the great role played by Stalin in defeating the greatest evil of the twentieth century, Fascism/Nazism which was the source of the worst forms of human rights violation in this century. Nor should they be squeamish in acknowledging the contributions made by other anti-fascists.

To get back to the Communists' allergy to Roy, during the M.N. Roy centenary celebrations, V.M. Tarkunde as the Chairman of the Roy Centenary Celebration Committee wrote to Jyoti Basu, the Chief Minister of West Bengal, for sanction of a financial grant to meet the expenses of the centenary projects, which included publication of Roy's selected works in six volumes, each volume of about 600 pages. Four volumes edited by Professor Sibnarayan Ray have so far been published by Oxford University Press (OUP). Although Tarkunde and Basu were mutually close on account of their shared resistance to the Emergency, his letter was not even acknowledged, not to speak of getting a grant! It was surprising, for I thought a *bhadralok* Bengali like Basu would at least acknowledge receipt of a letter apropos of Roy, even though Roy was a plebeian. Later, the Union Minister, Brahma Dutt, an old Radical Democratic Party member, spoke to Basu; and the latter promised to comply with the request and make a grant. I told Brahma Dutt that Basu would not live up to his promise, for if he did his party would expel him! Well, Basu remains in the party—and also the Chief Minister! I was Member Secretary of the Centenary Committee, and did not approach any other Communist leader after that experience.

To get back to Peter Hopkirk. He writes:

> Roy has been accused by his critics of intellectual arrogance, but no one has ever questioned his courage. He always said what he believed, and yet managed to survive... Prominent among the Asian delegates at the Congress [the Comintern's Second Congress] was a tall Indian revolutionary, highly intelligent, with revolutionary eyes, named Manabendra Nath Roy, the only one whom Lenin was prepared to take seriously.

Referring to Roy's intellectual honesty, and courage, Peter Hopkirk writes:

> Even his old friend Borodin, now back in Moscow from Mexico; had been exasperated by his lack of discipline—the highest Bolshevik virtue—while Chicherin, the aristocrat-revolutionary, now Russia's Commissar for Foreign Affairs, had sat up into the early hours trying to change the mind of his stubborn Indian. Men and women had been liquidated for a good deal less than this, even in those early days before Stalin's grim reign... On obtaining Lenin's go-ahead, Roy immediately began [invasion of India through Afghanistan] while the rest of the Comintern hierarchy attended the Baku Congress. This Indian had opposed this [the idea of having a Congress in Baku] from the start, arguing that it could only serve the cause of agitation, which alone was not enough to bring about a revolution in the East.

Bitterly anti-Bolshevik, the writer is, however, very angry that

> modern Indian historians do not credit two British Communists, [Phillip Spratt and Benjamin Bradley, both Englishmen] who were sent by the Comintern to India to help speed up the revolutionary process in India, with achieving much, while Roy himself, who had objected to their being sent in the first place, does not so much as mention them in his *Memoirs*.

They worked in India for two years before they were arrested by the British Indian police in the Meerut Conspiracy case; they were convicted. After serving the sentence, Benjamin Bradley left India; Phillip Spratt settled down in India. Later he joined the Radical Democratic Party and remained a colleague of Roy until the latter's death. He was the co-author with Roy of one of the most significant theoretical books, *Beyond Communism*. (At one point of time Roy felt so concerned about Spratt's financial condition that he wrote to a friend requesting him to fix up Spratt with *The Statesman* as a writer/journalist. According to Roy, Spratt was "an extraordinarily talented person".) What is surprising is that a senior and experienced observer of events like the correspondent of the *London Times* does not realize that the *Memoirs* ends before Phillip Spratt's arrival in India! I would not like to suggest that this British writer (as also Muzaffar Ahmad, as we will see later) misrepresented facts because of their intense prejudice against Roy—even if for different reasons.

Professor Ray refers to the "lion of Punjab", Lala Lajpat Rai, who wrote in his daily in June 1919, published in 1965, that of all the revolutionaries he met in New York, "the only one of the Bengali revolutionaries for whom I have had genuine respect is M.N. Roy". The rest of them left a "a very repulsive impression" on his mind, many of them spent a lot of money on luxuries and misappropriated and saved money for their future use, wrote Lala Lajpat Rai.

Jawaharlal Nehru writes in his *Autobiography*:

> I must say that I was not greatly impressed by most of the Indian political exiles that I met abroad... Of the few I met, the only persons who impressed me intellectually were V. Chattopadhyaya and M.N. Roy. Roy I met for a brief half-hour in Moscow. He was a leading Communist then, although, subsequently, his communism drifted away from the orthodox Comintern brand.

It should be clear that to write a biography of such a person is very difficult. However, a number of biographies exist: *M.N. Roy: The Man Who Looked Ahead* by A.K. Hindi (real name, Tayab Shaikh), the period covering up to 1928; *Roy: A Political Biography* by V.B. Karnik; and a few others written by M.N. Roy's followers. There is a large number of books and articles by European, American and Chinese scholars, and Indian political leaders who have given fairly detailed accounts of his life covering the period 1919–29. There are also several scholarly books, mostly by Western scholars, on Roy of this period. To mention a few: *M.N. Roy's Mission to China*, Berkeley, L.A. (1963) by Robert C. North and XJ. Eudin; *Communism and Nationalism in India: M.N. Roy and Comintern Policy 1920-39*, Princeton 1971 by J.P. Haithcox; Chinese Source Materials on M.N. Roy: A Report by Huang I-shu. Professor Ray has given a comprehensive list of all such books and scholarly articles. Another book, *Communism in India*, (the University of California) by Gene D. Overstreet and Marshall Windmiller, is a bit disappointing from the point of view of scholarship. There is a number of books by Indian political leaders—doctrinaire

Communists like Muzaffar Ahmad, to whose book I referred to earlier, and pathological anti-communists as, for example, M.R. Masani, who too wrote a book on the history of the Communist Party of India.

Professor Ray's biography of Roy is a scholarly and well-researched book of history. The author sets the tone in the very first paragraph of the book:

> At the Second Congress of the Communist International... a young Indian revolutionary representing the newly founded Communist Party of Mexico astonished the gathering of 217 delegates from 41 countries by introducing a set of supplementary theses on the National and Colonial question. Lenin was then at the height of his power and glory; his authority as the supreme theorist and tactician of the movement was beyond dispute; nevertheless the Congress on June 29, 1920 adopted both sets of these unanimously with three abstaining votes.

Professor Ray refers to almost all the writers and their many works about Roy—they are very many across the world. Future scholars working on this period, not merely on Roy, would remain indebted to Professor Ray.

Professor Ray's objective is

> to portray him (Roy) as an almost unique figure in our age of revolutions and political upheavals. Unique, because unlike almost any other of his contemporaries, he took an active and leading part in revolutionary movements in four continents (actually three, Asia, America, and Europe—Roy crossed through some African countries— Middle East—while returning to India overland in 1930).

Sibnarayan Ray writes in the Introduction:

> It is sad to reflect that although Roy was such a multifaceted personality and his life was so rich in dramatic events and changes, no really good biography has yet been written of him.

To write an account of the period up to 1929 is very difficult, for, as Professor Ray himself mentions, Roy's career during this period was spread over four continents. However well-researched the account might be, facts have often been distorted because of personal prejudices and ideological stances. As a sample, I will later quote passages from Muzaffar Ahmad's book by way of illustration.

Sibnarayan Ray's biography should be read in the background of what I have written in the foregoing. The present book is also important in that the biographer does not limit it

> exclusively to material which relates directly to Roy, but [has] also tried to provide, wherever necessary, the socio-historical background of the revolutionary situations in which he was placed in different countries at different times.

In Freedom's Quest can be divided into three parts, for the sake of the reader's convenience: (i) revolutionary period in Bengal, the search for arms outside India; (ii) landing in the USA, contact with Indian revolutionaries and freedom fighters; (iii) embracing Marxism-Leninism under the guidance of Borodin, invitation by Lenin to attend the Second Congress of the Comintern, on way to Moscow spending a few fruitful and instructive months in Germany, and then his fight for the freedom of India from Moscow, Central Asia, and Europe.

It is Professor Ray's thesis that Roy was a radical from the beginning of his political career and remained so until the end of his life:

> What would seem to run as a common thread through the different phases of his life is his consistent radicalism... It was his radical spirit which drew Roy in his early years to the hazardous path of militant nationalism... The same spirit drove him later to embrace first socialism and then communism in Mexico, and to emerge during the nineteen twenties as a major figure in the Communist International [at one point of time Roy was only next to Stalin in the hierarchy]... Finally, during the last phase of his life he was impelled by this spirit to formulate a philosophy and promote a movement which would go beyond both nationalism and communism and seek to place radicalism within a framework of humanist ideas and ideals.

The contributions made by Roy in this last phase "which has the greatest significance to many of his associates and followers" are not widely known. Even those few who are familiar with Roy's political philosophy in the last period and who have learnt from him hardly ever refer to him, Jayaprakash Narayan being an exception. This phase will be taken up by Professor Ray in his projected last volume of his biography. But since he refers to this in this volume, let me give a couple of instances.

A very well-known literary figure, who was a follower of Roy all his life, in the Radical Democratic Party days and also later, has hardly ever referred to Roy in the context in his writings in his mother tongue. He never spoke about Roy at any gatherings except in meetings of Royists. An anti-Fascist during the War days, he supported the War efforts in an active way. When he became a "famous" man he lost no opportunity in making efforts to wash off that "unpatriotic" past! A few years ago he said in a TV interview that he had joined the British Indian Army during the War to get secret information about the British! Another intellectual, at one time close to Roy, in his writings dealing with the subject of decentralization, power to the people, and partyless democracy has never found it necessary to acknowledge Roy's contribution to the theoretical aspect of this form of democracy and governance. Yet another prominent person, who now passes as an establishment intellectual, and a "VIP", was very close to Roy's political party (perhaps a member) and later his movement. This intellectual, during the Emergency and later during the M.N. Roy centenary celebrations, was terribly scared of meeting old colleagues and friends who were opposed to Indira Gandhi and her Emergency! Many such personalities used to meet their old friends who were openly opposed to the Emergency in 'burqas'! With some difficulty an appointment was fixed by V.M. Tarkunde for a meeting; at the last moment on some pretext the appointment was cancelled by the "VIP"!

A veteran Communist, the late Muzaffar Ahmad, writes in his autobiography, *Myself and the Communist Party of India 1920-29*, Calcutta, 1970 [he quotes extensively from M.N. Roy's Memoirs and accuses Roy's friends (who published M.N. Roy's Memoirs)]:

> The editors left out many portions from the original memoirs [first published in *Amrita Bazar Patrika* serially and then in the weekly, *The Radical Humanist*]... They omitted also the extract I have quoted above, (p. 88)

The fact is that Muzaffar Sahib's comrades misled him—the section referred to is there in the Memoirs on page 481.

Muzaffar Sahib's book is actually a biography of Roy! The period covered by Professor Ray in his biography is also covered by Muzaffar Sahib. What is most interesting in this book is Muzaffar Sahib's love-hate relationship with Roy. (Are there other Communists also like him?) He has some good words for Roy; his main grievance is that Roy should not have confided in people like Dange, people whom Muzaffar Sahib did not approve of, and that Roy did not send money which he received from the Communist International for developing the movement in India to Muzaffar Sahib and his trusted comrades or if he sent it, it was not adequate. A few passages may be quoted in order to indicate how subjective factors and ideological antagonism play a predominant part in writing about Roy:

> If Roy had carried out his tasks without committing any deviation, he would have never been expelled, (pp. 28–20). In April 1922 M.N. Roy and Evelyn Roy went to Berlin; which meant that the headquarters of the Indian Communist Party were transferred to Berlin. Of course, there were the Indian nationalist revolutionaries in Berlin [non-communist] who were opposed to forming a Communist Party in India. They were mentally prepared to send, if they could, Roy twenty fathom deep under water. There were many Indians in Berlin—nearly a hundred. But there were none who could really assist the Roys, man and wife. As for writing for the paper [*The Vanguard*], none were upto the task. Manabendra did not spend his time abroad as an exiled 'revolutionary' content with what he had learnt at the time of his departure from India. He developed his innate talents by hard study. Dr Bhupendranath Datta [Swami Vivekananda's brother], Roy's arch-enemy, lamented one day that the Indian revolutionaries abroad, with the sole exception of Manabendranath Roy, did not do any study at all... Those of Roy's contemporaries who returned to India from Germany said that the Roys used to live in big and expensive hotels in Berlin. I never enquired whether they did so actually. But we cannot in any way forget the hard work done in those days by Manabendra and his first wife, Evelyn, to build the communist movement in India. (pp. 255-256)

Even with a useless person like Jatin Mitra [who was thrust on Roy in Berlin], the Roys, man and wife, by hard labour wrote for the paper and brought it out timely. No delay, however slight, ever occurred. Books, manifestos, etc., were also published and circulated during the Berlin period. (p. 259)

Roy was guiding revolutionary work from Europe through correspondence. But did he check the *bonafides* of those to whom he wrote letters or those who wrote letters to him?... Take my case, for instance. Roy had received reports about who I was, my past, and present activities etc... Roy read, their [revolutionaries in India] letters and made instant assessment of who was fit and who was not. His assessment of S.A. Dange and Singaravelu Chettiar was based on this method... I mention their names together here because both of them chose to accomplish a noble mission by means of guile, (pp. 209 and 302) [Muzaffar Sahib calls them] two wily birds. (p. 306)

By recruiting cadres without checking on them, Roy caused immeasurable harm to our movement. (p. 309) I was working as a whole-time comrade, and I wrote to Roy repeatedly for money. But I did not receive any money from him in 1922. It is true that I felt neglected... There was a slight change in M.N. Roy's attitude in 1922. M.N. Roy tried to send me money by his own method, no matter whether the money reached me or not. (p. 314) [At one place he acknowledges that he received money from Roy but complains that the amount was insignificant.] [Muzaffar Sahib writes that many revolutionaries received a lot of money from Roy for revolutionary work.]

From M.N. Roy's subsequent behaviour it could be seen that he had been feeling a little inconvenienced on account of my absence. Perhaps, others were not as prompt as I in answering his letters. (p. 315)

Roy had asked Nalini to think of how to rescue Muzaffar Ahmad from jail and promised some monetary help for the purpose. (p. 316)

Without the knowledge of his correspondents, Dange would receive secret letters at the universally known address of his house and thus expose the identities and addresses of the comrades to the police. (p. 413)

[In the Chapter, 'Expulsion of M.N. Roy'] As regards India, Roy displayed extreme dishonesty. [For] he established contact through letter with people outside our movement, without making any attempt to find out whether or not" they were honest. (p. 482)

> After going abroad, Roy had by sheer industry educated himself, became a well-known writer in English and had even mastered mathematics. (p. 483)
>
> [The communist movement] benefitted greatly [from Roy's writings, but misappropriated [money because he sent money for the movement to wrong people]. Not to speak of many others, consider his three major recruits. They are S.A. Dange, Singaravelu Chettiar and Ramchandra Sharma. (p. 484)
>
> When the same Dange pocketed the passage money—a goodly sum [sent by Roy]... Roy must have found out Dange for what he actually was. Why did he, even after that, maintain contact with Dange? Why didn't he inform the other comrades about Dange? (p. 484)
>
> In 1924 I was in jail. Roy did not send a single pie to any of my comrades who were outside. [But] he sent money to people outside our movement. (p. 483)
>
> Roy had been expelled from the Party and I did not go to meet him in Calcutta. If he wanted to meet me, I might have met him after intimating the Party... (During his second visit) Roy expected that I would certainly call him, which I did not... This conceited [in the original Bengali version, the epithet is *ahankari*] man could have sent me word that he wanted to meet me... Was there any reason why I should have gone of myself to meet him? Although he was a famous man he had been expelled from the Party... My Party was my pride. (p. 489)
>
> I met M.N. Roy on February 19, 1939. [The Roys were invited to address a meeting of the Labour Party] and were waiting in a car below. I went downstairs at once. 'I am Muzaffar Ahmad', I said in Bengali. Roy seemed to be pleased. 'This is Comrade Muzaffar Ahmad' he said to his wife. Then they went upstairs. [He gave] a lecture in imperfect Hindustani... This was my first and last meeting with Manabendranath Roy.

I have quoted extensively from Muzaffar Sahib's book, for one thing that during the period covered by Professor Ray, Muzaffar Ahmad was one of the trusted contacts of Roy in India; for another, Professor Ray sets right the incidents and developments mentioned by Muzaffar Ahmad. Muzaffar Sahib's account of Roy indicates how irrational the Communists are apart from being subservient to the leadership and their inability to go beyond the textbooks. Ray's accounts set things right. And I would recommend Ray's book to Communists.

Muzaffar Sahib acknowledges, without any reservation, Roy's singular contribution, but he is sad and very angry that Roy acted "foolishly", and not in accordance with the ideals of a disciplined and unquestioning Communist like Muzaffar Sahib, and also that he ought to have remained subservient to the Communist International hierarchy of the time. Contrast this with what Peter Hopkirk wrote, as quoted earlier. Professor Ray refers to all incidents mentioned by Muzaffar Ahmad and adds that "it was Muzaffar who during this decade was to be Roy's principal communist lieutenant in Bengal". (p. 144)

As regards Muzaffar Sahib's venom against some other Communists—the usual phenomenon of Communists of one variety being deadly enemies of another—let me refer to a book, *Some Documents Relating to Early Indian Communists and Controversaries Around Them*, New Delhi, 1972 by D. Nandi which, as Professor Ray mentions, casts "serious doubts on Ahmad's integrity"!

*

Apart from Ray's account of Roy's ascendancy in the communist hierarchy from 1920 onwards, which is acknowledged, though grudgingly, even by the Communists to many of whom Roy's name is anathema, the author has given an excellent account of Roy's boyhood and adolescence in Chapter 11.

> From the age of twelve or thirteen Roy seemed to be burning with an inner restlessness and to have little attachment to the secure life at home or at school. He often disappeared on long lonely walks to distant places, and was known to frequent the local cremation ground on dark and deserted nights. He visited many ashrams and began to practice yoga. One Vaishnava sadhu, Ramdas Babaji, tried to make him a disciple, but presumably the cult of devotional humility did not suit either his Sakta background or his active and assertive temperament. He was more deeply influenced by another guru, Sivananda Swamy, who was a worshipper of the Sun god (*Suryasadhak*). The Swami gave him training in yogic disciplines, imbued him with an ideal of Hinduism which was free of caste taboos and discriminatory practices, and told him about the militant Hindu nationalist

> movement that had begun to develop in Maharashtra during the eighteen nineties... Although a Brahmin by birth, he had no respect for caste rules and taboos, being in this closer to Vivekananda than to Bankim [Chatterjee].

Ray's research leads him to the conclusion that already in his militant revolutionary period in Bengal, before he even heard of socialism and communism, Roy

> believed that history was made by men who refused to accept the established order as immutable and divinely ordained, and who sought to change it because their spirit was free in spite of their enslaved milieu.

Roy's whole life was devoted to change the enslaved milieu and quest for freedom.

I have known the author since 1948. Roy's followers—those who kept in constant touch with him after he disbanded his political party, the author is one of them—have treated me with considerable love and affection for I looked after the Roys from 1948 onwards although I was not a member of the Radical Democratic Party. An intellectual like Professor Ray does not have to depend on a reviewer to establish his scholarship. Yet, I must point out a few lapses in the book, which should, and could, have been avoided. Apart from the fact that the get-up is not befitting the subject of the book and scholarship of the author, it should have been edited by a competent professional editor. The chapters have no headings. So that serious readers—this book is written only for them—will find it very difficult to keep track of what is written in what chapter. The printing mistakes could not perhaps be avoided, for the average publisher in our country does not have any professional proof-reader nor do most publishers have professional editors.

I may also refer to a couple of other avoidable lapses. Professor Ray mentions in the Introduction that Roy had a third cerebral thrombosis attack which proved fatal. That is not correct. He was on the way to recovery from the second attack when he had a massive heart attack and died. He gives the date of the first cerebral thrombosis attack, but the date of the second attack is not mentioned. He had the second attack on 15 August, an important date (on which the Roys celebrated Mrs. Roy's birthday every year). Professor Ray also refers to his book, *The World Her Village 1979*, devoted to Ellen Roy and edited by him with a long introduction by him. It is possible that he might not have gone through some of the pieces written by people who knew Ellen Roy carefully; if he had he would not have published them without correcting, removing factual errors, and editing—some of the accounts given are not correct and truthful.

There are a few other things—not relating to the subject matter of the book—which too could have been avoided; I'll refer to them in another article if I live long enough to write!

Professor Ray points out a few errors in Roy's *Memoirs*, with regard to date, sequence, etc. Roy wrote his memoirs in instalments, week after week, and that too more than 35 years after the events, relying heavily on his memory—he did not keep a diary. The editor of the *Amrita Bazar Patrika* put pressure on him and Roy accepted the offer primarily because he had to earn his living. In spite of the few mistakes that the author mentions, the *Memoirs* remains the most authentic account of the period as acknowledged even by his severest critics, and it has been received very well even by those scholars who are his "arch-enemies". This is the only book written by Roy, the first edition of which sold 5,000 copies! Readers would have been happy, however, if all the instalments published in the *Amrita Bazar Patrika* and the *Radical Humanist* were included in the book (*Memoirs*).

In Freedom's Quest will remain the most authentic intellectual and scholarly biography of Roy written until now.

NOTE

1. When Acharya Narendra Deva contested a by-election in 1948—fourteen Congress Socialist Party members resigned their Assembly seats after the CSP became an independent political formation—from Faizabad constituency, his former colleague and friend Mohanlal Gautam was one of the principal campaigners against the Acharya—he was depicted as "*Ravana-roopea*" by Mohanlal Gautam and other leaders. (See, *Selected Works of Acharya Narendra Deva*, Vol. III, edited by Hari Dev Sharma, 1998) Roy felt very sad at the Acharya's defeat. In spite

of political differences Roy and the Acharya had considerable mutual regard. When Narendera Deva became the Vice-Chancellor of Lucknow University, he invited Roy to a symposium on Socialism at the University. Roy was not able to participate because of prior commitments.

[Courtesy: *Mainstream Annual 1999*,
25 December 1999, pp. 99–106]

****

CHAPTER 29

A Critical Voice on Gandhi

Gandhi had already become an international figure in 1909 before he became a national leader in 1919. His biography, written by Reverend Joseph J. Doke of Johannesburg with an introduction by Lord Ampthill, Chairman of the South African British Indian community, was published in London in 1909. Gandhi took a lot of personal interest in the writing, publication and circulation of the biography. Then came his most important work in Gujarati, *Hind Swaraj*, about that time. The English version, *Indian Home Rule*, came out in 1910. Gandhi sent these publications to eminent people, like Tolstoy across the world. Tolstoy appreciated his views and work in South Africa, specially in relation to the question of passive resistance, and wrote:

> Your work in Transvaal, which seems to be far away from the centre of our world, is yet the most fundamental and the most important to us, supplying the most weighty practical proof in which the world can now share and with which must participate not only the Christians but all the peoples of the world.

That was in 1910. (The biography and *Hind Swaraj* were published in India in 1919. For a detailed discussion, see Sibnarayan Ray's Introduction in *Gandhi, India and the World* edited by him, Bombay, 1970.) Thus Gandhi had come to be recognized as a thinker and a great activist by a number of intellectuals before he became the most important political leader in India during the period 1919-1920/22.

Almost immediately after the non-cooperation movement,

a large number of intellectuals from the West (like Romain Rolland, C.F. Andrews and Will Durrant) began to write on Gandhi appreciating his views and methods like non-violent struggle for independence, some of them declaring that Gandhi was the greatest man of the age. By 1939 (on the occasion of his seventieth birthday), intellectuals from across the world recognized Gandhi as the greatest man of his age.

With the outbreak of the Second World War, when the British came close to Jinnah for his support to the War efforts—the British could no longer treat him with indifference, in fact they came to lean heavily on him since Gandhi and the Congress declined to lend unconditional support and help to the War effort—Gandhi began to feel marginalized. (A careful reading of the nationalist movement inclines one to conclude that Gandhi felt marginalized after the outbreak of the War and then in 1946-48 when the Congress decided to accept the partition of the country behind his back and later after Independence, when the government led by Pandit Nehru said good-bye to all that Gandhi stood for: morality in politics, political practice and governance based on grass roots democracy and power to the people, that is, decentralization as against the parliamentary system, demilitarization, *ahimsa*, peace, back to the village, and so on.)

Since Gandhi and the Congress could not agree to the British proposals—namely, "self-government" after the War—Gandhi launched the "Quit India" movement. This was a disaster for various reasons—but for it India might not have been partitioned. Furthermore, it intensified the communal conflict. In fact, one of the heroes of the Quit India movement, Achyut Patwardhan, lamented on the twenty-fifth anniversary of the movement that the launching of the movement was a great mistake; India would have won independence without this movement—it was already said by a number of intellectuals including M.N. Roy, on the basis of a Marxian analysis, that once the allied forces defeated the Axis powers the British would be left with no other alternative but to quit all the colonial countries.

Gandhi died a disappointed man—a man who had brought

into the freedom movement millions of people, people of humble origin, the poorest of the poor, and instilled the spirit of revolt in them. We don't know of any other man in the world who ever succeeded in doing this—note, for example, nothing of this kind happened in dictatorial regimes like Spain and Portugal. It is true India became an independent country in spite of Gandhi and the Congress, but we cannot ignore his unique contribution to the freedom movement.

As for his effort towards solving some of the most important problems of India, like the Hindu–Muslim question, the Dalit problem, an examination of the problems that confront us even today is necessary.

Indian independence, Hindu–Muslim unity, and the removal of untouchability were the most important goals that Gandhi had set before himself. In fact, at times Gandhi gave more importance to the latter two than to attaining independence. The greatness of Gandhi lies in the fact that, unlike any other leader, he did not run away from these ugly realities but faced them bravely. In fact, checking communal riots during the period 1946 (Calcutta killings) to 1947-48 (Bihar, Noakhali and Delhi) in the last two years of his life—is his greatest achievement. This period, "culminating in his assassination", in the words of an American scholar and academic, Dennis Dalton, "contain the finest hours of his entire career". (As I write this note—1 March 2002—communal riots have flared up in Gujarat—the communal conflagration has spread like wildfire all over Gujarat. At such tragic times one remembers Gandhi.)

*

S.S. Gill in his book, *Gandhi—A Sublime Failure,* deals with the goals referred to above and other related topics, and finds Gandhi wanting. It seems to me, however, that Gill has written this book not with a view to denigrating Gandhi but to examine guidelines for dealing with some of the fundamental evils that exist in our society—communalism and the caste system—which, unlike any other leader during the freedom struggle, Gandhi had the courage and conviction to take up but regrettably failed to eradicate.

> It is quite easy to prove anything about Gandhi by selecting a set of his quotes which best serve your purpose.... There was the ever present hazard of my focusing upon such of his sayings and deeds as fitted into my 'thesis'. I have meticulously tried to overcome this temptation by applying two tests to my selections: one, how aptly a particular quote or event faithfully reflects the mood of the moment and is true to its context; and two, to what extent it is in consonance with Gandhi's overall thinking.

And yet blind admirers of Gandhi may not like to read this book—"reading it may not be a very comfortable experience". (p. xiii). For one thing, the very title, *A Sublime Failure*, will make them angry. (I must admit that I have felt uncomfortable with the adjective "sublime". What does the author wish to communicate? I am a bit surprised that even scholars, political leaders and Gandhians like Rajni Kothari, I.K. Gujral, Dr. N. Radhakrishnan with whom he had discussions and who had read some chapters of the book, did not comment on the title.)

However, those like this reader, who are concerned with massive societal human rights violations caused by communalism and the practice of the caste system, would read the book with interest—not for Gandhi's "sublime failure" but to analyze, as Gill has done, Gandhi's methodology and his perception which, according to Gill, were responsible for Gandhi's failure in eradicating the cancerous virus—communalism and untouchability. Past failures will enable us to evolve effective methodologies to tackle these evils. The human rights activists' main concern is to see how societal violation of human rights cause divisiveness and dissension and how such violations can be arrested. One can get an insight from Gill's book. Furthermore, this reader would also urge genuine Gandhians and activists to read the book, not because they must agree with him but to see how Gandhi can be studied and evaluated from different angles. And lastly, as Gill writes,

> it is a historical necessity to re-appraise once in a while every great movement, every great leader, to assess their contemporary relevance. (p. xiii)

In any case we will do great injustice to the memory of Gandhi if we write him off as a saint, which Gandhi never claimed to be.

It is in the above context that two chapters in the book—"Removal of Untouchability" and "Hindu–Muslim Unity"—are important, in that the problems concerning these two aspects need urgent attention from all thoughtful people. Gill's thesis is that Gandhi was "torn between two loyalties as in the case of caste versus untouchabilty", and since these two are "inherently irreconcilable" (p. 97) and as "Gandhi was convinced that caste performed a very useful social purpose" (p.98) he was destined to fail in eradicating this evil—an evil which has not recognized a section of our people even as persons. What is important is that we first tackle the question of *varnshramadharma*—the caste system. Gill maintains that Gandhi's perception of the problem and his methodology in tackling it was wrong. Gill does not, however, minimize Gandhi's concern.

> Gandhi's project to remove Untouchability was the great endeavour in the field of social engineering undertaken by any Indian. (p.110)

But, regrettably, the victims of the system have not been able to get out of the shackles of the system.

> Owing to the inherent limitations of his social outlook it produced only a marginal impact. It did arouse the caste Hindu consciousness and highlighted the indignities suffered by untouchables. But it did little to improve their social or economic status. (pp.110-111)

Gandhi was convinced that there was "no way of achieving anything in this afflicted country without unity between the Hindus and Muslims of India". And yet Gandhi failed in his mission. Here too Gill finds Gandhi's unscientific methodology and perceptions were wrong:

> Gandhi adopted a rather simplistic approach to bring the two communities together. He relied heavily on symbolic gestures, the 'brotherhood' approach......to remove communal venom.

Gill finds this wholly religious approach a cause for his failure. Communal harmony will always remain an unattainable goal in a climate of religious orthodoxy and fanaticism. Gill also refers to some of "Gandhi's observations about the Muslim community which hurt his crusade for communal harmony" (p. 173), like:

> The Muslim as a rule is a bully, and the Hindu as a rule is a coward.

The author draws our attention to the fact that the introduction of religion into politics (that is, desecularisation of nationalism) gave rise to communalism and widened the gap between the Hindus and Muslims. Another factor was the treatment meted out to Jinnah by the Congress.

Gandhi and the Congress all along treated Jinnah as a marginal leader, did not respect his genuine nationalist commitment, humiliated him repeatedly, and refused to concede even modest and reasonable demands made by him. No wonder, a highly egotistical and deeply wounded Jinnah took his revenge, by tearing to shreds his adversary's dream of Hindu–Muslim unity.

It is true that Gandhi failed in bringing about Hindu–Muslim unity and curbing communalism; it is, however, equally true, as we mentioned earlier, that Gandhi's greatest achievement lies in his checking the massacres during the last two years of his life, which culminated in his assassination. I may quote in this context M.N. Roy, who was for many years Gandhi's severest critic:

> Nationalism, heavily tainted by Hindu orthodoxy, bred Muslim communalism. Therefore, the ideal of Hindu-Muslim unity, placed before the country by the Mahatma, could not be attained. The failure in this respect must have been the greatest blow for the Mahatma. During his last days he staked his life for restoring communal harmony. He failed. Where he failed, smaller men with less lofty motive will not succeed. The cosmopolitan (non-communal) and humanist message of the Mahatma was never so-urgently needed by India as today. Caught in the vicious circle of the contradiction of his ideas and ideals, the Mahatma could not see the limitation of nationalism before it was too late. Will the martyrdom open the eyes of his followers? Will they know how to honour his sacred memory? That can be done by acting according to his message, more boldly than he dared himself.
>
> (*Independent India*, 8 February 1948)

The rest of the book deals with *ahimsa* and *satyagraha*, Gandhi's experiments in *brahmacharya* (celibacy), his concern about the poor and eradication of mass poverty, partition of India, freedom struggle. In all these, Gill "has taken up specific items of his programme and drawn up a statement of profit and loss account" (p. 229)—the balance-sheet shows enormous loss.

Yes, in a statement of profit and loss account, the "loss" may have been correctly drawn. Also, Gandhi was wrong in many matters relating to facts about religion; his view that "(sexual) union is a crime when the desire for progeny is absent" and many other such statements cannot appeal to a man of reason; he may be wrong in many other things, as Gill has pointed out in his book; and yet Gandhi will survive—for reasons that I have indicated very briefly in this review.

There are a lot of adulatory writings about Gandhi, most of which are specious and hypocritical. (Our Communists, for example, regret publicly that they did not join the Quit India movement!) Gill's book does not belong this genre—his is a critical voice. It is precisely for this reason that the book should be read by all those who want to relate India's problems to Gandhian thought, and who want to wage war on communalism and caste-based discrimination and untouchability.

[Courtesy: *Mainstream*, Vol. XL, No. 19, 27 April 2002, pp. 19–21]

****

CHAPTER 30

Opinion of Political Scientists on M.N. Roy and Gandhi*

Prof. Sudipto Kaviraj writes in his paper "Marxian theory and Indian politics" (a draft report) that M. N. Roy's prediction of a premature obituary of Gandhi's leadership of the Indian National Congress has gone wrong. I have always felt that it is dangerous to contradict political scientists particularly when they make statements like the one Prof. Kaviraj has done about Roy without oneself doing research, particularly if the subject matter relates to Gandhi and Roy. For one thing they start with the assumption that Gandhi could never make any mistake and that he never any made any mistake and Roy could never be correct in his criticism of Gandhi and Gandhism. In the context of criticism of Roy, I may refer to an incident in 1987 during the M. N. Roy Centenary year. At a seminar on Roy a participant was discussing Roy's war thesis (World War II). A senior professor of political science stood up and claimed that Gandhi was "more correct" and "Roy less correct". Even Prof. Amlan Datta, the great Gandhian ideologue who was presiding over the session did not ask the speaker what he meant by "more correct" and "less correct". Many of us present on the occasion were surprised that Amlan Datta also accepted that argument. It is very difficult to dismiss Roy on rational grounds. It is possible to do so through an irrational and unscientific approach

* This paper was presented at a seminar on M.N. Roy held at Jamia Millia Islamia organised by the Academy of Third World Studies on 29 November, 2006.

and immoral political practices which have tried to wipe out Roy from history. In this paper I will outline the many contradictions and failures in Gandhi's actions and contrast them with Roy's approach of scientific reasoning.

Gandhi

Gandhi faced two defeats at the AICC in a short span of time; at the Ahmedabad session of the AICC where the Swarajists led by Motilal Nehru and C.R. Das had their way on the question of council entry. Roy had dealt with this in an article, "Mr. Gandhi's Swan Song" published in *Imprecor.* I give below a summary account of how Subhas Bose met his political death. In 1939 when senior Congress leaders came to know that Subhash Bose was planning to contest the Congress Presidential election for the second time they made it clear that they did not want him. They asked Maulana Abdul Kalam Azad to contest, but he declined. Then Gandhi put up Pattabhi Sitaramayya, who had been recommended by the Andhra Pradesh Congress Committee. In the election Bose defeated Pattabhi Sitaramayya. Gandhi immediately announced that it was his defeat. He did not stop at that, he told his close associates (senior Congress leaders) that they had to choose between Bose and Gandhi.

In the AICC secession Pandit Govind Vallabh Pant moved a resolution that the Congress President should form the Working Committee in consultation with Gandhi. There was nobody, not even Gandhi, to point out that according to the Congress Constitution the President was not obliged to consult anyone. Gandhi then asked his close associates to start a vigorous compaign against Bose. Bose realized that these leaders of the high command would not allow him to act as President, so he resigned. Later the Congress Working Committee passed a resolution (drafted by Gandhi himself) barring Bose from holding any office in the Congress for three years. The resolution added that this was applicable to the Bengal Congress also. There were protests against this resolution, so much so that even Tagore sent a telegram to Gandhi to reconsider this stricture, but to no effect. It was thus that Bose was removed from the national scene. Gandhi and his disciples brought a charge of indiscipline against Subhash Bose. One would fail to understand what act of indiscipline Bose had committed except that he contested the election against Gandhi's nominee.

But for the immoral political practice adopted by Gandhi and his followers in throwing out Subhash Bose from the Congress, things might have been different in the sense that Gandhi might not have remained the absolute leader for a long time. After the election Gandhi saw to it that Subhash did not function effectively as Congress President and Bose was forced to resign.

If Prof. Kaviraj referred to M.N. Roy's *Imprecor* article, "Gandhi's swan song" in this context, I would only mention that Gandhi and his colleagues had been challenged by the Swarajists. It was the first time that the Mahatma's words had been questioned on an issue of national importance. The gauntlet had been thrown and even Gandhi had declared that if his programme was rejected he would retire from politics and devote himself to social reform. The choice was therefore, clear and unequivocal. He further announced that he would submit a resolution declaring that members who did not spin for half an hour a day and did not observe the five fold boycott of legislative councils, law courts, government schools, title and mill made cloth would have to resign from the All India Congress Committee. This resolution, if carried, would have automatically excluded the Swarajists from power and restored the leadership of the Congress to the orthodox non-cooperators. The AICC met at Ahmedabad, Mr. Gandhi's own province and seat of authority on 27th June, and continued its deliberations for three days. Gandhi submitted his famous self denying ordinance despite the heat of opposition by the Swarajists and even some of his followers who had sought to reach a compromise with the Swarajists beforehand. It was a dramatic moment. Mahatma Gandhi, the idol of the Indian people, defied by the opposition within Congress ranks. It fell to the lot of Pandit Motilal Nehru to state the case for the Swarajists who said, "We decline to make a fetish of the spinning wheel or to subscribe to the doctrine that only through that wheel can we obtain swaraj", he said. "Discipline is desirable but it is not discipline for the majority to expel the minority. We are unable to forget our manhood and our self respect and to say that we are willing to submit to Gandhi's orders. That Congress is as much ours as our opponents' and we will return with greater majority to sweep those who stand for this resolution."— With these words Pt. Nehru and Desh Bandhu Das left the hall taking with them 55 Swarajists. 110 remained when the resolution was put to the vote and was carried against 37 with 6 abstentions. This apparent victory of Gandhians was merely make-belief. Had the Swarajists remained in the hall, the resolution would have been defeated by about 20 votes.

However, Gandhi recognized his defeat and after hurried consultation with his followers agreed to drop his resolution on compulsory spinning and the fivefold boycott by members of the AICC making it only advisory in nature and with this and other concessions the Swarajists were persuaded to rejoin the Congress. Thus the defeat of orthodox Gandhism was complete and final. The Swarajists had won the day and Mr. Gandhi as leader of the Indian National Congress Struggle had sung his swan song.

Next I refer to Professor Bhiku Parikh who has written four books on Gandhi. The most important being *Colonialisation And Reforms; An Analysis of Gandhi's Political Discourse.* One fails to understand why Gandhi scholars and Gandhi devotees shy away from Gandhi's political thought centering round de-centralisation and village republics and partyless politics. One of the most important political documents pointing out reconstruction of Indian polity was the draft constitution of Congress which later came to be known as the last testament of Gandhi. In this, Gandhi recommends the dissolution of the Congress as a Political Party and that it should be converted into Lok Sevak Sangh. In this document Gandhi gives a broad outline of his political thought. Neither Bhikhu Parekh nor Raj Mohan Gandhi in his latest biography of Gandhi, *Mohandas,* make even a pale reference to this document. Political discourse in the context of Gandhi should include important political events which shaped the destiny of the country. Professor Parikh does not take into account such inportant events and analyse them.

Apart from the Bose and Swarajist episodes there is a number of other incidents of great national importance which Prof. Parikh does not analyse. For example, the Cripps offer during World War II. Why did the Congress and its supreme leader reject the Cripps offer which was acceptable to people like Aurobindo Ghosh and M.N. Roy? He may not be familiar with Aurobindo's opinion on the Cripps offer or perhaps Prof. Parikh's analysis would then lead him to draw the conclusion that if the Cripps offer were accepted India would not have been partitioned and the post partition holocaust would have been avoided. Then the most important event relates to the negotiations with Mohd. Ali Jinnah. What was it in Jinnah's demand that the Congress and its supreme leader found difficult to accept to accept? Why would independent India have suffered if Jinnah's demand were accepted? India would not have been partitioned.

I refer to all these things which Prof. Parikh has not dealt with in his book in the hope that in a future edition of the book—(the present edition is already out of print and I am sure the Publisher would like to print another edition of this popular book)—he will do that. In one of his books on Gandhi Prof. Parikh expresses his surprise why Gandhi who succeeded in bringing critics like M.N. Roy and Subhash Bose to his side failed to bring Dr. Ambedkar to his side. In fact, Prof. Parikh has given the reason himself when he called Gandhi a hypocrite in the context analyzing Gandhi's movement for eradication of untouchability and separate electorate. How does Prof. Parikh expect a man of Ambedkar's stature to follow and support a hypocrite?

Roy wrote an editorial in his weekly by way of paying homage to Gandhi in which he writes,— "inter-alia, communal harmony is not possible in the medieval atmosphere of religious orthodoxy and fanaticism. When the idea of individual liberty is precluded by nationalism which is a totalitarian cult it would be idle to pledge loyalty to the message of Mahatma Gandhi unless it meant realization of its contradiction and an intelligent effort to place the moral and humanist core of its teaching above the carnal cult of nationalism and power politics. Otherwise the Mahatma wore the crown of martyrdom in vain."— Prof. Parikh does not analyse this aspect of Gandhi's assassination. Nor does Prof. Parikh refer to the incident where Gandhi asked Roy not to write anything critical of Gandhi and Gandhism (Gandhi said in reply to a request for a message to render mute service). Possibly an analysis by Prof. Parikh would bring out the conclusion that Gandhi was actually intolerant of criticism. In any case, if Gandhi and Roy had lived another couple of years, Gandhi would not have asked Roy to render mute service but would have discussed with him, his theory of partyless politics and democracy, decentralization and village republic, gram sabhas and people's committees. (It would be a natural expectation that Prof. Parikh perhaps discuss these in another book *"The Political Philisophy of Gandhi"*). But regrettably he does not refer to this aspect of Gandhi's political philosophy.

Prof. Parikh does not analyse the Hindu-Muslim question nor the fact that Gandhi would not eat food cooked in a Muslim house. Did Gandhi quote any of the five injunctions in that context?

After the 1937, Provincial Assembly election during Gandhi's life time, Congress leaders started adopting immoral means to capture power. There was no evidence that Gandhi denounced these practices. I give below one incident: The opposition gave notice to the speaker of Assam Assembly for moving a no-cofidence against the Congress Government. What did the Congress leaders do? They made the Speaker adjourn the Assembly with a view to rescuing the Congress from certain defeat. Dr. Rajendra Prasad was greatly disturbed by this incident and wrote a letter to the Chairman of the Congress Parliamentary Party Sardar Vallabhbhai Patel saying that the Congress party should not adopt such immoral policies to capture power. Patel replied that these things happen in parliamentary form of Government. This must have been front page news in most of the dailies in our country and it is inconceivable that Gandhi did not know about this incident but we have no evidence that Gandhi intervened in the matter.

Could it be that he would not go against the 'Sardar'? I mention this only to refer to the very difficult task of Gandhi's insistence on practising morality in politics. I have made the above comments in the hope that Prof. Parikh would analyse these events in the next edition of his excellent book.

Prof. Parikh does not analyse the Quit India Movement which is said to be Gandhi's Brahmastra to drive away the British from India. In retrospect, some of Gandhi's own colleagues in the movement like the great socialist and intellectual Achyut Patwardhan came to realize that the Quit India Movement was not necessary to attain India's independence. Achyut Patwardhan spoke on the 25th Anniversary of the Quit India Movement from the same place (Gowalia Tank) where the movement had started.

Why is it Gandhi never liked to consult people outside his circle and even when intellectuals including his friends advised him, he rejected such advice summarily. When Gandhi first decided to visit Mussolini, his friend Romain Rolland advised him against this visit. Gandhi went to visit the fascist dictator. On his return, he even spoke very well of Mussolini and had a very good opinion of him. In the same way, it is quite possible that if Gandhi had condescended to give thought to other intellectuals' opinion relating to Cripps' offer and Jinnah's demands, India would have remained a united country.

On no other issue, however, he was as viciously attacked as on that of untouchability. When he mounted a systematic campaign to eradicate it, the *Sanatanists* were deeply alarmed. They feared his powerful hold over the Hindu masses and, since he attacked it from within the Hindu religious framework, they thought him a particularly dangerous enemy. Initially they argued with him, trying to convince him that untouchability was an integral part of Hinduism and that an attack on it threatened the very survival of the Hindu religion and social order. When that did not work, they published leaflets and wrote or inspired articles impugning his political integrity and dropping dark hints about his private life. He called it a campaign to frighten him away from his anti-untouchability work. Organised protests with the Sanatanists waving black flag and shouting slogans greeted him in major cities during his all-India anti-untouchability tour in 1934. A bomb was thrown at what was mistakenly believed to be his car, injuring seven persons. Pandit Lalnath tried to break up one of his meetings. In Karachi, a man wielding an axe rushed towards him, but was apprehended in time, In Benaras Baba Kalabhairav burnt his portrait and published scandalous and inflammatory leaflets against him.

While the Sanatanists denounced Gandhi for subverting the Hindu social order, Amdedker accused him of seeking to prop it up by making only token concessions to the unthouchables. In *What Congress And Gandhi Have Done To The Untouchables*, he observed, "Do the untouchables regard Mr. Gandhi as being in earnest? The answer is in the negative. They do not regard Mr. Gandhi as being in earnest. How can they? How can they look upon a man being in earnest who, when in 1921 the whole country was aroused to put the Bardoli programme in action, remained completely indifferent to the anti-touchability part of it? How can they believe in the earnestness of a man who is prepared to practice it against the Hindus for the sake of the Untouchables? How can they believe in the earnestness of a man who does nothing more than indulge in giving sermons on the evils of untouchability?

Do they regard Mr. Gandhi as honest and sincere? The answer is that they do not regard Mr. Gandhi as honest and sincere. At the outset of his campaign for Swaraj, Mr. Gandhi told the Untouchables not to side with British. He told them not to embrace Christianity or any other religion. He told them that could find salvation in Hinduism. He told the Hindus that we must remove untouchability as a condition precedent to Swaraj. Yet in 1921, when only a paltry sum out of the Tilak Swaraj Fund was alloted to the Untouchables, and when the Committee to plan the uplift of the Untouchable was unceremoniously wound up, he did not even raise a word of protest'.

Referring to Gandhi's fast against the Macdonald Award of 1931 granting a separate electorate to the Untouchables, which the Hindus regarded as one of his noblest and greatest,

Ambedkar remarked. "There was nothing noble in the fact. It was a foul and filthy act. The fast was not for the benefit of the Untouchables. It was against them and was the worst form of coercion against a helpless people to give up the constitutional safeguards of which they had become possessed under the Prime Minister's Award and agreed on the mercy of the Hindus. It was a vile and wicked act. How can the Untouchable regard such a man as honest and sincere?

After having gone on a fast unto death, he signed the Poona Pact. People say that Mr. Gandhi sincerely believed that political safeguards were harmful to the Untouchables. But how could an honest and sincere man, who opposed the political demands of the Untouchables, who was prepared to use the Muslims to defeat them and who went on a fast unto death, in the end accept the very same demands —for there is no difference between the Poona and the Communal Award—when he found that there was no use opposing, as opposition would not succeed? How can an honest and sincere man accept as harmless the demands of the Untouchables which once he regarded as harmful?'

Lest Ambedkar's criticism be attributed to his personal animus against Gandhi, it should be pointed out that they were echoed by many Harijan leaders, and were later reiterated by Kanshi Ram, a leader of the Harijan party, the Bahujan Samaj Party.

What has Gandhi done? He fought tooth and nail against the interest of the downtrodden people. In September 1932, he went on a fast against reservations. Later it was propagated that Gandhi was responsible for reservations. He was a great hypocrite, to my mind. He lived in a sweepers' colony and he told them, "Your job is very good and you are doing a very good job. If I am to be born again I would like to be born as a sweeper." He was told, "If you want to be a sweeper, we can fulfill your desire in this life itself. Come join us". But he never went. Why? Because was he a hypocrite then, just pleasing innocent people?

Roy

Prof. Kaviraj does not refer to other political events where Roy's predictions were correct. For example, Roy had predicted at the annual conference of the Radical Democratic Party in Lucknow in December 1942, at a time when hardly any Indian thought Hitler would be defeated, that the Axis powers led by Hitler would be defeated and that the British would be left with no other option but to leave the colonies after the war. The right to self determination had been promised to India with the greater assertion of British democracy on the situation. There was no reason to believe that the right would be withheld by any external agency or by any political formation in Great Britain during the post war period. He exhorted his colleagues to prepare for economic and political reconstruction of independent India. He brought out two documents, to that effect; (i) People's Plan for Economic Reconstruction of Independent India; (ii) A Draft Constitution for Free India. Then he predicted that in spite of the pact between Hitler and Soviet Russia the latter would be drawn into the war. It is now accepted by most historians across the world that but for Stalin joining the Allies, Hitler might have not been defeated.

Roy had also said (predicted) in a lecture delivered at University Institute at Calcutta on February 5, 1950 that the future of democracy in India was not very bright and that it was not due to the evil intentions on the part of the politicians but because of the system of Party politics. He wrote,— "Perhaps in another 10 year demagogy will vitiate political practice. Scramble for power will continue to breed corruption and inefficiency... They want a short cut. The short cut to power is always to make greater promises than others; to promise things without the competence or even the intention to implement them". This is perhaps the reason why there was not even a polite reference to Gandhi's political ideas of decentralization and village Republics in the Constitutent Assembly when the Constitution was first being framed. This was in spite of the fact that there were a number of Gandhian members in the Constituent Assembly. Roy also said that, "The future of democracy in our country depends on people who are either outside politics today or who have the courage and vision to step out of the indecent scramble for power. They will have to act in a manner which may not attract the practical politicians." In another lecture also at Calcutta on January 30, 1947 Roy said, "When political power is concerted in the hands of small community, you may have a facade of parliamentary democracy but for all political purpose it will be dictatorship even if it may be paternal and benevolent, How many people realize that the drift in national politics is leaning towards dictatorship? Beyond the politics of power to make democracy effective power must always remain vested in the people effectively not periodically but from day to day. Automised individuals are powerless for all practical purpose." Roy advanced the idea that, "those who are against me must see a new social order, the economy of which will be for production for use and distribution. It will be based on direct participation of the entire adult population through people's committees/gram sabhas. Its culture would be based on universal dessemination of knowledge and have minimum control and maximum scope for an incentive to scientific and creative activities. The new society being founded on reason and science will necessarily be planned. But it will be planning with the freedom of the individual as its crux. The new society will be democratic, political, economic as well as cultural. Consequently, it will be democracy which can be defining itself,"—These ideas remind one of Gandhi's ideas, it is therefore important that political scientists do a little research to find out why even Gandhians did not make any reference to Gandhi's ideas and why our leaders to whom power was handed over by the British decided to go on the beaten track (namely Parliamentary from of Government). Why was Gandhi totally ignored by his followers.

Democracy has been treated as an ideal for a long time. But before it has ever had effective chance of practice, people are beginning to question whether democracy is at all possible. As a matter of fact democracy appears to be a widely discredited ideal and will be possible and practicable if the "State becomes coterminous with society". So long as the State is coterminous not with society it remains an instrument in the hands of a minority and when power is concentrated in the hands of any minority or any one section, big or small, it necessarily becomes an instrument of coercion and democracy becomes impossible.

Philip Spratt, a British Communist leader who was sent to India by the Communist International to help the communist movement in India, was arrested by the British Police and made an accused in the Meerut Conspiracy case. He was sentenced to 4 years' imprisonment. After release from jail he did not return to U.K. He joined the Radical Democratic Party and become Roy's colleague and friend. He was one of those few whose advice Roy had sought in the formulation of the 22 theses of radical democracy and in the publication of the quarterly magazine *The Marxian Way* later renamed *The Humanist Way.* He wrote the foreword to Roy's book *New Orientation* (published in 1946). Spratt said that no other practical politician or merely an observer was more consistently correct a prophet than M. N. Roy. He said that because Roy had been dealing for twenty five years with European, Indian, Chinese and world politics, there was hardly any major issue on which his analysis and prediction were disproved by events. Roy was not merely a writer. Probably many journalists could claim a fairly impressive record of predictions come true-if only because they have written so much that they are bound to make a lucky fit now and then. Roy has always written not as a journalist but as a political stategist concerned to know what is happening so that he can act appropriately. There is therefore nothing journalistic about his writing; no ornamentation, no tub-thumping, no irrelevancies, no evasion. It is functional writing, consistent and responsible; and that such writing, should prove to be so unvaryingly right must be almost unique and is certainly noteworthy. It is strange therefore that in a country so given to hero-worship, Roy should not have become a popular idol. Not that his merits as a political thinker are entirely unrecognized. They are admitted even by some who disliked him-people who would not be found dead with a copy of *Independent India* yet like to know what Roy was thinking about things. It is rather that the truth hurts, and hurts in particulars all those who control public opinion in India.

But there is another factor in this conspiracy to ignore a

man who should be among the foremost in public life; and here is perhaps a justification for the present introduction. Roy, as I have said, was not a journalist. He wrote for a limited circle who understood his style of thought and his background of ideas, and seemed unconcerned whether he was intelligible to outside or not.... India is a part of world and is involved in the revolution. Roy thought about those solutions which applied first to the world as a whole and then applied to India with the necessary modifications which were often not too great. This has always annoyed the nationalists, who at the bottom do not think of India as part of the world; they think India is unique, that foreign or western ideas do not apply to the country and presumably, therefore, that she happens to be having a private revolution of her own. This of course is a way of saying that they want to confine the revolution to its nationalist aspect, whereas Roy said that it was merely a small beginning hardly worth calling a revolution at all. He said that, "It is good in so far as it removes a mental obstacle to further changes; it satisfies the demand for equality of status among the nations, which has always been a main factor in nationalism; but clearly that does not get us very far."

It is interesting to note that Roy had been saying this for more than twenty years. He was clear on the main ideas years earlier, but the first I remember of it is an article in The Communist International about 1924, in which he pointed out that after the 1914-18 war and particularly since 1923 the export of British capital to India had fallen to zero. This and other facts led him to infer that in due course a peaceful transfer of political power to Indian hands would take place—not through the British ruling class, or the democratic convictions of the British ruling class, but by virtue of a shift of economic power. And it followed that as regards the real problem of the revolution that transfer of power would mean nothing. The old order would remain; only the personnel at the top would change. Now this was not just a brainwave, a bright idea for an article, to be written. Roy thought about it seriously, discussed it with Lenin (who disagreed), and finally decided it was true and stuck to it when probably no one else in the world accepted it. He made it an essential part of his diagnosis of India's condition and it determined his attitude to all subsequent problems. In particular it helped to decide his attitude during World War II, when after Churchill became British Prime Minister in 1940, he saw that the consummation he had prophesied could take place at any time if only the Indian National Congress would adopt a responsible attitude to the war. He saw that Congress opposition, was what betting men would call hedging, a provision against the eventuality of an Axis victory. He said that in the circumstances it was merely not permissible but obligatory for a sincere opponent of fascism to support the war and therefore, the Government, should do so. Now that everything he predicted has taken place and the erstwhile incorruptible revolutionaries are cooperating, they should admit their error. But perhaps that is too much to expect. He said, "India being part of the world and involved in the revolution like the rest of it, we have to consider the same sort of solution to the problem it sets. One type of solution we can rule out without any doubt is the type we call 'fascist'. Fascism is theoretically a solution only in the form of the conquest of the world by a single fascist power. If two or more major powers went fascist they would fight, and that is no solution. In any case the solution is a highly undesirable one. But though we need not hesitate to reject, it needs some discussion." Roy's assertion that in time all nationalism is potential fascism, is true of Indian nationalism too, and thus Gandhism is a fascist ideology. Roy was highly critical of Gandhism from the very start, from 1920, and never altered his opinion. He had, of course written much about Gandhism at one time and another, and he had said many penetrating things about it. Yet it is true, I think that he failed to make its criticism intelligible to the Indian reader. His approach to Gandhism seemed that of an outsider, and an unsympathetic foreigner. He never tried to get under the skin of the Mahatma or his admirers to see where that extraordinary power came from.

Roy not only conducts social analysis, he judges values, and I may say that I regard his judgement of value as no less sound than his judgement of facts. He says that this dilemma is intolerable. As between Gandhism and Communism, the former is better, doubtless, but its success is most unlikely and it is not good enough. We have seen communism tried out, we can tell where and how it went wrong, and we ought to be able to avoid its worst errors. Any ultimate solution of the world's trouble must be either socialist or collectivist. That is inescapable. We can therefore build on the socialist movement. But that movement in both its divergent branches has reached a dead end. A policy adequate to meet the world's needs must avoid the errors of the traditional socialist parties. It must get away from the lifeless, uninspiring formalism of the social democrats; and the direction in which it can look for reminders is to bring the rank-and-voter into intimate, permanent contact with the administration, more or less in the way the original Soviets did in Russia. How this may be done is suggested in Roy's Draft Constitution for India. On the other hand, though it accepts the Soviets, it rejects the illiberal doctrines and practices which have caused the communists to be so strongly opposed; their reliance only on the industrial working class and the poorer peasant, and hostility to other classes, their intolerance of all ideas but their own, their repudiation of free election and of civil liberties, and their demand for a single party dictatorship. The condition which made this narrow policy plausible thirty years ago have been destroyed by subsequent events, and over large parts of the world only a really liberal but dynamic socialism can now appeal confidently to all classes except the few remaining rich. There are indications that the communists are changing their policy in the direction, but how genuine the change is, remains to be seen and even if it is genuine they will have to overcome immense doubt as to their good faith before they can make it effective. To sum it up in, a slogan form, to Roy's three objectively necessary factors in a solution set forth above, we must add a fourth-freedom. (1) Peace; (2) Collectivism; (3) Material well-being; (4) Freedom. His Draft Constitution states the kind of the state structure in which these ideas can be realized.

In the end, I may revert to Max Eastman. He distinguished three impulses behind the socialist movement- for freedom, for fraternity and for order. Roy points out a fourth which is conspicuously present in all the socialist movements and thinkers-the moral motive, the demand for a better order.

CHAPTER 31

What Led to the Two-Nation Theory and Partition?

What led to the "two-nation" theory and who was responsible for the partition of India in 1947, which led to human rights violations of the worst kind caused by communalism? Some young historians, like Ayesha Jalal (*The Sole Spokesman*, Cambridge University Press) and Joya Chatterjee (*Bengal Divided: Hindu Communalism and Partition 1932–47*, Cambridge University Press)[1] have, in recent years, shown remarkable objectivity and scientific outlook—shunning all journalistic flourish, common in our country—in answering this question, which is not the conventional revisionistic view of history. According to Jalal, Jinnah did not want the partition of the country, which conclusion is reinforced by Chatterjee who gives conclusive proof from her research that it is the *bhadralok* Hindus of Bengal (including the Congress and Hindu Mahasabha) who wanted Bengal to be partitioned. Older generation of scholars, like H.M. Seervai, who hold the Congress responsible for the partition of the country are rare.

For those who witnessed the partition, who were actors and participated in the tragedy, for whom partition is not mere history—many of whom have been searching their hearts to muster courage to come out with the truth—it is not an easy job to do so, though. Kuldip Nayar is one of those making valiant efforts to face the truth, through his regular widely published columns on the subject. One of these, "The Two-Nation Theory" was published in May-June 1997. In this piece he refers, among other things, to the Congress approach to the Second World War, the Quit India stir, M.N. Roy apropos of support to the war effort, the Gandhi-Jinnah stand on the partition of India, etc.

Nayar does not give any definitive opinion about Jinnah's role in the partition of the country, or what led to the two-nation theory. His only comments are:

> Both Gandhiji and Jinnah stood poles apart as much in dress as in thoughts. Jinnah was elegantly dressed with a stiff white collar even in hot weather. Gandhiji wore only a doubled-up dhoti. For one the two-nation theory was a knife to cut the Gordian knot of the subcontinent's independence question, for the other the two-nation theory was the perpetuation of the subcontinent's ills. 'Vivisect India,' Gandhiji said. Jinnah was 'Mr. Jinnah' to the closest of his followers but Gandhi was Gandhiji even to non-Congressmen.

Nayar appears to contradict himself with regard to the question of the 'Quit India' stir, and is, at places, rather ambivalent. At one place he criticizes the Communists and M.N. Roy for their support of the War effort (that is, for being anti-Fascists) and for not joining "Sardar Patel (who) had envisaged an underground movement" against the British. At another place he writes:

> Many years later when I met Patwardhan (Achyut Patwardhan was one of the young heroes of 1942, and was also one of the first to have been disenchanted with political parties and their corrupting influence) to commend his role during the 1942 agitation, he regretted it. He said that the 1942 stir was *not necessary because the British would have anyway left*. This turned out to be a correct assessment. (emphasis added) (Achyut Patwardhan, as is well known, said so in public—in a public lecture on the 25th anniversary of the 'Quit India' resolution, he declared at the August Kranti Maidan in Bombay, that the British had no other alternative but to leave India after the War and that the 'Quit India' stir was unnecessary.)

My purpose is not to make any attempt to demolish Nayar's arguments—I value his friendship highly—but to give another side of the coin in a forthright manner, without any ambiguity—

and no journalistic flourish. Furthermore, Nayar and I have one thing in common—we both came from Pakistan, and we both were nationalists at one time. In any case, most Bengalis and Punjabis were devotees of Subhas Bose. (Many *bhadralok* Bengalis hailed Hitler as an *avtar*!) We both witnessed the partition. And I am sure, like me he did not contribute to the partition of the country. In any case, I for one, even now feel nostalgic about "East Bengal". (Although I do not approve of the kind of treatment that is meted out to the Biharis who have been left behind in Bangladesh—in fact, no civilized man can approve of that, if Pakistan does not accept them, Bangladesh must accept them as their own. How can Bangladeshis, who claim to be the inheritors of a culture propounded by Tagore and Nazrul Islam, treat the "Biharis' as foreigners? They should be generous and cosmopolitan, as Tagore and Nazrul Islam were.)

I may strike a personal note. My father, who was a plebian was opposed to the partition of Bengal in 1947, but my maternal uncles, who were big landholders and feudal in their behaviour, wanted partition—they could not dream of being under a Muslim Chief Minister! My parents did not leave East Pakistan—they lived there until 1960. They left, persuaded by their Muslim friends, only when they were very old and could not look after themselves— to join my elder brother in India.

Another personal note: I had the pleasure and opportunity of working, in an honorary capacity, in a project, Documentary History of Partition of India, in Hamdard Institute of Historical Research in Delhi. The first volume (which, I am told by the editor, is being published soon) covers the period 1937–40 (Lahore Resolution of the Muslim League). A number of documents, hitherto unpublished, are revealing, but I cannot quote from them since that was the understanding between the editor and me.

II

Nayar refers to M.N. Roy, although he does not appear to be familiar with Roy's ideas, his War thesis, his views on fascism, imperialism, democracy, the Hindu–Muslim problem, and

Jinnah's role, which are very relevant in the context of partition of India. (Nayar refers to M.N. Roy, "a radical humanist"; in 1942 Roy had not propounded the philosophy of radical humanism, he did so in 1946. In 1942, Roy was a radical Marxist/Communist.) However, this reinforces the fact that Roy is not widely read.

Roy became unpopular with the Congress leaders mainly because of his War thesis, and with Hindu nationalists because of his approach to the Hindu–Muslim problem. Roy felt deeply concerned and disturbed by two evils—communalism and fascism—constant threats even today. While in jail (1931–36) he wrote two books: one, the *Historical Role of Islam,* with a view to indicating the way to a solution of the Hindu–Muslim problem; two, *Fascism: Its Philosophy, Profession and Practice* to warn against the dangers of this monstrosity. These were published after he was released from jail. (These have been reprinted in the *Selected Works of M.N. Roy* Vol. IV, edited by Professor Sibnarayan Ray and published by Oxford University Press, 1997.)

The Historical Role of Islam and the Hindu–Muslim Problem

Roy maintains that in spite of the fact that Islam had played out its progressive role before it penetrated India, Islam was welcomed as a message of hope and freedom by victims of the Brahmanical reaction which had overthrown the Buddhist revolution resulting in a state of chaos in Indian society. How is it that, he posed the question, the Mohammedans, though not large in numbers, managed to rule a vast country for such a long time, and millions of people converted themselves to the new faith? The fact remains, Roy maintains, that the Mohammedans satisfied certain objective requirements of Indian society. Roy therefore appealed to his fellow Indians to undertake a

> dispassionate study of this chapter (which) is of great importance in the present fateful period of the history of India... With us, today in India, particularly with the Hindus, a proper understanding of the historical role of Islam and the contribution it has made to human culture has acquired a supreme political importance... Indeed, there is no other example of two communities living together in the same country for so many hundred years and yet

> having so little appreciation of each other's culture. No civilised people in the world is so ignorant of Islamic history and contemptuous of the Mohammedan religion as the Hindus... The prevailing notions could be laughed at as ridiculous, *were they not so pregnant with harmful consequences...* A proper appreciation of the cultural significance of Islam is of supreme importance in this crucial period of the history of India... *Unless a radical change of attitude is brought about by a sober sense of history, the communal question will never be solved... On the other hand, few Muslims of our days may be conscious of the glorious role played on the stage of history by the faith they profess,* (emphasis added)

Roy concludes with the hope that

> Indians, both Hindus and Muslims, could profitably draw inspiration from that memorable chapter of human history. Knowledge of Islam's contribution ... would shock the Hindus out of their arrogant self-satisfaction, and cure the narrow-mindedness of the Muslims of our day by bringing them face to face with the true spirit of the faith they profess.

It is hardly necessary to emphasize the point that the above observations remain eminently relevant even today—after partition; and social activists like Kuldip Nayar, more than anyone else, should give their thought to what Roy wrote, if they are serious about eradicating communalism.

Anti-Fascism and 'Quit India' Stir. Not many Indians knew, or know even today, particularly those who think that he was wrong in his thesis about the anti-Fascist character of the Second World War, his support to the War effort, as also his scientific analysis in 1942 that the Allied Forces would win, British Imperialism would be liquidated and India will be a free country after the War, that Roy was an uncompromising opponent of Fascism throughout his life. Roy traces the origin and ancestry of Fascism in the book that he wrote in jail (referred to above). He appealed to "those Indian nationalists who can think, who are not simply swayed by prejudice, or who are not conscious reactionaries, that is, potential Fascists, themselves" not to be proud of philosophy which will bring disaster. (This writer gave a fairly detailed analysis of Roy's War thesis in an article published in this journal, March 22, 1997).

Roy chose between freedom and perpetual slavery: If the Axis Powers won, the question of even fighting for independence would not arise. As is well known, Pandit Nehru and Maulana Azad had decided to "fight against the mortal enemy of all freedom", but could not muster courage to challenge the rest of the Congress High Command, Nayar acknowledges this:

> Nehru and Abul Kalam Azad did not want to embarrass the war efforts which, they knew, were directed towards fighting Fascism.

And yet he must criticize Roy for his fight against Fascism! Nayar does not also make any effort to explain why, in spite of their commitment to anti-Fascism, the Congress leaders lent their support in passing the 'Quit India' resolution, while in effect it meant support to fascism. The fact remains that there was, and is no relational explanation.

Roy's thesis in 1942— "prophecy": In December 1942, Roy announced:

> The War is going to end in 1944 when the Fascist Powers will be comprehensively defeated, and that Indian freedom fighters must bear in mind that 1943 or 1944 cannot be 1939, and that whatever be in the mind of a Churchill or a Roosevelt, none will be able to bring the world back to 1939.

He made the further prophecy, "Japan will be defeated, and after the war Britain will be seriously weakened in every respect". He declared, "in view of the fact that British imperialism will have no power to retain India, *transfer of power was inevitable" because British imperialism was bound to be liquidated* (emphasis added).

It is in the background of the above that Patwardhan's regret about the launching of a wholly "unnecessary stir in 1942"—in fact, it was a disaster—and Nayar's agreeing with this assessment, referred to above, is statesmanlike. But how does it reconcile with what he writes at another place:

> Patel was amazed when (the Communists) said 'no' to his offer of an underground movement. And not only they, M.N. Roy, a radical humanist, accepted funds from the government and help War efforts?

Apart from the fact that the language used sounds like that of a small-time politician, one can only say, echoing Sophocles, how thoughtful people can think so thoughtlessly!

It may be added that outside the Congress there were a large number of distinguished, freedom-loving and patriotic Indians like Dr Ambedkar, and many others who had actively supported War efforts and were part of the government during the War. Their services were eagerly solicited by Pandit Nehru and his government and on whom he relied heavily. (For quite a few years, Pandit Nehru could not find a Finance Minister from the Congress party.) They never regretted their active cooperation with the British in the fight against fascism. History of the sub-continent would have been different—for the better—if the Congress had supported the efforts and fought against Fascism, and in the process solved the Hindu–Muslim problem. One might added that in the fight against Emergency, against communalism, and against other fascistic tendencies today, Nayar has been working with and actively cooperating with one of those, V.M. Tarkunde, who "accepted funds"—he was the General Secretary of M.N Roy's Radical Democratic Party during the War. (Incidentally, a specific amount was allotted, a meagre Rs 12,000 odd per month to the Indian Federation of Labour of which M.N. Roy was General Secretary, in the budget of the Central Government, for carrying on war efforts to fight Fascism, the destruction of which enabled India to gain independence—there was nothing secret about this amount.)

Nayar and "patriotic liberal nationalists" like him might remember that it was those Second World War anti-Fascists who stood up against the fascistic and authoritarian regime imposed by the Party and its leaders in 1975 who boast of launching the 'Quit India' stir, and who during the 1975 Emergency, let loose a reign of terror, barbarism, and violence and it is they who justified violations of all standards of morality, justice and freedom on ideological grounds; and no wonder, therefore, they did not fight against Fascism during the Second World War. Our "liberal nationalists" (whatever this expression may mean), at least those who strive to put a curb on the rise of Fascism in our country (manifested by communalism and authoritarianism), might shed their unnecessary patriotic arrogance and learn to respect those anti-fascists who contributed their mite in defeating Fascism in 1939-45, as a result of which India became an independent country.

Communists (of the ruling groups) have, in recent times, pretty often expressed their regret that they isolated themselves from the "Quit India" stir. Which means, logically, that they now regret their fight, against fascism. Whatever they may now say about Stalin, the fact remains that but for his valiant and heroic fight, the Axis Powers could not be defeated—a truth which is acknowledged even by most irrational and rabid anti-communist historians in the West. And if the Axis Powers were not defeated, India could not become an independent country. Sophisticated scholars and crafty liberal-nationalists will, of course, tend to dismiss this as a very simplistic conclusion!

Role of Jinnah and Congress attitude towards him: In the light of recent writings on the partition of the country, a lengthy quotation from Roy on Jinnah written in September 1948 is appropriate:

> Mohammad Ali Jinnah was the most maligned and misunderstood man. That experience made him bitter and it was very largely out of spitefulness that he pursued an object, the attainment of which placed him in the most difficult position. Jinnah was not an idealist in the sense of being a visionary; he was a practical man possessed of great shrewdness as well as of more than average intelligence. Such a man could not be blind to the difficulty which was to follow his highly problematical success. During the latter part of his career, politics was a gamble for him; having played a game of poker with high stakes, he could not pull out. He had to go to the bitter end, so to say. Bitter, because he must have been frightened by the spectre of success when it came within the reach of possibility. But then it was too late to retreat. It was a case of a man getting inextricably entangled in power-politics without having begun with the lust for political power. Few would agree; yet, that is a fact which will win the recognition of impartial and dispassionate historians...... Jinnah was temperamentally not a professional politician. He began as a liberal for whom politics was a holiday pastime. Being a man of outstanding merit, he could not remain a back-bencher. Unfortunately, his coming to the front rank of politics synchronised with the desecularisation of nationalism,

> which doubtful development introduced communalism in politics. The responsibility for that fateful turn in the political life of the country must be judged by history. But ever since then, politics became a game of wits for Jinnah. Successful in that game, thanks to his own cleverness, he won the opprobrium of being a henchman of imperialism. The fact, however, is that, if distrust and hatred of the British were the hall-mark of patriotism, Jinnah was always as staunch a patriot as any other Indian. *The more that fact was willfully ignored by his opponents and he was maligned and misrepresented deliberately, the more was Jinnah naturally embittered* (emphasis added). But even then his ambition was not to gain political power, but avenge the wrong which he believed had been done to him. ...But he was not the devil of the drama, as he was made out to be. He is no more with us. Let justice be done to his memory. ...The homeland for the Indian Muslims was a Utopia; and territorial division was bound to leave many millions of them out, in a very delicate position of being regarded as aliens, suspected of disloyalty to the land they must live in. An intelligent man like Jinnah must have foreseen this tragic consequence of what he demanded. Therefore, I for one do not believe that he really wanted partition of the country (emphasis added). Like a gambler, overconfident of his wits, he staked high, believing that the other party would compromise on his terms. *That would have been for the best of all concerned. But the latter having taken up the attitude of all or nothing, Jinnah was driven to the bitter end*—of gaining a victory he himself dreaded and which he did not survive, (editorial in *Independent India*, September 19, 1948).

Historians will go on exploring: who was responsible for the partition of India? Meanwhile, we may take a sane and civilized view and insist on our textbook writers and columnists to give up the "hate campaign" against Jinnah, and against those who fought against Fascism. In any case, invectives cannot substitute for logical debate and discussion.

Finally, this distorted view of history involving hatred will always stand in the way of a normal and healthy relationship between the two countries, India and Pakistan.

NOTE

1. This is what Joya Chatterjee writes in the chapter "Conclusion" in her book, *Bengal Divided: Hindu Communalism and Partition 1932-1947*;

"The inwardness of Partition cannot be fully understood through a study of the motives of those in Delhi and in London. ... Nor do investigations into Muslim separatism tell the whole story. ...When push came to shove (in Bengal), *bhadralok* Hindus preferred to carve up Bengal rather than to accept the indignity of being ruled by Muslim. ...(I have) attempted to challenge the prevailing wisdom about Partition on a number of counts. Partition is generally believed to have been a consequence of his separatist politics of Muslim minorities, but in the case of Bengal, Hindus evolved a parallel separatism of their own. The Congress High Command is widely, but wrongly believed to have acquisced only reluctantly to Partition. This study suggests that, on the contrary, not only was the Congress High Command ready to pay the price of Partition in order to strengthen its hold over an unitary India, but that the Bengal Congress campaigned successfully for the vivisection of its own province on communal lines. ...The United Bengal Plan had no takers on its home ground, culture was deployed as a mark of difference rather than evidence of traditional unity in the region, and *bhadralok* Bengalis, far from launching agitation against it, actually fought for the Partition which gave them a separate homeland of their own. Partition was not imposed by the centre on an unwilling province. ..(This book) has shown how the Communal Award and the Poona Pact deprived the *bhadralok* of political power at a time when agrarian depression damaged their economic position and gave new opportunities and power to some Muslims. The measures enacted by successive Muslim governments demolished, step by step, the structures that had long sustained *bhadralok* dominance. Hindu communal mobilisation emerged as the most powerful of the competing political strategies that were evolved in response to this series of challenges. Secular strategies of a populist sort were also devised by an emerging left but these failed to carry the bulk of *bhadralok* opinion, which grew ever more parochial, more concerned with preserving narrow self-interest and more virulently communal. The 'Hindu' communal discourse of the *bhadralok* articulated the deeply conservative world view of an embattled elite, determined to pay whatever price it had to in order to cling to power and privilege. It was a discourse that was deeply communal in intention even when it did not invoke religious imagery or deploy sacred symbols. ...the arguments set out in this book may have some relevance to another debate which continues to dominate thinking about

India's political future. A central theme of this work has been the idea of a *shift* from nationalism to communalism. Whatever similarities in style and idiom between nationalist rhetoric and Hindu communal posturings, the differences are critical. Nationalism was directed against imperialism, and gave top priority to anti-British action. The communalism of the *bhadralok* was directed against their fellow Bengalis. History for the one was the struggle against British rule; for the other, it was the celebration of British rule as an age of liberation from the despotism of Muslims. Its key political objective was to prevent this 'despotism' from returning when the British left India, and to deny that Muslims could be Bengalis, and by extension Indians.

The Hindutva version of the history of the last decades of the Raj has it that Congress was 'anti-national' because it consented to Partition and surrendered to Pakistan the soil of the motherland; that Communists were 'anti-national' because they collaborated with the British during the War effort. Only the Hindu organisations, in this account, remained true to the cause of the nation. The pernicious consequences of self-serving doctrines of this sort have gone much further than the division of a province; now once again they threaten the very future of the nation, (pp. 266–268)

[Courtesy: *Mainstream*, Vol. XXXV, No. 43,
4 October 1997, pp. 17–20 (pp. 266–268)]

****

CHAPTER 32

Was Partition of India Inevitable?*

On a black Saturday evening my family and I switched on the TV and heard the sad news of Pakistan coming under emergency rule, which meant Martial Law.

We changed channels but all channels were telecasting the same news. I said, to the great annoyance of my wife, for she does not like my criticism of Gandhi, in Hindi, "*Yeh sab Gandhi ki meharbani hai.*" What I wanted to say is narrated below.

If Gandhi and the Congress had accepted the Cripps' offer, the country would not have been patitioned. There are two aspects of his question: one, that partition could be prevented, two, whether or not unified India would have been a better place to live. I am dealing with the first question. One thing is clear, namely, that if there were no partition, Gandhi would not have been assassinated in 1948 and there would have been no Kashmir war. The main grievance of the few Hindu nationalist militants who had been planning to kill Gandhi was that Gandhi was pro-Pakistan and pro-Muslim. The Kashmir war that has been going on since 1947 in one form or another has cost us a lot of money, which could have been used for social development and welfare. The immediate provocation to give a fresh look at this question was provided by news of Pakistan coming under the Martial Law. One can be reasonably sure that if India were not partitioned, this situation, and also that

* This paper was presented at a discussion group on the subject organised by the Academy of Third World Studies, Jamia Millia Islamia on 29 April, 2008.

Pakistan has been under more or less perpetual military rule, would not have arisen.

Instead Gandhi launched the Quit India movement. One fails to understand why Gandhi scholars like Prof. Bhikhu Parikh and Raj Mohan Gandhi do not analyze as to why Gandhi resorted to starting Quit India movement in spite of opposition from his colleague Maulana Azad.

It would not be wrong to suggest that Gandhi expected to regain the supremacy of his position in the Congress through a movement like the Quit India movement.

Let us give a quick look at what happened to the movement. One heroic figure of the Congress Aruna Asaf Ali wrote, "We know ours is the voice of lost souls that championed a lost cause." Another heroic figure of the Socialist Party Achyut Patwardhan told the veteran journalist Kuldeep Nayar that it was not necessary to have the Quit India movement to attain India's Independence. Maulana Abul Kalam Azad writes in his book *India Wins freedom* that after serious consideration he had tried to dissuade Gandhi from launching the Quit India movement. But Gandhi then wrote to him to resign from the Presidentship of the Congress and also withdraw from its Working Committee. It was, however, Patel, who had no special love for Azad though, who pressurized Gandhi to withdraw the letter. The veteran Congress leader, C. Rajagopalachari, too did not join the Quit India Movement and thus remained out of jail.

The well known historian R.C. Majumdar has written in his book *The History of Freedom Movement in India*, "That the Movement was crushed within two to three months and there is no doubt that it failed to achieve any tangible result not to speak of the end for which it was launched there is no doubt."

On another occasion when Lord Wavell become Viceroy of India, he met Jinnah. What the British government wanted to do in India was to install an interim government in Delhi, which would have the support of the Muslim League, i.e., Jinnah and the Congress, i.e., Gandhi so that the British could transfer power to this government in Delhi after World War II (after defeating the Axis powers). So when Lord Wavell met Jinnah, the latter's main demand was that Muslim ministers should be selected by the Muslim League, i.e., Jinnah proposed that the government would be nominated by the League and by nobody else. Wavell then met Gandhi and asked him to show statemanship** and accept Jinnah's demand for the sake of peace but Gandhi would not. If Gandhi had accepted Wavell's plea united India would not have suffered any loss except that men like Maulana Abul Kalam and Rafi Ahmed Kidwai, who were the Congress's Muslim candidates for ministership and would in no case have been nominated for the post by the Muslim League led by Jinnah, would not have become ministers. But in that case the partition of India would have been avoided and thousands of people would not have become victims of that tragedy. In 1940, the Congress in the provinces resigned. Instead of resigning if the Congress had invited the Muslim League to join the Congress to form coalition governments, the British rulers would have got a clear signal that the Muslim League and the Congress had come together. Neither Gandhi nor Jinnah made any efforts in this regard. On the contrary Jinnah announced that the resignation of Congress government be celebrated as deliverance day.

A young friend of mine, who was till recently a card-holding member of the CPIM, one day asked me what has been Jyoti Basu's contribution to the politics and government of Bengal that he has been the uncrowned king of West Bengal for such a long time. I said that the most important contribution made by him is that he was a party to the decision to partition Bengal. As you know all the Hindu members in the Bengal Assembly, including the communist members, voted for partition. The reason was that in United Bengal a Muslim would almost always have been the Chief Minister, and the *Bhadralok* Hindus did not want to live under a Muslim Chief Minister.

This reminds me of my very kind friend the late Justice Dorab Patel of Pakistan making a comment at lunch at my place in Delhi, that the whole tragedy was that we did not have any statesman in pre-partition India and that we had only clever and crafty politicians.

Jinnah did not want India to be partitioned. Let me quote

M.N. Roy in his context, "Unfortunately Jinnah's coming to the front rank of politics synchronized with desecularisation of nationalism, which doubtful development introduced communalism in politics. If distrust and hatred of the British were the hallmark of patriotism, Jinnah was always as strong a patriot as any other Indian". In the General Council meeting of the League held in the Imperial Hotel of New Delhi to endorse the plan of partition, Jinnah concluded his speech by declaring, "I have won Pakistan for you. Now do what you can do with it." If Jinnah had known that his men would rule Pakistan through emergency and Martial Law he would have perhaps given a second thought to the idea. What I suggest in this brief article is that Partition could have been avoided and undivided India would have been a less unhappy place than what these two countries are today.

It was the *Hindutvavadi* leader Savarkar who first propounded the two-nation theory. Veer Savarkar, while presiding over the 1937 session of the Hindu Mahasabha, said in plain and simple words, advocating the two-nation theory, " I warn the Hindus that the Mohammedans are likely to prove dangerous to our Hindu nation. India cannot be assumed today to be unitarian and homogeneous nation. On the contrary there are two nations in the main, the Hindus and the Muslim in India," (Source—*Mohandas* by Raj Mohan Gandhi, p. 411). Another important thing, which has prompted me to give a fresh look at this question, is to explore the possibility of bringing about peace between India and Pakistan. (In fact, the matter came up in a short discussion at a meeting organized by Jamia Millia Islamia under the aegis of the Academy of Third World Studies recently). I don't believe, like some Gandhians and RSS ideologues, that there can be peace between India and Pakistan only if Pakistan joins India in a Confederation. What a well-known Gandhian and others like him want to say is that the partition should be undone, then only there would be peace and there is nobody to question him why Gandhi did not prevent partition when he was in a position to do so as I have argued in this article. Also there is nobody to question him if India is truly a federation. That Gandhian intellectual wrote an article in a national daily, wherein he pleaded for Pakistan to join India in a confederation. Subsequently, while presiding over one session of an annual conference of the Indian Radical Humanist Association he advanced the same argument. I questioned him and wanted his permission to speak on the subject. Later in the course of a private discussion I asked him why was it that Gandhi did not accept Jinnah's demand?

It is for intellectuals like the one I have referred to above to enlighten us on how Gandhi reacted to one ruler of a Muslim majority state signing the treaty of accession with India, and also when Jinnah wanted to go to Kashmir for a holiday, why the Maharaja said that he would not allow Jinnah to enter Kashmir. It was only after this that Pakistan leaders had a meeting and decided to send infilrators as secret agents to Kashmir to evaluate the situation and determine the Maharaja's real intentions.

This was one of the greatest tragedies in Indian history and I have to say with the deepest regret that a large part of the responsibility for his development rests on Jawaharlal Nehru.

Sardar Vallabhbahi Patel was India's quintessential politician. He ran the machinery of the Congress party. I was surprised when Patel said that whether we like it or not there were two nations in India. He was now convinced that Muslims and Hindus could not be united into one nation. It was better to have one clean fight and then separate, than have bickering everyday. It was surprising that Patel was now an even greater supporter of the two-nation theory than Jinnah. He may have raised the flag of partition but now the real flag bearer was Patel Jawaharlal Nehru, the firm opponent of partition had become, if not a supporter at least acquiescent to the idea. (Source—*Crisis in the Indian Subcontinent: Partition; Can it be Undone* by Lal Khan, Aakar Books, Delhi). So far as Gandhi was concerned, Mountbatten told Gandhi that the Congress was not with him, it was with Mountbatten, to which Gandhi replied that the Congress might not be with him, but the country was with him.

In fact in India those who advocate directly that the partition be undone may read this book. It is a well-researched and scholarly book. The book has relevant quotations, for example,

Trotsky's critical comments on Gandhi and relevant quotations from Abul Kalam Azad's book *India Wins Freedom*. One such important quotation, which relates to Sardar Patel and his advocacy of the two-nation theory, has been referred to above.

A more improbable leader of India's Muslim masses could hardly be imagined. The only thing Muslim about than Mohd. Ali Jinnah was his parents' religion. He drank, ate pork, religiously shaved his beard each morning and just as religiously avoided the mosque each Friday. God and the Koran had no place in Jinnah's vision of the world. His political foe, Gandhi, knew more verses of the Muslim Holy Book than he did. Jinnah had been able to achieve the remarkable feat of securing the allegiance of the vast majority of India's Muslims without being able to articulate more than a few sentences in their traditional tongue, Urdu.

Jinnah despised India's masses. He detested the dirt, the heat and the crowds of India. He delighted in touring India's Muslim cities in princely processions, riding under victory arches on a kind of Rose bowl style float, preceded by silver-harnessed elephants and a band booming out "God save the King" because, Jinnah observed, it was the only tune the crowd knew. Jinnah had only scorn for his Hindu rivals. He labelled Nehru a Peter Pan, a "literary figure" who "should have been an English professor, not a politician", "an arrogant Brahmin who covers his Hindu trickiness under a veneer of Western education". Gandhi, to Jinnah, was "a cunning fox", "a Hindu revivalist." Jinnah never forgot the sight of the Mahatma in his mansion, stretched out on one of his priceless Persian carpets with his mudpack on his belly.

In most of the words of Partition, Gandhi is portrayed as the crusader of unity. Azad, his close associate and the former president of Congress, in *India Wins Freedom* said about Gandhi's position on Partition:

> But when I met Gandhiji again, I had the greatest shock of my life to find that he had changed. He was still not openly in favour of Partition but he no longer spoke so vehemently against it. What surprised and shocked me even more was that he began repeating the arguments which Sardar Patel had already used. For over two hours I pleaded with him, but could make no impression on him.

When Patel was convinced, Lord Mountbatten turned his attention to Nehru. Again according to Azad:

> Jawaharlal was not first ready for the idea and reacted violently against the idea of Partition. Lord Mountbatten persisted till Jawaharlal's opposition was worn down step by step. Within a month of Mountbatten's arrival in India, Jawaharlal, the firm opponent of Partition had become, if not a supporter, at least acquiescent to the idea. I have wondered how Jawaharlal was won over by Lord Mountbatten. He is a man of principle but he is also impulsive and amenable to personal influences. I think one factor responsible for the change was the personality of Lady [Edwina] Mountbatten. She is not only extremely intelligent but has a most attractive and friendly tempeerament. She admired her husband very greatly and in many cases tried to interpret his thoughts to those who would not at first agree with him.

NOTES

* I can't define Statesmanship but I would refer to two instances of great Statesmanship.

1. When Hitler attacked the Soviet Union, Churchill announced on the BBC that he would fight with Stalin in the air, on the sea and on land and destroy the common enemy of human culture, civilization and democracy. Some of his friends asked him how he could do so for he had been opposed to the Soviet Union and Communism all his life. Churchill replied that if Hitler attacked Hell, his friend should not be surprised if he were in alliance with the Devil to destroy the evil.
2. A few months before Abraham Lincoln was tragically assassinated in a theatre hall, some of his friends asked him about his views on the system of slavery to which his reply was that his first concern was the Union, and to keep it steady and if for that he was required to support slavery he would do that and if he was required to oppose it would do that.

V. Essays on Politics and Other Thorny Issues

CHAPTER 33

Mischiefs of Party Spirit

REFLECTIONS ON THE OCCASION OF INDEPENDENCE DAY (1998)

The conflict between morality and political practice, between party politics and grass-roots democracy, is not new; in fact it is as old as politics. And today, at least in our country, people have stopped expecting morality in political practice and moral conduct from our politicians. More about this a little later. Meanwhile, a happening narrated by this writer for about 38 years to first-year college students who read with him:

> I had occasion to enquire in a town which was the way to Mahatma Gandhi Road, upon which the person whom I spoke to, instead of answering my question, called me a young puppyish cur, and admonished me—who made Gandhi a Mahatma? I, being in some confusion, enquired of the next I met, which was the way to Gandhi Road; but was called prick-eared cur, and instead of being shown the way, was told that he had been a Mahatma before I was born, and would be one after I was hanged. Upon this, I did not think fit to repeat the former question, but going into every lane of the neighbourhood, asked what they called the name of the lane. By which ingenious artifice I found out the place I enquired after, without giving offence to any party.

After narrating this accident, I would "lecture" on such a dreadful spirit of division:

> This division gives the impression that we belong to several different nations in the same country. A furious spirit like the one I have experienced may break out in falsehood, detraction,

> calumny, and a partial administration of justice. The minds of many good men among us appear soured with this principle of 'division', and alienated from one another in such a manner, as seems to me altogether inconsistent with the dictates either of reason or religion. Furthermore, if this spirit has so ill an effect on our morals, it has likewise a very great one upon our judgements. What is light to one, is darkness to another. Knowledge and learning suffer in a particular manner from this strange prejudice, which at present prevails amongst all ranks and degrees. For example, calumnies that have never been proved, or have been often refuted, are the ordinary postulates of infamous scribblers, upon which they proceed as upon first principles granted by all men, though in their hearts they know they are false, or at best very doubtful. If this shameful practice of the present age endures much longer, praise and reproach will cease to be motives of action in good men.

The narration and the "lecture" would end here. I would then add at once that while the story is original in that I hold on to the views expressed, it was "told" by Sir Roger de Coverly while narrating his accident in finding out St. Anne's Lane to his creator Joseph Addison in early eighteenth century in the essay, "Mischiefs of Party Spirit", and that I was influenced by this essay about the futility of party politics and the evils it generates. The danger envisaged by Addison may not have engulfed the United Kingdom; but almost everything written in this essay was envisaged by Gandhiji, and remains relevant today for us in India. (We could replace 'Mahatma Gandhi' and 'Gandhi' by 'Dr. Ambedkar' and 'Ambedkar', and so on.)

Party politics has become an unnecessary evil in India, as also in many other countries where morality in political practice has been completely and neatly done away with under the garb of parliamentary democracy, in which system politicians have been playing unspeakably dirty and diabolical games of barbarity and savagery.

Gandhiji gave considerable thought to the evils of party-politics. He also gave the utmost importance to morality in political practice. If, however, we judge Gandhiji's ideology by the political atmosphere that has prevailed in our country since

Independence, it has not made any impact in any sphere of life, particularly in introducing morality in political practice and genuine decentralization. For one thing, almost immediately after Independence thousands of "Gandhians" left him, for another of his disciples who got into power forgot almost immediately after assuming power, his message and the codes of conduct laid down by him.

The fact that Gandhian ideology has failed to introduce morality in politics should make the thoughtful section of our people—particularly those who are aware of the "mischiefs of party spirit"— wage war on the mad race and lust for power.

A number of concerned citizens had hopes from another quarter. They thought that after the collapse of communism in Soviet Russia and the rise of free-market socialism in "communist" China, the Communists in our country would involve themselves in some intellectual exercise in this regard. But the history of the communist movement in our country would indicate that they are incapable of undertaking any fatiguing exercise. Presently they are as good or as bad nationalists as any other. Is there any difference between the political practice of non-communist parties and the Communists in power? Both are engaged in the "serious" game of capturing power—for the sake of power—through any means. The Communists too have "sold" their souls to the god of power.

The clash and conflict between morality and political practice that I referred to, could be done away with by introducing a different system of politics and governance based on decentralization of power as advocated by Tagore and Sri Aurobindo, by Gandhi and M.N. Roy, and later by Jayaprakash Narayan.

I started with Addison's essay only to suggest that partyless democracy is neither utopian nor something new. There have been thinkers like Addison who saw the mischiefs of party-politics, and they too suggested formation of a people's movement that could blaze a new trail. Since I started with Addison, let me also conclude with the "manifesto" of the people's movement that he gave in the essay:

> We do so solemnly declare, that we do in our conscience believe two and two make four; and that we shall adjudge any man whatsoever to be our enemy who endeavours to persuade us to the contrary. We are likewise ready to maintain with the hazard of all that is near and dear to us, that six is less than seven in all times and all places; and that ten will not be more three years hence than it is at present. We do also firmly declare, that it is our resolution as long as we live to black, black and white white. And we shall upon all occasions oppose such persons that upon any day of the year shall call black white, or white black, with the utmost peril of our lives and fortunes.

Addison then asked:

> Do we have such a combination of honest men and women who would endeavour to extirpate such infamous hypocrites, that are for promoting their own advantage under colour of the public good; with all the profligate immoral retainers to each side, that have nothing to recommend them but an implicit submission to their leaders? If we don't, this furious evil spirit will expose us to the derision and contempt of all the nations about us. It gives me a serious concern to see such a spirit of dissension... For my part, I am sometimes afraid to discover the seeds of a civil war in these our divisions; and therefore cannot but bewail the miseries and calamities of our children.

We might succeed in arresting the rot if we implement a system of governance based on decentralization of power. Let power be wielded by the people, but not for the people. Our hopes that we had dreamt on 15 August 1947 lie in this system.

[Courtesy: *Mainstream*, Vol. XXXVI, No. 34,
15 August 1998, pp. 13-14]

****

CHAPTER 34

Ramblings on "Minor Foibles"

APROPOS PRIME MINISTER I.K. GUJRAL

Going by the kind of invective used by distinguished chief editors/editors of newspapers these days, it would appear that while journalism is literature in a hurry, literature itself is invective at its worst. As students, we were taught that the use of invective is a social foible; today it is no longer so. It is central to a new style of editorial English.

For reasons of space I'd limit myself to a couple of instances. From day one when I.K. Gujral assumed the office of the Prime Minister, the chief editor (CE) of a national daily (which I read by habit), began to use the choicest "epithets" for him. According to him, Gujral is "one-man demolition brigade" in the ranks of the United Front "to achieve disrespectful ends"; he is "unscrupulous"; he is a man "without a sense of shame"; he is a "dangerous man", and so on. Obviously the CE is very angry with Gujral, and one can be sure that the CE has his good reasons into which I don't wish to pry since, by habit, I like to maintain a safe distance from feuds amongst politicians and between politicians and their seemingly "scientific analysts", and also for the reason that political parties are unnecessary evils in our country and have persistently stood in the way of the growth of a decentralised democratic system.

The CE is convinced that a liberal use of such "epithets"—we were taught that the use of adjectives in the English language is a dangerous thing, Charles Lamb being one of the very few exceptions—is the only way to make a point or to give expression to his "anguish". For example, once when the Bahujan Samaj Party (BSP) leaders made critical comments about Gandhiji, the CE used the following "epithets" to characterize them: the BSP is a pack of wolves, shameless, loud-mouthed gadflies, intellectually retarded, suffer from inferiority complex, street ruffians, devoid of commonsense, hypocrites, the loud and insignificant insects, and so on.

Gandhiji must have turned in his samadhi both out of shame and anger since he cannot come back to life to reply to the CE like what he did, for example, in the 1930s when he wrote:

> Dr Ambedkar has every right to be bitter. That he does not break our heads is an act of self-restraint on his part. He has had to suffer humiliations and insults which should make any one of us bitter and resentful. Had I been in his place, I would have been as angry.

Aren't these apt examples of invective being literature in a hurry? In any case, one can't but admire the CE's astounding ability to inveigh against people whom he does not like or does not agree with.

Another example of invective and journalism used interchangeably by journalists today. One senior editor of a national daily got so angry with the Supreme Court judges that he thundered:

> Some recent strictures passed by the Supreme Court against the law-enforcing agencies in Punjab suggest that the learned judges of the nation's apex juridical authority may be in need of psychiatric counselling.

Once a senior editor of a popular periodical described V.P. Singh, when he was the Prime Minister, as "Machiavellian" (and many other similar "epithets"), of course, without giving any instances. (A former academic and colleague of mine, I happened to meet him one day and asked the meaning of the word, Machiavellian—he changed the topic!) Another CE of a national daily described V.P. Singh, again when he was the Prime Minister, that he was "another Hitler in the making" because he introduced reservation for the other backward casts (OBCs)! In a discussion session one of them raised the question of truth and asked: "What is truth?" several times, but never once waited for the answer!

These gems of literature remind one of an incident in which a young aspirant for a journalist's job was politely asked by Lord Morley about his qualification. Pat came the reply: he excelled in invective! The CE and the senior editors referred to above must forgive me if I got this impression about them.

To get back to Prime Minister Gujral in the context of his failures/action referred to by the CE. In a long Doordarshan interview sometime back, Gujral, while replying to a number of questions and criticisms— quite a few valid criticisms—made an un-Indian, but pleasant to hear, observation, and also refreshing for a change, namely, that he did not seek the office of the Prime Minister nor is he going to do so in the future. There are some, he said, who offered themselves for the job. [One of them has been maintaining for years now that he is the only person in the country who is competent to hold the office of the Prime Minister! Once again he is in the field.] Gujral does not offer himself, he said; and one is inclined to believe that at least in this respect he is un-Indian. In reply to another question, he said that any Prime Ministerial aspirant must be a secular person, and must have a thorough knowledge of Indian secularism. True, but neither the interviewer nor the PM elaborated on what was meant by secularism and how Indian secularism was different from other varieties. Also, a man of his background and experience ought to have added that a basic knowledge of Indian sociology (apart from Indian history)—given the extreme complexities of Indian society and life—is a must.

The significant achievements of Gujral as External Affairs Minister—and a very tragic failure on the part of the United Front Government led by him and earlier by Deve Gowda—were not raised in the interview, nor are these mentioned in the media. Obviously, they are neither relevant nor important for they concern the common man and woman of the country, not the middle-class intelligentsia. Most of our rulers have almost always wanted to solve India's problems and disputes with her neighbours by pursuing the policy of establishing India's hegemony in the region. The fact remains that we have too many arrogant people both in the foreign service and among ruling politicians, who betray a lack of intellectual equipment, and one cannot expect sound judgment from such people. Gujral has been different from such people and pursued a different policy. Accord with India's immediate neighbours, most importantly Bangladesh, with whom our relations had soured during the last 16/17 years, must be hailed as a significant contribution. That Gujral was able to reach an agreement with Bangladesh, and which Bangladesh itself has hailed as a unique achievement, in spite of West Bengal Chief Minister Jyoti Basu's known stand on the water-sharing issue, deserves to be acknowledged by alibis, foes and friends. For too long a period India has been obsessed with its relationship with the big countries of the West at the cost of good neighbourliness with its immediate neighbours, and for too long a period successive governments in India forget the textbook knowledge of foreign relations being determined by internal conditions and realities. It seems Gujral has revived this old textbook formulation.

One wishes he took a bolder step with regard to Pakistan. Friendship with Pakistan will bring tremendous relief to the common man and woman in our country.

One of the major failures, hardly referred to by critics, relates to the non-implementation of the provision of Article 45 of the Constitution (compulsory primary education). In his August 15, 1997 speech from the Red Fort he did, however, announce his agenda in which he put universal primary education, the girl child, and gender equality first in the list of priorities. It was refreshing to hear Gujral propounding that no development is possible without introducing universal primary education. And also refreshing to recollect is the fact that he was the first Prime Minister to have announced this agenda of priorities in his independence day pronouncement from the Red Fort. But, like the average Indian politician, did he also mean, when he made the announcement, that the operative part of the pious sentiments are not meant seriously?

Nobody suggests that compulsory primary education could be accomplished in six month's time, but the steps taken by the

Human Resource Development Ministry of his government do not indicate that the government was at all serious about this all important social welfare programme. The only "contribution" made by the United Front Government was to introduce a Bill to make primary education a Fundamental Right and fundamental duty! The fact, however, remains that it was already made a Fundamental Right by a Supreme Court judgement in 1993, and legislation on the subject was not strictly necessary. The fundamental duty aspect amounts to playing a fraud, to put it mildly, on the part of the government and specially the HRD Ministry. The operative part of this provision is that both, violation of fundamental duty (by the state) and violation of fundamental duty (by parents), are cognizable offences. Has the state ever been punished for violating Fundamental Rights, and in this case, provision of Article 45 which was made a Fundamental Right by the Supreme Court in 1993?

Another failure, which too has not been referred to by any analyst and critic, refers to transparency in matters relating to human rights. Soon after Gujral became External Affairs Minister, he assured activists that he would soon permit the Amnesty International to visit the State of Jammu and Kashmir, Punjab, and other parts. (As is known, the Amnesty International does not send any team as tourist, as do some other international groups.) It is sad and unfortunate that Gujral has not done this. One fails to understand why Gujral and his colleagues should think that heavens would fall if the Amnesty International is permitted to visit various places in the country? Or, is it that Gujral was not able to bring round the Army authorities who are known to be against permitting any human rights groups from abroad? Gujral, more than anyone else, knows that the world today is a big village, and nothing can be kept a secret. Democratic culture and transparency, one should have thought, enhance the prestige of a practising democracy.

I may refer to an incident revolving round Gujral, for whatever it is worth. The Independent Initiative, an NGO founded by

Justice Krishna Iyer, Justice Rajindar Sachar, Professor Rajni Kothari and others, deputed me to observe the polling in the Patna parliamentary constituency on 20 May 1991. I undertook the task with trepidation because the then Chief Election Commissioner (CEC), T.N. Seshan, had already forecast a bloodbath on the election day in Patna. In fact, it was the dire prediction of the all-knowing Seshan which prompted the Initiative to opt for Patna for observation. (The CEC countermanded the election even though both the Congress and BJP leaders and workers had demanded repoll only in 50/60 booths and did not ask for countermanding the election as a whole. Incidentally, it was a scoop of sorts, for I reported that the CEC had countermanded the election even before he received the report from the Election Officer at Patna or from his own team of observers! It was published in the newspapers of May 22.) On my return journey on May 21, Gujral was the Janata Dal candidate from the Patna constituency and I sat side by side in the plane. I recognized him from his beard—I had not seen him in person before! From the badge I put on, he came to know of my identity. We talked about the "weather"; never once during the journey did he ask me anything about my findings. Well, a gentleman is one who does not embarrass you nor does he inflict pain on you!

[Source: *Mainstream*, Vol. XXXVI, No. 8, 14 February 1998, pp. 13–15]

****

CHAPTER 35

An Unwarranted Outburst

PRIME MINISTER'S VERBAL OFFENSIVE IN PARLIAMENT

One is reminded of Prime Minister Atal Behari Vajpayee's political guru, a great parliamentarian, Dr. Shyama Prasad Mookherjee's repartee on Prime Minister Jawaharlal Nehru's unwarranted outburst and anger at Dr. Mookherjee in Parliament in the early 1950s. Dr. Mookherjee's very brief intervention, and a very effective one at that, was: "It is not the birthright of the Prime Minister to lose his temper."

Regrettably, there was none like Dr. Mookherjee in the Congress party and other Opposition formations during the joint session of Parliament on 26 March 2002 to tell Prime Minister Vajpayee that his outburst and verbal offensive at the Congress party's leader, Mrs. Sonia Gandhi, was unwarranted, and that his anger was made up. Even Mrs. Gandhi's speech-writer (if he/she was present in the joint session) could not think of an effective intervention, except to bring all the Congress MPs to their feet—and some came into the well of the House. Mrs. Gandhi's party no doubt has "shouting brigades" and scheming small-time politicians, but they do not make good parliamentarians nor can "shouting brigades" and small-time scheming politicians govern a vast country like India. That, however, is a different question.

On some occasions Vajpayee would be on the offensive to demonstrate his oratorical skill, but not on 26 March. He hardly said a word about the subject—the POTO (anti-terrorist) bill, to pass which the joint session of Parliament was called. In fact, none of the government spokespersons could make out a cause in favour of POTO. A few Opposition members, like the CPI-M leader Somnath Chatterjee's arguments against POTO were very effective.

We are not here concerned with the Opposition leader or her ability; we take note of what Mrs. Gandhi spoke which "engaged" Vajpayee.

"Will the Prime Minister be submissive and weak in his leadership or will he uphold the prestige of the high office he holds? His moment of reckoning has come. He has to decide whether his primary duty is to the people or the party," Mrs. Gandhi said. The words "submissive" and "reckoning", to which Vajpayee took objection, are not unparliamentary nor insulting. (A man of Vajpayee's learning and "seniority" should not have failed to notice that Mrs. Gandhi's speech was written by a skilfull writer.)

Vajpayee may not be submissive, but then men of his persuasion, culture, tradition and learning have always been both arrogant and submissive, now this, now that. He might, for example, have been against the demolition of the Babri Masjid, but he could not and cannot go against the RSS and the like, he has to rely heavily on them for his political fortune. He is right when he said in the joint session that he does not owe his Prime Ministership to Mrs. Sonia Gandhi and her like. But he did not mention that he owes this to his Sangh Parivar cadres, and also to his thoroughly unprincipled and unscrupulous political allies. Furthermore, to say, "I do not work under pressure from anyone", is a tall if not vainglorious claim. Vajpayee has to submit not only to his party cadres (RSS) but also to other power-hungry colleagues from other formations. A few months ago he removed one of his senior Ministers from his department and placed him in another department, under pressure from BJP and RSS cadres; and that with a view to winning elections in Delhi. Is this political morality?

Mrs. Sonia Gandhi questioned the "moral integrity" of Vajpayee's government. "Is this language to be used against the Prime Minister? What does it ('moment of reckoning') mean?

Am I being put in the dock?" Well, one has to follow the games of the institution of Parliament in the parliamentary form of government. Vajpayee seems to think that the Prime Minister is above Parliament and nobody can question him. His contention that "our intentions and bonafides are being suspected—these are personal charges", is misplaced . In the recent past, elections in UP, Uttaranchal, Punjab, (and now in Delhi where the Prime Minister's party has been wiped out) clearly indicate that the vast majority of the people suspect the intention and bonafides of the present government. If the election results are any indication, the common men and women of our country are greatly worried about the Prime Minister and his men's agenda: draconian measures in the name of anti-terrorism and anti-Pakistan climate; construction of Mandir and destruction of Masjid; terrorising minorities. He wanted their votes on this agenda; they have rejected the agenda. The common men and women do not care whether Mrs. Sonia Gandhi or some other leader "suspects the intention and bonafides" of the government; they have given a clear signal, outside Parliament, that they do suspect. It is for Vajpayee to decide whether or not he is obliged to take note of the signal and decide his future course of action. If he is brave and upright, as he claims to be, he must resign and ask for the people's verdict.

Mrs. Gandhi accused

> the government of manipulating the process of Parliament for promoting a divisive ideological agenda. ... In any case, for an issue such as POTO, a joint session can never be a satisfactory solution. It is even more unacceptable when it is used to pass a draconian law in the backdrop of communal tension, or murder and looting in Gujarat, a divisive Ayodhya campaign and an outrageous attack on the Orissa Assembly by activists of the *Sangh Parivar*.

One does not know whether the Congress or any other political party will be against a draconian law when they come to power, but certainly our common men and women, who have kept democracy going in spite of the dominating middle class with an authoritarian mindset, have stated in no uncertain terms that they do not want any draconian law.

To get back to the question of "moral integrity". All that has happened during the last two-three years and Vajpayee's reaction to these happenings, do not indicate that he is "milky white" as he claims. And, also that because you are a very senior member, your intentions must not be questioned, falls on the borderline of moral coercion.

When the Christians were under attack in different parts of the country, he chose not to come down heavily on the attackers (members of the *Sangh Parivar*); he wanted to solve the problem of attacks through a debate on conversion. (Interestingly, he did not want a debate on the caste system, which has been the primary cause of conversion in our country).

Vajpayee does not appreciate the fact that the Chief Minister of Gujarat, Narendra Modi, and his colleagues and cadres have been responsible for the cruel killings of Muslims in Gujarat, and that they have contributed enormously towards creating a polluted climate of dissension and divisiveness, thereby threatening the unity of the country and also threatening Hinduism—Hinduism is in danger in the hands of the *Hindutvavadis*. The Prime Minister wants POTO to keep India united. His "seniority" in politics should have made him see reason, namely, that so long as the polluted climate is not tackled the country will head towards disintegration, and that no draconian law has ever kept a country united.

In any civilized country, a man like the Gujarat Chief Minister would have been chargesheeted and tried in a court of law for crimes that he has committed: of making efforts deliberately to destroy the unity of the country; and the horrendous crime of not preventing rampaging mobs who murdered innocent people (Muslims) in cold blood. It is reported that two of his Ministers led a mob. (It is understood the National Human Rights Commission is coming out with a detailed report on the Gujarat coverage within the next couple of days. The Commission' report is not, it is understood, going to be a pleasant one for the Gujarat Government.)

The minimum that one expected from Vajpayee is to dismiss this Chief Minister. And yet his loud claim that he does not submit nor does he work under pressure. This is what one calls unnecessary arrogance, which we have inherited from our tradition. I appreciate that it is too late for Vajpayee to disown this ugly heritage.

I cannot say why Vajpayee went on the arrogant verbal offensive that we watched on television on 26 March; one may, however, hazard the guess that Vajpayee has been, for sometime, resorting to the defence mechanism. Ayodhya, the BJP's defeat in the recent elections (he had been lucky on 26 March that election results came in a day later of the Delhi Municipal Corporation where the party has been wiped out), Gujarat carnage—all these have brought down his image both here and abroad; and he knows it. The outburst was a reaction to the poor image. He has not, however, succeeded in improving his image through the unwarranted and arrogant outburst.

[Courtesy: *Mainstream,* Vol. XL, No. 17,
13 April 2002, pp. 19-20]

****

CHAPTER 36

Contempt of Court—A Dicey Question

The Contempt of Courts Act 1971 defines contempt (in Section 2-C-1) as the publication of any matter or the doing of any other act which scandalizes or tends to scandalize, or lowers or tends to lower the authority of any court. Despite this definition, it remains a dicey question. There has been a number of cases under this law before the Supreme Court/High Courts. The latest before the Delhi High Court is against the editor of a magazine, *Wah India*. The Bar Council of Delhi was so terribly outraged that it lost no time in petitioning the High Court against the magazine and its editor. The editor-in-chief of the journal tendered an apology when the hearing started.

The *Wah India* magazine published in its 16–30 April 2001 issue a "ranking" given by fifty senior advocates about Delhi High Court judges—their manners in court, general reputation on personal integrity, quality of judgement, knowledge of law, punctuality, receptiveness in the arguments addressed. With the Court ordering confiscation of copies of the particular issue of the magazine, reproduction of the contents is not possible. Having read the impugned article (before the Court passed its order), I will raise a couple of issues, certainly not with a view to "questioning the credibility of the judiciary". The credibility issue, we shall consider later.

One, why should the Bar Council be so aggrieved? Over the years have the members of the Bar Council (or at least a majority of them) behaved like officers of the Court, as they are expected to do? Two, do the apologies tendered in contempt cases flow from the heart or they are prompted by the need to escape from the consequences of conviction?

A few years ago, a contempt case was instituted against the editor of a metropolitan newspaper for the following comments in an article:

> Some recent strictures passed by the Supreme Court against the law-enforcement agencies in Punjab suggested that the learned judges of the nation's apex juridical authority may be in need of psychiatric counselling.

Hauled up for contempt, the writer and the editor of the daily tendered apologies and were let off. Must we take it that the writer became a transformed person? Apart from its outrageous suggestion that judges who passed strictures on the Punjab Police for killing suspected militants in fake encounters should have their heads examined, the article betrayed a mindset which is incompatible with democracy, the rule of law and human rights. This ideology is upheld by many in our country. An apology, in such cases, is rendered only to wriggle out of the trouble. In this case the Editors Guild of India planned to take a deputation to the Chief Justice of India to protest against the harsh remarks of a Supreme Court bench against the writer and the newspaper. The Editors Guild members, with their knowledge of law and commitment to its rule, did not consider it necessary to view the matter in a larger light than in trade union terms of defending one of their tribe for his indiscretion.

I, therefore, suggest, with all respect for the High Courts and Supreme Court that apologies may not be entertained, much less demanded in all such cases because it renders apology into a mere formality. Section 2 (c)(1) of the 1971 Act, I suggest, may be struck off the Statute book. With respect for our judges I maintain that heavens will not fall if this law is struck off, and that the credibility of the judiciary cannot be damaged by such writings, even if such writings are "irresponsible and dangerous", nor can credibility be restored through apologies or through punishment, credibility depends on many other factors like commitment to democratic culture and law, human rights, civil liberties and freedoms. The common men and women—the so-called illiterate people of our country—are not "dangerous", they showed their courage and commitment to human values in the general election of 1977. Let us remember that democracy and human rights have been kept alive in our country by the common men and women. They were greatly disappointed by the judiciary during the Emergency (1975–77). One wonders if the middle class has contributed towards the growth of democracy or if it has any respect for human rights and freedoms.

We also suggest that contempt of the courts and law should not be formal but should cover transgression of the spirit of the Constitution and the rule of law and human rights it enshrines. But then the question arises: what about judges who uphold executive actions clearly violative of the rule of law and human rights as happened during the Emergency in 1975–77. I refer to the historical event—the infamous 28 April 1976 (*ADM Jabalpur vs. Shukla*) apropos of suspension of Fundamental Rights during Mrs Indira Gandhi's Emergency regime when four judges (including the then Chief Justice) of the Supreme Court dealt a severe blow to the whole concept of rule of law, democracy and human rights. [Three of them were elevated, subsequently, to the position of Chief Justice! And one of the three, who goes about as a 'great' human rights activist and is courted even by human rights groups and activists, wrote a letter to Mrs. Indira Gandhi, hailing her on her becoming the Prime Minister in 1980! (Have you ever heard of a judge in a democratic country prostrating before a politician!)]

What did they say to a simple question, despite the Presidential proclamation of the emergency in 1975: can a High Court admit a habeas corpus petition filed by a person challenging his detention (to which quite a few High Courts said, yes)? They (the Supreme Court), with a solitary dissenting voice, said: No. ["In view of the Presidential Order dated 27 June 1975 no person has any locus to move any writ petition under Article 226 before a High Court for habeas corpus or any other writ or order or direction to challenge the legality of an order of detention on the ground that the order is not under or in compliance with the Act or is illegal or is vitiated by *mala fides* factual or legal or is based on extraneous consideration (in the case referred to in all law reports as *ADM Jabalpur vs Shukla*)."] Can there be anything more disappointing than such a pronouncement? This Presidential Order referred to above was issued during the Emergency 1975 declaring that the right of any person to move any court for enforcement of the rights conferred by Articles 14, 21 and 22 of the Constitution shall remain suspended during the Emergency period.

The dissenting judge, at one stage, asked the government (through its Attorney General): "Life is also mentioned in Articled 21 and would government argument extend to it also?" "Even if life was taken away illegally, courts are helpless," was the answer of the Attorney General. The four "distinguished" judges of the Supreme Court agreed! At one stage the chief Justice admonished the counsel for the detenues for referring to Nazi gas chambers. Now, if I severely criticize this judgement, as I have done in the past and will continue to do, shall I be prosecuted on the charge of contempt?

Let me quote a couple of gems! One judge said (while commenting on the condition of persons placed in jail during the Emergency): "We understand that the care and concern bestowed by the state authorities upon the welfare of detenues (those who were put in jail, like, for example, Jayaprakash Narayan and Bhimsen Sachar) who are well housed, well fed and well treated, is almost maternal." Yet another luminary crossed all limits in his eulogy: "Counsel after counsel expressed the fear that during the emergency, the executive may strip and starve the detenue and if this be our judgement, even shoot him down. Such misdeeds have not tarnished the record of free India and I have a diamond-bright, diamond-hard hope that such things will never come to pass."

I may end this article with what the "Human Rights Judge" (referred to above) said in this case: "I do not think it would be right for me to allow my love of personal liberty to close my vision as to persuade me to place on the relevant provision of the Constitution a construction which its language cannot reasonably bear." How does one evaluate such "craft"?

In short, the Supreme Court judgement is incompatible with democracy, the rule of law and human rights. And yet I do not remember any occasion when our judges made any comments about the four judges for their total disregard for rule of law and human rights which is to be preserved by the higher courts. We have been ruled by preventive detention laws in independent India since 1947—politicians and bureaucrats move such laws and they are happy when their adversaries are placed in jail without trial; that judges on whom our citizens depend for their life and liberty should have given their seal of approval to such laws during the Emergency should be a cause for anxious thoughts—should they hold the high position in a democratic country. Finally, did the Supreme Court judgement add to the credibility of the judiciary? (23 May 2001)

Postcript: The above article was written before the High Court judgement in the *Wah India* case delivered on 28 May. According to reports (*The Statesman*, 29 May), the Court unanimously held that "prima facie contempt has been committed by the respondents". Three judges (majority) accepted unconditional apologies tendered by the editor-in-chief. One of the two other judges said: "It appears to me that the apologies have been tendered to avoid punishment and are not genuine." The other judge said: "Apologies tendered were not made in good faith." He further said: "Mere parrot-like repetition of regrets in about identically worded affidavits does not convince me that the respondents are really remorseful or repentant." These two judges were of the view that action should be taken against the contemners. (1 June 2001)

[Courtesy: *Mainstream*, Vol. XXXIX, No. 26,
16 June 2001, pp. 27–28]

****